When Protest B

Anthropology, Culture and Society

Series Editors:
Jamie Cross, University of Edinburgh,
Christina Garsten, Stockholm University
and
Joshua O. Reno, Binghamton University

Recent titles:

When Protest Becomes Crime

Politics and Law in Liberal Democracies

Carolijn Terwindt

First published 2020 by Pluto Press
345 Archway Road, London N6 5AA

www.plutobooks.com

Copyright © Carolijn Terwindt 2020

The right of Carolijn Terwindt to be identified as the author of this work has been asserted by her in accordance with the Copyright, Designs and Patents Act 1988.

British Library Cataloguing in Publication Data
A catalogue record for this book is available from the British Library

ISBN   978 0 7453 4005 0   Hardback
ISBN   978 0 7453 4004 3   Paperback
ISBN   978 1 7868 0607 9   PDF eBook
ISBN   978 1 7868 0610 9   Kindle eBook
ISBN   978 1 7868 0608 6   EPUB eBook

Typeset by Stanford DTP Services, Northampton, England

Simultaneously printed in the United Kingdom and United States of America

Contents

Series Preface

As people around the world confront the inequality and injustice of new forms of oppression, as well as the impacts of human life on planetary ecosystems, this book series asks what anthropology can contribute to the crises and challenges of the twenty-first century. Our goal is to establish a distinctive anthropological contribution to debates and discussions that are often dominated by politics and economics. What is sorely lacking, and what anthropological methods can provide, is an appreciation of the human condition.

We publish works that draw inspiration from traditions of ethnographic research and anthropological analysis to address power and social change while keeping the struggles and stories of human beings centre stage. We welcome books that set out to make anthropology matter, bringing classic anthropological concerns with exchange, difference, belief, kinship and the material world into engagement with contemporary environmental change, the capitalist economy and forms of inequality. We publish work from all traditions of anthropology, combining theoretical debate with empirical evidence to demonstrate the unique contribution anthropology can make to understanding the contemporary world.

Jamie Cross, Christina Garsten and Joshua O. Reno

Preface

During the research for this book, I closely followed three different political struggles in three different countries. I studied the grounds for the disputes and looked at the various groups and individuals involved on either side: the mainstream and fringe activists, their political opponents and the targets of actions. I looked at protest tactics as well as actions of defense against such protest, and ensuing confrontations with law enforcement agents. These formed the context for my real interest: the way in which criminal law and criminal justice measures and institutions were used, called upon, legitimated and criticized in the course of those interactions.

Ultimately, we are dealing with the grand subject of justice and injustice. During my research I have often been outraged by particular cases of injustice. I could not be indifferent when listening to someone who recently lost his father because he was a prosecutor in Madrid. I found it impossible to be unconcerned about the issue of living continually with personal bodyguards, a necessity for many in the Basque Country. And I was deeply disturbed when I learned that the Spanish state had colluded with paramilitaries to kill its own citizens. I was moved listening to four elderly Mapuche men living in the utmost poverty, who did not understand the legal reasoning in the Chilean criminal proceedings when they were convicted. I was affected when I saw the pictures of the inundated area for a hydroelectric dam where only a year before a Mapuche woman had proudly shown me her land. I was not indifferent either to the fear of a young Chilean child growing up in his parents' house in the countryside who felt unprotected against attacks by a neighboring Mapuche community. I was profoundly sad when Eric McDavid was sentenced to 18 years in a US prison, with the full weight of a terrorism enhancement upon his alleged crime of conspiracy, turning him into an example for others. And in the course of my research, I have come to care for the struggle against cruelty inflicted upon animals.

The list of past and current cases of potential injustices is inevitably long and they form a core part of each of these political conflicts. Whereas each of the examples may have been moving when taking the point of view of the suffering person, this does not mean that what happened was "unjust" by all standards. The common feature in each of the episodes studied was that opponents held different standards, which was the starting point of my research. These diverging standards for justice are embedded in different worldviews. As a researcher I continuously switched between these worldviews in order to learn and describe their constitution, features and differences. These competing worldviews at times fit the cliché "One man's terrorist is another man's freedom fighter." So I have spoken with people who consider ETA (Euskadi Ta Askatasuna) militants to be terrorists, and with people who consider them to be freedom fighters. But worldviews are more complex than that simple juxtaposition and to do them justice requires an in-depth understanding of a wide range of issues.

As Howard Becker pointed out in his essay "Whose side are we on?" (1967), by taking seriously the standards of justice as advocated by a group like ETA, for example, I run the risk of being suspected of taking their side. My interest in this project was not, however, in any of these conflicts or their actors in particular. I am an outsider to each of them, even though I feel more closely involved after having spent much time listening to the people who have a real stake in them. And, of course, I also developed my own opinions regarding the disputes at hand. Instead of supporting a particular position, though, the goal was to go beyond any of these episodes and to obtain a better understanding of the way in which criminal justice systems in liberal democracies work.

Criminal proceedings in each of the episodes studied became a major site of political mobilization and contention. In this project, I attempted to unearth what that means, both in terms of the overall dynamics of political contention and for the liberal promise of criminal justice through proceedings according to the rule of law. While this book may not necessarily offer new information to those familiar with a particular episode, my hope is that the comparative approach and novel analytical framework will enable readers to view the development and operation of prosecutorial narratives in those episodes in a new light. The analysis calls for a heightened awareness of the critical role played by narratives promoted by interest groups. As prosecutorial choices are based on such narratives, the choice of a prosecutorial narrative and contextualization of an alleged crime is far more political than the common proclamation of a simple application of the law would make it seem.

Acknowledgments

When Protest Becomes Crime is a book that has been many years in the making and I am immensely grateful to the many people who have played a role in its development. I am indebted to all who have helped point me toward relevant information, enriched my understanding through interviews, and sharpened my analyses through discussion and feedback. Research involving fieldwork inevitably becomes deeply personal. In the months I spent in the countries where the analyzed criminal prosecutions took place, I spent many hours with people involved as defendants, victims, prosecutors, lawyers, or supporters for one of the parties. My deepest gratitude, therefore, goes to all of those who were willing to share their experiences with me. I also want to thank the friends who offered me a place to stay during my travels to prisons, trials and interviews, especially those who became sparring partners in thinking through my research. For the inspiring and rich discussions, I would particularly like to thank Pedro, Myka, Iñi, Eneko and Jaime.

The research for the book was conducted with the support of my doctoral dissertation committee at Columbia University: Jeffrey Fagan and Daniel Richman from the Law School and Elizabeth Povinelli from the Anthropology Department. Thank you all for opening up intellectual doors and the many engaging discussions. My writing further benefited from the Contentious Politics Workshop initially led by the late Charles Tilly from Columbia and then by Jim Jasper and John Krinsky from CUNY (City University New York), which fostered a unique vision of and dedication to collective scientific enterprise. I am also grateful for the grants that made my field research possible. A Columbia grant enabled my US travels, while a Marie Curie Fellowship permitted my stay at Deusto University in Bilbao and a fellowship from the International Institute for the Sociology of Law in Oñati allowed a return research visit to the Basque Country. Thanks also go to the Max Planck Institute for Comparative and International Criminal Law in Freiburg, Germany, where I received a scholarship to support my writing and joined the International Research School on Retaliation, Mediation, and Punishment.

Finally, I thank Daniel Augenstein, Mark Barenberg, Gur Bligh, Hanspeter van den Broek, Ruben Cañadas, Christian Davenport, Jolle Demmers, Zoltán Fleck, Mario Fumerton, Laura Gasiorowski, Daniel Gregor, Csaba Györi, Wolfgang Kaleck, Sun Chul Kim, Javier Martín, Matthijs Nelemans, Suzanne Nievaart, Phil Parnell, Patricia Richards, Richard Rottenburg, Christian Schliemann, Claire Tixeire, Wouter Veraart, Matija Vlatkovic, Vera Wriedt as well as the anonymous reviewers for commenting on my research design, fieldwork results and draft chapters. Indispensable for the process of turning the dissertation into a book has been my work with Allison West, who provided valuable substantive suggestions and thorough editing of the entire book. Her encouragement and insightful proposals made everything better.

Carolijn Terwindt
Berlin, May 2019

Abbreviations

AEPA	Animal Enterprise Protection Act
AETA	Animal Enterprise Terrorism Act
ALF	Animal Liberation Front
AVT	Asociación Víctimas del Terrorismo
BVE	Batallón Vasco Español
CAM	La Coordinadora de Comunidades en Conflicto Arauco-Malleco
CONADI	Corporación Nacional de Desarrollo Indígena
CORMA	Corporación de Madera
ELF	Earth Liberation Front
EPPK	Euskal Preso Politikoen Kolektiboa
ETA	Euskadi Ta Askatasuna
FARC	Fuerzas Armadas Revolucionarias de Colombia
FBI	Federal Bureau of Investigation
GAL	Grupos Antiterroristas de Liberación
HLS	Huntingdon Life Sciences
IACHR	Inter-American Commission for Human Rights
MLNV	Movimiento de Liberación Nacional Vasco
PETA	People for the Ethical Treatment of Animals
PNV	Partido Nacional Vasco
SHAC	Stop Huntingdon Animal Cruelty
SOFO	Sociedad de Fomento Agrícola

Mapuzugun (Mapuche language)

Lonko	Community chief
Winka/ huinca	Pejorative word for "Chilean" – literally: thief

1

Introduction

Molotov cocktails and terrorism in the Basque Country

After a street demonstration in 1992 in the city of Bilbao, Yulen and his brother threw a Molotov cocktail into the offices of Spain's national train company. It was a time of widespread *"kale borroka"* in the Basque Country, the territory claimed as homeland by the Basque people who straddle modern state borders in the north of Spain and southwest of France. This Basque-language term, which translates roughly to "street struggle," was widely used in Spain to refer to actions in which Basque youth aired their political frustrations in the streets by destroying cash machines, throwing stones at party offices or smashing the windows of agencies for temporary employment. In explaining their decision to throw the Molotov cocktail, Yulen cited the brothers' anger at the disproportionate use of force by police earlier that day against participants in a public demonstration by the Basque left-nationalist movement, a group in favor of an independent and socialist Basque Country (Interview S-23).

At the time when the brothers threw the Molotov cocktail, instances of property destruction in the context of *kale borroka* were usually brought before local courts as cases of public disorder, generally leading to fines for misdemeanors or short jail sentences (Annual Report of the Attorney General Spain or *Memoria Anual* [MA] 1993:416). Indictments in these instances usually focused on the economic damage inflicted through *kale borroka* protest actions (MA 1993:147). Yulen and his brother, however, met with a different legal response. Investigative judges from the Audiencia Nacional (National Court) in Madrid stepped in and claimed jurisdiction over the brothers' case. This specialized court for certain types of serious crimes, such as terrorism and money laundering, sentenced the two brothers to ten years in prison each – while not being members of ETA – for having "collaborated with the goals and objectives of ETA," the notorious underground organization Euskadi Ta Askatasuna that has advocated using armed struggle to achieve an independent Basque Country and killed numerous officers of the Guardia Civil (Spain's national military police force) and later also politicians and journalists to further this aim.

The brothers' case set a new precedent, kicking off a battle between defense lawyers and prosecutors over the jurisdiction of the Audiencia Nacional in incidents related to *kale borroka*. Key to their success in obtaining jurisdiction, the Madrid prosecutors did not describe the brothers' acts of vandalism as separate and isolated events. Instead, they labeled participants in *kale borroka* as "groups of support to ETA" in order to categorize their actions as a terrorist offense (for example, MA 1994:156). This trend continued and by the end of the 1990s, it had become routine to qualify acts of *kale borroka* as terrorism, with such cases automatically going to the Audiencia Nacional. A new law in 2000 (LO 7/2000) cemented this development by turning "material destruction" into a terrorist crime, even if the perpetrator did not belong to an armed organization, as long as it was done with the goal to "subvert the constitution" or "change the public peace."

Since the Audiencia Nacional's founding in 1977, the court has tried ETA militants for carrying out or collaborating in armed attacks. Even though *kale borroka* actions had always been viewed as springing from the general milieu around ETA, they were not prosecuted as terrorism before the 1992 case. The move to bring these cases to the Audiencia Nacional fitted with a prosecutorial theory that claimed – based on ideas attributed to ETA leader "Txelis" – that ETA needed constant low-level sabotage during the times when its commandos were not active to keep up pressure on selected targets (for example, court houses or political party offices). In the words of an investigative judge at the Audiencia Nacional, *kale borroka* was thus part of ETA's strategy to maintain a "permanent coercive effect on citizens" (Case Kale Borroka, 19 October 2007). According to this narrative, ETA actually orchestrated *kale borroka*, a view that gradually became institutionalized through court decisions. Supporters of the Basque left-nationalist movement, a collective of parties and grassroots organizations and groups whose common denominator is the nationalist and socialist project, criticized the new portrayal of *kale borroka* by prosecutors. Many left-nationalists denied the existence of ETA-coordinated protest groups and – even though some *kale borroka* actions were actually claimed in communiqués (Van den Broek 2004:719) – emphasized the often spontaneous participation of frustrated youth in *kale borroka*.

This book focuses on the key role that "prosecutorial narrative" – the official accusation and explanation of what makes certain conduct a crime delivered in court by a prosecutor tasked with the authority and responsibility of representing the public interest – plays in reproducing and legitimizing certain societal views, while marginalizing others. By choosing to describe conduct in a particular manner in the courtroom, prosecutors can enable changes in the way conduct is defined judicially, with significant impact on criminal prosecution and sentencing. Classifying *kale borroka* actions as terrorism, for instance, not only results in higher sentences (up to 18 years in prison) than for public disorder, but also opens up the possibility for incommunicado detention and the dispersion of the convicts across Spain. The example of the changed label for *kale borroka* further shows that prosecutors do not simply apply the law – as if the law is static and straightforward – but rather play a key role in shaping the way events are legally qualified and taken to court. As this book endeavors to demonstrate, this is not only the case with regard to prosecutors in Spain in the special situation of its long-standing struggle against ETA, but is part and parcel of the application of the law in contested socio-political terrain.

The application of law involves, however, what I call "prosecutorial narratives," which imply the choice of a context, selection and interpretation of the facts, and the choice of certain perpetrators. Defendants, their supporters and their critics all struggle to define this narrative, which not only becomes the key to influencing the initiation, scope and course of criminal proceedings, but also a major truth-producer publicly communicating about political events, grievances and identities. Prosecutorial narratives simultaneously provide the basis for the choices made in specific criminal prosecutions and fulfill the function of legitimizing the very endeavor of dealing with the issue at hand in the criminal justice arena.

Unlike in authoritarian dictatorships, the legal institutions of liberal democracies rest on the assumption of a society in consensus, in the sense that society is expected to be made up of free and equal citizens, and where dissent can be solved in parliament or civil lawsuits. In such a society, the prosecutor is expected to act in the public interest. In reality, as criminal law professor Alan Norrie (1993:222) has pointed out, society is divided and criminal law functions as a mechanism of social control. The existence of social and political conflicts in democratic societies is ignored in the ideology of liberal legalism and crime conceptualized as "the result of individual calculations" (Norrie 1993:58). While prosecutors are expected to act in "the public interest," Norrie cautions that "The law embodies a logic of individual right to be applied universally, but is in reality applied to one group by another" (Norrie 1993:31).

What do prosecutors do when the public is divided and interest groups advocate for radically different understandings of what is criminal and how to apply the law? In such instances, the prosecutorial narrative becomes the focus of discursive action and mobilization by groups in society claiming victimhood and seeking to define certain conduct as criminal, while those facing criminal charges counter-mobilize to challenge the claims and/or assert the legitimacy of their actions. By comparing episodes of such "contentious criminalization" across three well-established liberal democracies – Spain, Chile and the United States – this book attempts to shed light on what happens when political contestation moves into the criminal justice arena, where the issues, demands and actors become co-determined by the logic and language of criminal law and procedure. Rather than assuming that the criminal justice system and its performance are fixed and natural, this book follows sociologist David Garland (1990:4) in suggesting that it may be challenged and subsequently change.

In Spain, the book traces the shifting and contested prosecutorial narratives about ETA and its alleged support network in the Basque left-nationalist movement, which represents a broader struggle for a free and socialist Basque Country that clashes with the political and territorial unity inscribed in Spain's Constitution. Established in 1959, the armed organization ETA was originally founded to fight against the Franco dictatorship. In 1973, members of ETA killed General Carrero Blanco, the supposed successor of Franco, garnering significant popular support for the armed Basque organization. Even after Spain's transition to democracy, however, ETA continued its deadly attacks, justified by what the organization and its sympathizers saw as an undemocratic state of exception in the Basque Country, where the Basque people faced repression and lacked a political path to independence. In 1978, almost half of Spain's Basque citizens viewed ETA members as idealists or patriots, as compared to just 7 percent who considered them criminals (Alonso and Reinares 2005:267). According to the annual reports of the prosecutor's office, during this time period the Spanish state viewed ETA as an opponent in a war (MA 1979:65), though this changed over the course of the 1990s, when the criminal justice system became the main venue for encounters between the state, ETA, and its supporters. At the same time, by implementing the Statute of Basque Autonomy, passed on 18 December 1979, significant powers were transferred from Madrid to the regional government of the Basque Country in areas including health care, policing and taxation. In 2010 ETA announced a permanent ceasefire and in 2018 its leaders dissolved the organization.

In Chile, the book explores prosecutions set in the context of the so-called "Mapuche conflict," in which Mapuche indigenous groups demand the return of lands from which they were dispossessed by the Chilean government in 1883. These lands are now predominantly in the hands of timber companies and large-scale farmers, who argue that their forestry plantations serve the public interest, as they claim they create jobs and benefit the country's economic growth while also protecting native forests. Mapuche activists, on the other hand, question who the plantations really benefit, emphasizing their historic right to their ancestral lands and highlighting how the industrial plantations create water shortages for adjacent Mapuche communities. In the face of protracted political inertia on the issue of land redistribution, Mapuche activists began to stage occupations of disputed lands, leading to criminal prosecutions against them. In other cases, Mapuche activists have been accused of arson of plantations. The book shows how the present-day landowners successfully mobilized to influence prosecutorial narrative by appealing to law and order in cases of property destruction and portraying themselves as "victims" of a radical minority who sought to leverage their Mapuche identity for personal gain. However, the oscillation in these cases between viewing Mapuche land occupations as criminal conduct to seeing them as a form of legitimate civil disobedience shows how prosecutorial narrative is not neutral, but inevitably reproduces and elevates certain arguments and power relations in society, marginalizing others.

In the US, the book traces the discursive battles surrounding prosecutorial narratives on "eco-terrorism" in the context of animal rights and environmentalist activism against practices like animal testing, fur farms or tree logging. While mainstream conservationist and animal welfare organizations receive widespread support in American society, the more radical ideas of animal rights and nature-centered demands have been viewed with skepticism. In 1979, animal rights activists for the first time broke into a lab in order to release caged animals. In 1980, the radical environmentalist group Earth First! was founded, a group that engaged in tree-sits and came up with wilderness proposals. For a long time, protest actions like the release of animals from fur farms or testing laboratories were not a priority for US law enforcement agencies. In 1998, the

Director of the Federal Bureau of Investigation (FBI) Louis Freeh said that "[e]co- and animal rights terrorism [...] was not an issue, not a priority and not on the agency's 'radar screen.'" Fur farmers were outraged by the lack of attention to the activist raids they experienced, so they mobilized and lobbied the FBI for more protection. Just seven years later, on 24 August 2005, a top FBI official declared the "eco-terrorism, animal-rights movement" to be "the No. 1 domestic terrorism threat" in the US (Schuster 2005). This threat assessment was accompanied by a proactive approach to investigating activist groups, including the use of FBI informants, conspiracy charges, and a prosecutorial demand for higher sentences as a deterrent to other activists. By 2009, the release of animals in the context of animal rights activism had transformed into a terrorist offense and two activists were convicted and sentenced to 21 and 24 months respectively, under the Animal Enterprise Terrorism Act (AETA) for the release of 650 mink from a fur farm in Utah.

My long response to a Chilean prosecutor

The idea for this book emerged while attending a trial against three Mapuche activists in Chile in April 2003. Rather than focus narrowly on the three defendants and the particular criminal actions imputed, the prosecutor's opening statement traced Chilean–Mapuche relations from the 19th-century war that forced the indigenous group into reservations, ending with an analysis of how the defendants "abused" their indigenous Mapuche identity to get away with arson at a plantation simply because it was on disputed land subject to historical Mapuche claims. The politicization of the trial and evident centrality of criminal justice proceedings within the dynamics of the so-called "Mapuche conflict" in Chile sparked my interest in processes of criminalization in complex situations of protracted socio-political contestation.

Shortly thereafter, in an interview with Esmirna Vidal, the regional prosecutor for the 9th Region in the south of Chile, she stressed to me that her job was simply "to apply the democratic mandate of the law" (Interview 2003, C-10). Her reference to the law as the basis and final arbiter of her job supposedly closed the discussion about the choices she made and the way she conducted criminal proceedings in an obviously challenging political context. Newspaper headlines at the time speculated about the impending outbreak of a "Mapuche Intifada." Graffiti in the streets of Temuco threatened the prosecutors that "if they apply *winka*

[Chilean] law, there will be Mapuche justice" (see Photo 1). Clearly, "just applying the law" was more complicated than she made it out to be. Her remark sparked my desire to understand more profoundly the dynamics in and role of prosecutorial offices, and to go beyond the simplicity of her evasive resort to her legal mandate to explain her decisions. This book is, in that sense, a lengthy response to Prosecutor Vidal, in which I argue that "applying the democratic mandate of the law" is the beginning rather than the end of a much larger discussion on the role of prosecutorial narrative in situations of contentious criminalization in liberal democracies.

Photo 1   Picture taken in the streets in the southern city Temuco, Chile, April 2009

Of the prosecutors I interviewed in Spain, Chile and the United States, many acknowledged the different ways in which fitting facts to existing norms is a more complex process than simply "applying the law." Yet, to maintain their authority and legitimacy as unbiased representatives of the public interest, prosecutors often rely on and reproduce notions of "the law" as an uncontroversial and established body of norms that enjoy societal consensus, enabling them to hide choices they make by insisting that all they do is "apply the law." This book is about the fuzzy frontier that prosecutors negotiate as they attempt to remain neutral and avoid politics, but also take into account the context in which crimes occur. In liberal democracies, people are supposed to be prosecuted for what they do rather than who they are or what they stand for. Echoing these precepts, the spokesperson of a regional prosecutors' office in Chile wrote:

> The Public Ministry is a technical organism, whose function is to investigate crimes, in the execution of which one cannot take into consideration general circumstances that motivate or are the basis for the commission of a given illegal action. If that were the case, how dangerous would the prosecution of crimes become, which would become subject to subjective considerations whose reach no one is in condition to foresee. (García 2002)

This reasoning places the police and the prosecutors, as law enforcers, outside of politics, incapable of resolving the grievances that constitute the "Mapuche conflict," which hinge on claims of injustice related to existing laws and policies outside of the domain of criminal law. Regarding Mapuche demands for land redistribution, law enforcers defer to the political arena as the proper realm of contestation, where dialogue, negotiation, persuasion, political party activity, elections, and parliamentary procedure can influence law- and policy-making. However, in the face of decades of setbacks and inertia in the political arena, Mapuche protest, civil disobedience and arson incidents propelled the conflict into the criminal justice arena, making the courtroom the primary site of interaction between present-day owners of disputed lands and Mapuche activists.

Even though one Chilean prosecutor admitted that a Mapuche activist burning down a plantation was not the same as a random pyromaniac, he insisted that the context of Mapuche land claims should not influence his categorization of the conduct as a crime (Interview 2003, C-12). Trial observation and transcripts show a different picture, however. Since the 1990s, the context of the "Mapuche conflict" has come to play a key role in the Chilean prosecutorial narrative, with major consequences. The criminal definition of certain conduct was substantially altered by the changed narrative and the prosecutor became an important voice in the ongoing political dispute by adopting and thus strengthening one discourse and set of arguments over another.

This book traces how, contrary to carrying out a simple and straightforward "application of the law," prosecutors in Chile, the United States and Spain significantly changed their charging narratives over time in relation to incidents enmeshed in ongoing episodes of socio-political contention.

It demonstrates how interest groups successfully influence the prosecutorial portrayal of events by creating alliances and leveraging victimhood claims, and shows how discursive shifts result in real penal consequences regarding who goes to prison and for how long. Set in and around the courtrooms of liberal democracies, this book offers an in-depth study into the social construction of criminality, processes of legitimization, and the power of categorization, contextualization and narrative in liberal criminal law frameworks.

Research question and design

When Protest Becomes Crime constitutes an in-depth study of what the criminalization of social protest means beyond the fact that people may end up in prison or a movement's resources and focus may be diverted. It relies on ethnographic research in three liberal democracies – Chile, Spain and the United States – to explore how competing definitions of harm, public interest and legitimacy feed into the struggle of interpretation that is part and parcel of initiating and building criminal prosecutions in liberal democracies. By focusing on the construction and broader effects of prosecutorial narrative in contentious politics, it digs into the multiple layers constituting the shift from political protest to criminal treatment of an issue, activists, or a movement.

This book emphasizes on-the-ground perspectives of different actors as they participate in the process of labeling actions, defining crimes and mobilizing support in favor of or against governmental responses. It constitutes a multi-sited ethnography not only because it covers contentious episodes in three different countries, but also because it includes interviews with various actors and traces the temporal development of contentious criminalization in each episode over several decades. This research explores how similar patterns and mechanisms of prosecutorial narrative-making hold across distinct types of political protest cases in different democratic contexts. For analytical purposes, the book examines prosecutorial narrative in separate contentious episodes within larger "streams of contention" in each country, which sociologist Charles Tilly defines as "connected moments of collective claim making that observers single out for explanation" (2007b:204). Thus, whereas the Chilean–Mapuche territorial conflict is a "stream of contention" that has been running ever since the Chilean army fought against Mapuche communities in the 19th century and subsequently forced them onto reservations, the analysis here is limited to the contentious episode that began in 1990, when a democratic government was installed after the referendum that rejected the Pinochet regime. The relevant episode in Spain runs from the democratic transition in 1978, while the starting point of the US episode coincides with the first documented break-in and release of animals from a North American lab in the name of animal rights in 1979 (Jasper and Nelkin 1992:33). I trace the discursive battles over prosecutorial narrative in each episode, with most detail until 2009, the year in which I concluded my fieldwork interviews and trial observations. This in-depth analysis was complemented with some of the most relevant events and judicial proceedings that occurred between 2010 and 2018 on the basis of newspaper accounts, judgments and reports.

The processes of contentious criminalization analyzed here are not unique to the chosen countries. For example, similar developments have also characterized prosecutorial narratives in Germany against left-wing militants of Rote Armee Fraktion and their supporters in the 1970s and 1980s (for example, the criminalization of sympathizers in §129a of the criminal code). Also, in the trial of 13 young Muslims (generally referred to as the "Hofstadgroep") in the Netherlands allegedly planning attacks on politicians and constituting a terrorist organization, the prosecutor started his statement by setting the case in the context of fear which had emerged after 9/11 (Amsterdam, 23 January 2006). He then spoke at length about the differences between an acceptable moderate Islam and a problematic radical Islam in order to prove the terrorist objective of the defendants (25 January 2006: 43ff.).[1] The defense lawyers called the prosecution a witch hunt and criticized the criminalization of religious thinking, meetings and conversations.

This book highlights features of contentious criminalization characteristic of liberal democracies. To that end, it selects three liberal democracies with highly different socio-political contentions: animal and environmental rights in the United States, Basque political independence in Spain, and land redistribution in Chile.[2] In each of the cases, the contention was

---

1   Requisitoir van de officier van justitie in de zaak 'Arles', arrondissementsrechtbank Rotterdam, case against N. Adarraf et al., Amsterdam 23 and 25 January 2006, prosecutors A. van Dam and J. Plooy, on file with the author.
2   The countries were selected from a pool of countries that received the highest of relevant rankings during the relevant time period, such as www.worldaudit.org/democracy.htm (division 1); Polity IV Project, www.systemicpeace.org/polity/polity4x.htm (predominantly level 9/10); https://freedomhouse.org/content/freedom-world-data-and-resources (predominantly level 1/2). Although the environ-

ongoing for a period longer than 20 years and I could speak the language in order to conduct the interviews and follow trials and their transcripts. There is clear variation in these cases. In Chile and the United States, there is no comparable organization to the armed ETA in Spain nor such a high number of deaths. Further, while most of the Mapuche people live in extreme poverty without any form of (officially recognized) autonomous government, the Basque people are economically comparatively well-off and have an autonomous, if not independent, regional government. Frequently coming from white middle-class backgrounds, US animal rights and environmental activists are not generally in a disadvantaged position either. Finally, whereas economic considerations play a dominant role in the interests of present-day landowners in Chile and fur farmers in the United States, this is not the case for victims of ETA violence mobilizing to put pressure on prosecutors in Spain.

I have purposefully selected three highly different cases in order to explore the common phenomenon of "contentious criminalization," the process in which the criminal justice arena is politicized as it becomes the site of and subject to collective claim-making. What counts for the comparison is that the mobilization by challengers of the status quo – and in Spain and Chile also by the defenders of the status quo – was perceived as a considerable threat to public order in the media, by groups in society, and by the government. Furthermore, the political demands to change the status quo were shared by larger constituencies and, in each of these episodes, significant groups of challengers of the status quo lacked faith in political or judicial routes to meet their goals. Activists turned to disruptive or illegal tactics to call attention to or directly enforce their claims. For example, ETA commandos killed political opponents, Mapuche activists occupied their ancestral lands, and US animal rights activists released animals from factory farms. Making matters more complicated, in Spain, paramilitary groups have also killed suspected ETA members, while landowners in Chile have spoken publicly about creating armed groups and Chilean police have killed young Mapuche protesters. All of these incidents have been brought to the attention of prosecutors and are

---

mentalist and animal rights concerns are sometimes viewed as a "single issue," US activists invariably emphasized that their demands to give rights to animals and change the relation between society and nature challenge the economic and political system – and the core parameters of the social contract – as fundamentally as the demand for independence in Spain or land redistribution and autonomy in Chile would.

subject to different interpretations, accusations and justifications. The chosen episodes thus offered different contexts to study development of prosecutorial narrative.

The resulting processes of criminalization in these liberal democracies can fruitfully be compared to explore three highly different trajectories of the application of criminal justice procedures in episodes in which the defendants and victims are likely to have the support of a larger constituency. At stake in these prosecutions is not only the appropriate dealing with a specific incident, but the legitimacy of state institutions and the rule of law more generally. This raises the question of how prosecutors, as state representatives, balance the need to establish order by punishing legal transgressions, while maintaining or regaining legitimacy of the state and its rule of law (Weber 1972; Balbus 1973; Thompson 1975).

There is a long-standing debate inside as well as outside of academia about the nature and capacity of law to shape and regulate a state's use of force. In this book, I contend that criminal prosecutions do not simply reproduce the interests of the powerful elite, as some would argue. If that were the case, criminal proceedings in the contentious episodes selected here would occur more often, lead to more convictions, and yield higher sentences. Prosecutions and convictions, however, are also not explained by a simple reference to the law and a straightforward application of its provisions, as legal positivists would have it. Were that so, profound changes in the interpretation and application of the rules would not be explicable. To analyze the process of criminalization more satisfactorily, I build upon the notion that law and politics should be seen as "distinct but interdependent" (Abel and Marsh 1994). Research in this spirit typically indicates the paradoxical workings of the law as both constraining and legitimizing for the state (Thompson 1975; Ron 1997). As McBarnet puts it, laws do not so much constrain judicial decisions as they constrain the *justification* for them (in Lacey and Wells 1998:16).

This tradition can be traced back to the so-called legal realists, a group of scholars in the early 20th century who emphasized the empirical study of law and were followed by the law and society movement and critical legal theorists, who focused on power hierarchies in society on the one hand, and law on the other (Tamanaha 2001). Placing this book within that approach, I understand the court as an institution that is continuously socially constructed and reified in the interaction of people (cf. Berger and Luckmann 1967). As legitimating mechanisms, courts and the claims they make need to be believed as "true." This capacity of truth-production is challenged in the episodes under examination here.

Instead of asking *whether* politics plays a role in these cases, this book focuses on *how* politics plays a role and what it means for the law, those who execute it, and their claims to objectivity and authority. It critically examines how the state constructs its courtrooms as the correct venue for dealing with the accusations leveled against defendants, that is, how the state turns criminal procedure into the legitimate (and only) avenue to respond to the actions of the challengers or defenders of the status quo. Prosecutorial narratives play a key role in drawing the imagined boundary between the political and the criminal justice arena, and thus give meaning to the "political" and the "criminal" in any given society. These narratives are construed and can be analyzed at the micro-level of single proceedings, trials, or even at the level of single documents, such as an indictment. Such analysis allows for enhanced understanding of a single case and can trace, for example, the patterns of interaction between prosecutor and defense lawyer in a particular trial, or gauge specific nuances in discursive take-up from one site to another by comparing two documents. The chosen unit of analysis to analyze processes of contentious criminalization in this book, however, is the episode. This allows for the observation of trends in prosecutorial narrative over longer periods of time, as well as trends in societal discursive mobilization and action. Such analysis thus enables inquiries about the relation between different criminal investigations, trials, legislative changes, societal mobilization, "criminalizable events" (Hulsman 1986) and subsequent prosecutorial discourse.

The research question was straightforward: in the course of a contentious episode, does a shift in the prosecutorial narrative occur, and if so, when (as a result of which processes and factors?), how (what changes in criminal doctrinal devices constitute that change?), and what narrative does the prosecutor adopt? This involves understanding what audience prosecutorial narrative addresses, which constituencies push this narrative in society, and what alternative narratives are silenced by it.

It is not my concern here to explore the dynamics within prosecutorial offices or engage with the personal considerations of individual prosecutors. Prosecutors cannot all be put in one box and the state is not a monolithic enterprise either. Prosecutors may act in contradiction to other state actors, such as judges or politicians. Migdal (2001:16) suggests conceptualizing the state as a "field of power marked by the use and threat of violence" and shaped by a combination of an image of a "coherent, controlling organization in a territory, which is a representation of the people bounded by that territory" and the "actual practices of its multiple parts." This book studies the practices of prosecutors as state actors who draw upon, defend or reproduce a particular image of the state and its relation to the people.

While prosecutorial errors, biases and flaws may be responsible for parts of the process of contentious criminalization, all prosecutors expressed a firm adherence to the rule of law, their responsibility toward the larger public, and the importance of democracy. Precisely because of that, I am interested in the structure and ideology with which prosecutors in liberal democracies inevitably work: the criminal law system and its ideology of liberal legalism. This system presupposes a functioning liberal democracy, a common public interest and a shared public order that should be defended. Each of the political struggles studied here, however, challenges exactly those assumptions.

In the cases in this book, prosecutors, police, juries, judges and even stenographers participate in imagining and producing the space in which the criminal justice logic, framework and discourse is accepted as the correct vocabulary for communication and interaction, in which the roles and identities of defendants, victims and law enforcers are given form. How are political motives brought into proceedings, ignored or rejected? How do political identities inevitably come to play a role because of certain prosecutorial choices, such as the prosecution of a collective? How does the structure of criminal law sometimes favor decontextualization and at other times require the construction of a pattern to put the harm in context? The complexity and unintended consequences of such choices in criminal prosecutions, as reflected in distinct episodes across three countries, are at the heart of this book.

Methodology for data collection and analysis

The fieldwork in Spain was conducted between January and June 2008, with a return visit in January 2010. Data collection in Chile took place between November 2002 and April 2003, as well as between March and May 2009. Research in the United States occurred between September and November 2007. The materials consisted of interviews, trial transcripts, judgments as well as newspapers, books and websites. Many materials were originally in Spanish. All translations in this book are mine.

In the conceptualization of criminal prosecutions as communicative acts, the book traces the trajectory of the prosecutorial narratives throughout each contentious episode. These narratives consist of the charging decisions as well as the evidentiary choices made. An overview of the criminal cases that were selected in order to analyze the trajectories of prosecutorial narratives can be found in my dissertation (Terwindt 2012:901–36). Collecting the relevant information required access to judicial databases, indictments, opening statements, witness examinations, closing arguments, verdicts, information from government websites, and public statements or press releases by prosecutors, public ministries, investigative agencies and police, as well as crime statistics.[3] In addition to a collection of "traces" of the prosecutorial narrative throughout the years, a deeper understanding of such traces was also sought by personal attendance at trials and interviews with prosecutors and investigative judges.[4] Limitations existed due to the lack of digitalization of judicial records in earlier years of the episodes, especially in Chile. Where online databases were insufficient, access to transcripts was obtained through court archives and contact with defense lawyers.

The prosecutorial narratives were compared with narratives put forward by challengers and defenders of the status quo. These (alternative) narratives were explored in written material, such as the numerous press declarations, newspaper interviews, books and public statements on websites in which many of the actors actively presented their narrative about events that were subjected to criminal prosecution, as well as incidents that, to their outrage, were not subjected to prosecution. Again, a deeper understanding of these narratives was sought in person. Semi-structured interviews were conducted with government representatives as well as business farmers and forestry companies in Chile; Mapuche activists and community members in Chile; left-nationalist activists in

---

3   A list with the legislation, indictments, trial transcripts, prosecutorial allegations, defense arguments and judgments which were used for analysis can be found in my dissertation (Terwindt 2012:792–95 for Spanish documents; 812–15 for Chilean documents; 829–31 for US documents). In sum, I conducted 125 interviews, attended 6 trials (25 trial days) and analyzed the trial transcripts and verdicts in 46 criminal proceedings.

4   Tilly (2007a:47) argues that in any empirical research you always need a theory embodying explanations of the evidence concerning that phenomenon. First, how does the phenomenon under investigation leave traces? Second, how can analysts elicit or observe those traces? Third, using those traces, how can analysts reconstruct specified attributes, elements, causes, or effects of the phenomenon?

the Basque Country; representatives of right-wing parties in Madrid; and animal rights activists in the United States. As it turned out that many of these actors actively mobilize with a claim to victimhood or in support of defendants in the criminal justice arena, further written "traces" were collected from those involved in criminal cases. These traces were complemented with semi-structured interviews with defendants, (former) prisoners, defense lawyers, public defenders, prisoner supporters, representatives of victim organizations, and lawyers for victim organizations.

Access to interviews was sometimes hindered by security concerns or distrust. For example, in the United States, the companies Huntingdon Life Sciences, Novartis, and Life Sciences Research refused to grant me an interview about the animal rights protests against their animal-testing businesses. They justified their refusal by citing security concerns, illustrating just how seriously they assess the threat posed by such protest activities. The FBI also turned down a request for an interview after having considered that they would not be able to disclose much information. In Chile, when I asked current landowners to speak with me about the criminal justice system's performance in cases related to the Mapuche conflict, I was invariably transferred to the lawyers working on their cases. This would have been helpful had the lawyers actually had authority to give me information. Instead of talking about law and criminal justice with landowners, I got to talk with their lawyers, who, as soon as I touched on more political questions, referred me to their bosses. The superficial separation, but intimate connectedness between law and politics was rarely more obvious than in this play of sending me in circles and avoiding the subject.

The prosecutorial narrative not only speaks by initiating criminal prosecutions, but also through silences, or a lack of prosecutions. This meant collecting traces of the entire pool of criminalizable events. The approach was to collect available information from official crime statistics and from reports by self-identified victims and their organizations, as well as lists provided by activists. The latter type of list was posted on the website Indymedia in 2008, for example, by an activist in the United States who wrote that at least 80 actions were claimed in the name of the Earth Liberation Front or Animal Liberation Front, or otherwise attributed to them. The username was "ELF supporter" and, in the introduction to the long list, the person bragged: "Something like 12 ELF activists ever have been arrested. Look at this list. Then tell me who's winning, pig" (ELF Supporter 2008).

It was not always easy to obtain information about incidents or crime statistics. It was, for example, difficult to get access to statistics on the number of criminal complaints filed by forestry companies in Chile. I asked one of the major forestry companies as well as the Governor of Malleco, in Chile, for their data on the criminal complaints that they had brought, respectively, and the results of these complaints (investigations, prosecutions, trials, convictions). While they confirmed having this data, in both cases they denied access to it. The reason given by forestry company Mininco was that it was too sensitive and could have a deleterious effect on their relations with the Public Ministry.

Given the significant differences between the countries under comparison, a note on the legal systems is warranted. The criminal law systems of Spain and Chile are highly similar, as they are both rooted in the continental law tradition. Both Spain and Chile have a Public Ministry which provides the necessary bureaucratic organization for the country's prosecutors and is in charge of developing the criminal policy. The US has a common law system, which includes, for example, the use of jury trials. While common law is known for the emphasis on case law, the US relies on statutes for its criminal law, which thus resembles the codification of continental law. A key difference between the traditions is the opportunity principle in common law systems that allows prosecutors discretion in their decision to prosecute, whereas continental prosecutors are guided by the so-called "legality principle" of mandatory prosecution.[5] However, this doctrinal contrast has lost much of its significance over time; by the 1990s, adaptations in the systems had largely eroded the differences in practice (Kyprianou 2008:16). Even though the systems have different features, analysts of comparative criminal law have emphasized more similarities than differences between common law and continental law (Vercher 1991:14; Fletcher 2007). Most relevant for the approach taken here is the shared basis of Enlightenment values and the philosophy of liberalism and the rule of law that underlies these criminal justice systems (cf. Vercher 1991:278).

Questioning the very things that lawyers often take for granted, this research is far more anthropological than it is legal. It does, however, engage closely with criminal law doctrine and legal documents, which are all too often shunned by anthropologists, as such texts are assumed to be

---

5   This principle "commands that every case in which there is enough evidence and in which no legal hindrances prohibit prosecution has to be brought to court" (Kyprianou 2008:14).

too impenetrable for "outsiders," perpetuating the convenient myth that law should be left to lawyers. The concern with the prosecutorial production of reality reflects an interest in describing powerful elites as much as the powerless, in line with the "studying up" approach to create ethnographic studies of sites of power as advocated by Gusterson (1997). At the same time, the anthropological approach is relevant to lawyers, legal scholars and particularly prosecutors, as the findings in this study pertain directly to their daily practices and contribute to a better understanding of the ways in which law works.

Chapter overview

This book consists of two parts. The first part – "Law, Politics and Legitimacy in Liberal Democracies" – covers the complexity of the contentious episodes, the challenges for prosecutors who operate in such a demanding setting, and the mobilization of interest groups attempting to influence the prosecutorial narrative. Chapter 2 traces decisions by certain groups to take justice into their own hands, while openly challenging democratic proceedings and the state's monopoly on the legitimate use of force. Chapter 3 fleshes out in more detail the construction of the prosecutorial narrative and distinguishes between a decontextualized approach assumed to be the default mode and the politicization that occurs once this default is replaced with a narrative that emphasizes and reframes the context in which criminalizable events occur. Such shifts in the application and framing of context primarily serve to enable prosecutors to respond to the demand by targets of protests to (re)establish order by punishing lawbreakers. Chapter 4 highlights the role played by those claiming victimhood, who seek strong alliances to increase pressure on the state to take their interests seriously, in turn influencing prosecutorial narrative. Finally, chapter 5 analyzes mobilization by supporters of those facing criminal prosecutions, against perceived undue state repression and their attempts to challenge the state's definition of their protest actions as crime.

The second part of the book – "When Prosecutors Respond: Narratives in Action" – highlights specific instances in which prosecutorial narratives in each of the examined episodes shifted in response to discursive mobilization efforts. Chapter 6 analyzes the significant change throughout the 1990s in Spanish prosecutors' conception of ETA in relation to its network of sympathizers from the Basque left-nationalist movement. By redefining the terrorist organization as a network, prosecutors enabled the rounding-up of many activists in Basque left-nationalist groups, both social and political, that previously remained outside the purview of the criminal justice system. A new law passed in 2000 in Spain made it possible to prosecute approval or praise of ETA militants as "glorification of terrorism" or the "humiliation" of ETA's victims. Chapter 7 describes how this led to a flurry of legal complaints in which the criminality of common practices of the left-nationalist movement in the Basque Country came to be negotiated in courts.

Chapter 8 describes how Chilean prosecutors have vacillated between lenience and harshness in their response to Mapuche protests, at times staying silent and at other times applying anti-terrorism legislation. This reflects the challenge of dealing with historical grievances that many, both in Chile and internationally, recognize to be legitimate, while the government fails to offer satisfactory solutions in the political arena. Chapter 9 analyzes how Chilean prosecutors respond to allegations of racism and repression of "the Mapuche people" by denying that certain Mapuche defendants "really" represent the Mapuche people, even going so far as to accuse some of "abusing" their identity. These cases show how prosecutors in Chile get drawn into contestation over identity politics, as their courtroom narratives become part of a broader societal conversation on citizenship and minority rights.

Chapter 10 turns to the emergence of the concept of "eco-terrorism" pushed by a coalition of so-called "animal enterprises" and lobby groups like the Center for the Defense of Free Enterprise as the foundation for contentious criminal cases in the 2000s in the United States. It highlights how the narrative primarily concerns perceived danger and risks of ideological radicalization, pushing the FBI to turn to proactive investigations of anarchist-leaning animal rights and environmentalist movements in the United States and the subsequent shift among prosecutors to indicting activists under conspiracy charges. Chapter 11 examines the case against activists of a campaign called "Stop Huntingdon Animal Cruelty" (SHAC) and how the prosecutor narrated a pattern in order to hold known defendants responsible for criminal acts committed by unknown others. The prosecutorial narrative legitimized the charges by drawing a line between an "educational campaign" and criminal "intimidation."

The concluding chapter returns to the question of how prosecutors deal with the challenge of conducting criminal prosecutions that balance the state's need to punish those transgressing existing laws, while having their decisions to prosecute viewed as legitimate by all relevant constituencies, including the defendants and their sympathizers. Are prosecutors in liberal democracies making their decisions to prosecute or not dependent on popular support (and if so, how)? This book demonstrates that prosecutors do indeed engage with the narratives proposed by partisan interest groups. They respond to public pressures to obtain convictions and then seek to justify their prosecutions, focusing on those audiences whose approval they deem important. This is not a failure on the part of particular prosecutors, but built into the discursive nature of the application of law and the prevalent belief in liberal democracies that order is established through punishment resulting from criminal prosecutions, which must be viewed as legitimate. The book thus goes beyond diagnosing an incidental "gap" between ideal and practice. It argues that the contentious processes described in the construction and functioning of prosecutorial narrative are built into the very premise of the rule of law.

Resorting to the criminal justice system to solve socio-political problems in democracies is all too common, despite the structural inability of the liberal legalist framework to address the complexities inherent in long-running conflicts on which no clear consensus exists. In liberal legalism, criminal law is designed to reduce complex situations to concrete acts committed by single perpetrators against one or more specific victims. Addressing this tension head on, this book uses in-depth ethnographic material to make an important theoretical contribution to understanding protest, prosecution and the politics of contentious criminalization in liberal democracies. Because crime is not a pre-given category and because liberal legalism is not necessarily able to provide substantive as opposed to procedural justice, criminal proceedings become an important arena for collective claim-making, polarization and conflict escalation, sparking a potentially infinite reframing of events and innovation of criminal vocabulary.

PART I

LAW, POLITICS AND LEGITIMACY
IN LIBERAL DEMOCRACIES

2

When Groups Take Justice into Their Own Hands

> We wanted justice and we gained the rule of law.
>
> (East German artist Bärbel Bohley on the
> reunification of Germany; *Economist* 2010: 91)

The dilemma of establishing order while maintaining legitimacy

Liberal democracies share a basis in the rule of law and the notion that citizens have a say in influencing the legislation that governs their conduct. In a rule of law, the exercise of power by state authorities and private individuals is subordinated to well-defined and established laws. In his essay "What Is the Rule of Law and Why Is It So Important?," legal scholar Sellers (2014:4) distinguishes between legalistic "rule *by* law" and the "rule of law." Whereas mere legalism can actually serve arbitrary power when one person or faction uses positive law to impose their will, the rule of law is always supposed to serve the common good of society as a whole. Given that people may disagree about the common good, it is important how laws are enacted, interpreted and implemented. In a democracy, government means "rule by the people," while "there is some form of *political equality* among the people" (Held 1996:1, emphasis in original).

In liberal democracies, then, people have access to democratic debate or legal proceedings in order to address private disputes and public grievances. Even if this does not always lead to the desired outcome, people may be satisfied with having had their chance in court or parliament according to procedures that are recognized as fair and equally accessible for all. Though designed to arrive at just resolutions through clarity of laws and procedural consistency, in and of itself legal reform or private adjudication do not necessarily ensure (substantive) justice. When prevailing laws or their particular application are deemed by those subject to them to be unjust, their enforcement may be perceived as problematic. In Chile, a member of a Mapuche community explained their demands for land reform, noting: "We did not make these laws [granting land to foreign immigrants]; we did not participate in the process" (Interview C-22).

Even democratic societies can be deeply divided on key questions of governance, such as the independence of a portion of the country, the use and ownership of natural resources, or the extent of minority rights. Yet, the formal procedural tools of liberal democracies for resolving political conflict – parliamentary deliberation, legislative reform, round-table negotiation, constitutional amendment, and legal adjudication through civil lawsuits – may fail to deliver a solution that adequately meets everyone's needs and interests. Those unhappy with the status quo may decide that the stakes are too high or urgent to abide by such slow and uncertain procedures. Instead, they may take justice into their own hands, bringing their grievances to the street in public forms of protest or organizing in underground resistance movements. Their actions may include anything from public rallies to educational campaigns, the physical occupation of buildings or lands, symbolic or strategic property destruction, and even killings in the context of armed struggle. While assassinations and property destruction are among the most notorious forms of illegal protest action, many other protest activities have also been challenged through criminal prosecution. Examples covered in this book include offering fugitives a place to sleep, writing press communiqués, organizing honoring ceremonies for ex-prisoners, making alternative national identity cards, spray-painting shops or houses, releasing animals from factory farms and research facilities, and shouting offensive slogans.

To justify illegal protest activities, challengers of the status quo claimed the legitimacy of their grievances, argued the urgency of their actions, and cited the deficiencies of existing legal avenues for resolution. Many liberal democracies have rich histories of activists demanding rights through civil disobedience (the intentional transgression of laws deemed to be unjust, while accepting any subsequent criminal proceeding against them). Rosa Parks refusing to give up her seat to a white passenger on a Montgomery bus despite prevailing racial segregation laws in the United States is but one famous example. It has been argued, though, that civil disobedience only serves to challenge "minor and easily correctable," not "pervasive and systematic" injustices (Duff 2017:497). Thus, struggles about "deep political disagreement" (2017:497) were almost always accompanied with protest tactics that went beyond civil disobedience. This is how slavery and racial segregation were questioned and how women won the right to vote.

In the episodes studied here, some actors carried out illegal protest activities, including the use of arms to achieve their goals, guided by the belief that the ends justify the means. A Chilean supporter of Mapuche demands for land restitution accused of burning a truck on the highway emphasized this point in relation to having exhausted legal avenues for change: "How many years have we been demonstrating? [...] It has already been 150 years. For some, the violence doesn't do anything, but I think that is because we are too few [doing such actions]" (Interview 2009, C-63). Following a similar logic, in July 2009, the Mapuche organization Coordinadora Arauco Malleco (CAM) publicly claimed an attack on a bus demanding the "purchase and transmission of the terrains seized by señor Jorge Luchsinger to the Mapuche community Yeupeko-Filkun. Without any quick response to our demands, we will radicalize our actions" (Neira 2009).

Open justifications of private violence in protest or self-defense, as well as declarations of armed struggle, challenge the state's monopoly on the legitimate use of force. Liberal democracies assume the existence of a social contract as an "accepted legitimating myth" (Engle 2008), whereby citizens give up their right to private violence in exchange for state protection. If the government does not abuse its position by repressing the population, the resulting pacification is supposed to bolster its legitimacy. However, the fiction of the social contract can only be upheld and lead to continuing obedience as long as the government fulfills its obligation to provide security. People who feel threatened by disruptive protest actions often call upon the state to protect them and punish the perceived wrongdoers. For example, a Chilean senator explicitly argued: "Facing these types of conflicts, State intervention is logical and demandable, as the State has the legitimate use of force at its disposal and is the guarantor of the rule of law. The absence of the State in the solution of this conflict [...] justifies self-protection, which is the basis of barbarity" (Comisión de Constitución 2003:22).

Impunity for criminals poses a problem for liberal democratic states. A widespread belief that the state allows crimes to be committed with no consequences implies that the state is failing to uphold its end of the bargain to protect those under its authority. When targets of social protest feel truly unsafe, they may take their protection into their own hands, leading to additional illegal conduct. For example, in Spain in the 1980s, private citizens formed right-wing commando units like the Basque-Spanish Batallón Vasco Español and Triple A to target and kill presumed ETA militants. In Chile, private landowners founded a retaliation commando unit to protect against harassment by Mapuche activists.

In cases where procedural justice fails to provide substantive justice, liberal democracies that base their power on popular sovereignty and an ideology of individual liberty rely on public protest and civil disobedience to resist oppression, overturn unjust laws and renegotiate the social contract. How does the liberal state maintain order and retain its legitimacy during such a process? How does it satisfy the demands of those seeking state protection from protesters, without further stirring up discontent and alienation among the protesters and their constituencies? The criminal prosecutions that are the subject of this book lie squarely within this quandary of balancing the simultaneous and at times competing interests of "order" and "legitimacy" during such political struggles in liberal democracies. What do prosecutors tasked with initiating criminal proceedings in the public interest do when the public is divided and interest groups advocate for radically different ways to apply the law? This chapter illustrates this dilemma in the context of the contentious episodes in Spain, Chile and the United States that form the basis of this book.

Basque separatists challenge the Spanish state

Since its transition to a democracy in 1978, the Spanish state has faced a constant challenge to its sovereignty from the population of the Basque Country (Euskadi or Euskal Herria), where popular support for independence has been significant and constant. After the death of Franco, who ruled Spain as a one-party military dictatorship from 1939 to 1975, the new government set out to build liberal democratic institutions. At the same time, specific sectors of the Basque Country demanded independence from Spain, including the organization Euskadi Ta Askatasuna (Basque Homeland and Liberty, or ETA), which had begun an armed struggle for independence under Franco. ETA emerged in 1959 as a student group that sought more radical resistance than that offered by the moderate Basque Nationalist Party (Partido Nacional Vasco, PNV). As part of its armed struggle for independence, ETA waged its most deadly campaign in the early 1980s – it killed 92 people, mostly Civil Guards, in 1980 alone. During the 1980s, few people in the Basque Country openly criticized ETA's armed struggle. At the same time, paramilitary violence in retaliation for ETA attacks also received public support. The 1990s saw fewer deaths overall, but ETA's killings were often more spectacular, targeting high-level politicians, journalists and judges.

The goal of ETA and the broader Basque left-nationalist movement is a free and socialist Basque Country. Basque self-determination in this sense is incompatible with the Spanish Constitution, which claims Spain to be united and indivisible. Even the proposal for a referendum in the Basque Country to decide on the matter is perceived as a strong challenge to Spanish unity, as it would imply that the Basque people alone could decide the matter. In 2008, the Constitutional Court ruled that a referendum planned by the president of the Basque Country was unconstitutional and thus illegal. One Basque left-nationalist activist commented upon this decision: "We don't even have the right to lose. They say that we will lose. OK, we'd like to see that. Democracy means that everyone can try to persuade the people" (field notes, June 2008). Whereas many moderate Basque nationalists have long accepted a certain degree of autonomy instead of total independence, left-nationalist activists have generally regarded the Spanish state and its claim to govern the Basque Country as illegitimate. Refusing to participate in the collective imagining of the nation-state, they never refer to "Spain," but always to "the Spanish state."

The Autonomy Statute of 1979 clarified the relationship between the Basque Country and the Spanish state, including the former's new autonomous competencies, such as the Basque police, the Ertzaintza. Throughout the 1980s, ETA's armed struggle put the moderately nationalist PNV in a better negotiating position regarding the implementation of these rights in the Basque Country. As the Basque Country became more autonomous in practice and, for example, the Basque language came to be promoted by governmental institutions, ETA's discourse about the need for an armed struggle became less convincing. At the same time, Basque nationalists of all stripes continued to criticize the Spanish state's slow process of deferring the autonomous competencies granted to the Basque Country under the statute.

For decades, the Spanish state did a poor job establishing its legitimacy in relation to Basque nationalist protest and its military struggle against ETA. Its attempts to maintain "order" were perceived as unjust repression of the Basque people as a whole, while at the same time, ETA continued its violent campaigns. To complicate matters, the Spanish state also faced a number of challenges to its liberal democratic framework from groups beyond those demanding Basque independence. In 1981, General Antonio Tejero Molina attempted a military coup and almost succeeded, providing a strong incentive for the government in those years to appease right-wing concerns for the unity of Spain – possibly for this reason several right-wing paramilitary groups were not reined in.

During the first years of the transition to democracy, the Batallón Vasco Espanol (the Basque-Spanish Battalion) and "Triple A" (Apostolic Anti-communist Alliance) engaged in the killing of suspected ETA members and people close to ETA. From 1979 until 1987, an estimated 80 persons were killed by these extremist right-wing groups (Calleja and Sánchez-Cuenca 2006:97). The Spanish government conveniently labeled these groups "uncontrollable" (for example, MA 1978:70). Only in the 1990s were criminal prosecutions pushed through against the paramilitary group "GAL" (Grupos Antiterroristas de Liberación or Anti-terrorist Groups of Liberation). The judicial investigations revealed that the Spanish government was itself deeply involved in the so-called "Dirty War" against ETA: between 1983 and 1987, GAL killed 27 people, including the head of the political party Herri Batasuna (Popular Unity), torturing several others. Only 14 of those killed actually belonged to ETA (Calleja and Sánchez-Cuenca 2006:97).

In 1988, an alliance forged by a treaty known as the "Ajuria Enea Pact," signed by the major Spanish and Basque political parties, replaced the common framing of the dispute as "Basque nationalists versus Spanish parties" with an alliance of "democrats versus terrorists." This new framing led to the isolation of the left-nationalist political party Herri Batasuna for its refusal to condemn ETA's violence. While the government defined ETA's actions as terrorism and prosecuted ETA militants accordingly, ETA's popular support was high enough and its capacity to wreak havoc significant enough that the Spanish government participated in three formal attempts to negotiate with the group, in 1989, 1998 and 2006. For decades, these negotiations failed.

Throughout the years, many left-nationalist activists have maintained a "state of exception" discourse to justify ETA's use of violence, reasoning that as long as there was neither democracy nor the rule of law, the armed struggle remained justified as a defense against oppression. For example, since the banning of the Batasuna party (successor to Herry Batasuna) in 2003, left-nationalists argued that the legal means to fight for their political project had been taken away. ETA and its sympathizers often used war arguments to justify ETA actions, arguing that attacks were done in defense or retaliation, and against military targets. They also held that the state was implicated in terrorism, not ETA, as ETA's attacks were not indiscriminate, but targeted specific persons.

Continued support for ETA's armed struggle, combined with the use of violence by private paramilitary groups and torture of suspected ETA members by state agents, posed a severe challenge to the young Spanish democracy and its legal institutions. Indeed, the erosion of legitimacy of state institutions, and particularly the criminal justice system, has been such that interviewees on all sides perceived the criminal justice system to be partial and failing. "There is no criminal justice system here," said a businessman when I told him the subject of my research (Interview S-31). He was forced to pay ETA's "revolutionary tax" for years and claimed: "We are the losers, we are the poor bastards [*los pringados*]." Sympathizers with ETA in the Basque Country, in turn, have mobilized weekly demonstrations for decades calling for attention to the suffering of Basque "political prisoners" and deaths they attribute to the Spanish state.

Within this context, prosecutors have faced a number of challenges in their role of upholding the public interest. In 1993, the Spanish Attorney General urged restraint regarding criminal prosecutions of "verbal manifestations" in support of ETA and its actions. He wrote that prosecutors must act with "great prudence and flexibility [...] having to react penally only against conduct with especially grave and intolerable results, because experience has shown that 'hyper-criminalization' in this terrain usually produces effects contrary to those intended" (MA 1993:406). Indeed, actions of *kale borroka* (street struggle by Basque youth) were at times a response to perceived repression. Similarly, in a newspaper interview in 2007, ETA explicitly justified its actions as a response to repressive criminal justice measures:

> Don't attack Euskal Herria. Don't pass measures such as the Parot doctrine to target Basque political prisoners. Don't prosecute and imprison Basques like Iñaki de Juana. The trials of large numbers of Basque youths, and so on and so forth, are all further examples of the exceptional state of affairs in our country. Let all this stop and ETA will have no need to react. (*Gara* 2007)

While prosecutors have thus sought not to be overzealous in their prosecution, they have also sought to ward off allegations of fostering impunity. Recognizing the danger of such criticism, the Spanish Attorney General wrote in the Annual Report of 2007:

The permanent criticism on the actuation of the judicial organs and the prosecutor's office in the struggle against terrorism, with unfounded accusations of giving up (*césion*), passivity and/or inactivity, have contributed to creating a climate of social tension and a lack of confidence in the normal functioning of the institutions. (MA 2007:161)

In an interview in 2008, the chief prosecutor at the Audiencia Nacional recognized this "double criticism," where victims of ETA claimed that the state did not do enough to destroy terrorism and left-nationalist defendants argued that they were persecuted for their ideas. He defended his role as a prosecutor to "apply the law," which in a constitutional state (*estado de derecho*), he pointed out, "also includes respecting the rights and guarantees to citizens [...] including the rights of the worst terrorists" (Interview S-21). He said that "justice is based in the application of the law" (Interview S-21). His emphasis on procedural justice echoed not only the precepts of liberal legalism, but also reflected the far more comfortable position of the Spanish judicial system in 2008, shortly before the defeat of ETA. He refused to have any sympathy for "Guantánamo Bay-like" practices of counter-terrorism. At the same time, he did not fear the possibly counter-productive effects of hyper-criminalization, which had been present during the 1980s and 1990s. In 2011, ETA conceded and laid down its arms, and in March 2018 publicly apologized to its victims. This step was hailed by the Spanish government as proof that ETA had been defeated "with the weapons of democracy and the strength of the rule of law" (Jones 2018). A month later, ETA announced it had dissolved all of its structures, while emphasizing that the political conflict remains: "This decision ends ETA's 60-year historical cycle [...] But it does not bring an end to the conflict between the Basque homeland and Spain and France. The conflict did not begin with ETA and will not end with its dissolution" (Jones 2018).

Mapuche territorial claims in Chile

The Mapuche people are the largest indigenous group in Chile and live in the south of the country, predominantly in the 8th, 9th and 10th Regions. The 9th Region is also known as the Araucanía region after the large Araucaria tree which grows there. Temuco is the region's capital and informally understood as the main Mapuche urban center. The so-called "Mapuche conflict" has turned into a major national concern over the past three decades, often making the headlines of national newspapers. It has been visible in a large number of concrete disputes over local and regional development projects, including the building of an airport, waste dumps, a viaduct, hydroelectric dams, a coastal highway and a paper factory, as well as further development of the salmon industry and expansion of forestry plantations. The larger label (and misnomer) "Mapuche conflict" lumps together a host of different disputes and incidents involving different actors, targets and motivations, thereby assuming that, instead of questioning whether, they constitute one phenomenon with one explanation. Mapuche activists further argue that this terminology perpetuates the notion that Mapuches are the problem and that they are to blame. Instead, they prefer to call the conflict the "forestry conflict" or "territorial conflict." Still, most actors refer to the "Mapuche conflict," which is also the label adopted by prosecutors.

The Mapuche movement, as it is called in Chile, is a loose network of urban and rural organizations, as well as community leaders and members who organize on the basis of Mapuche identity to make demands, such as calling for land restitution. Activists in the Mapuche movement seek recognition for the Mapuche culture and language and raise awareness regarding socioeconomic inequality, demands for more autonomy, and claims for the restitution of lands taken from the Mapuches at the end of the 19th century. Mapuche activists also oppose the detrimental effects of commercial tree plantations, including erosion, water pollution through pesticides, the disappearance of medicinal plants, a decrease in groundwater reserves, and the reduction of biodiversity (Seguel 2002). In summer, the government has had to ship water into some Mapuche communities, due to extreme water shortages caused by nearby plantations (Richards 2010:68).

In contrast to indigenous peoples in other parts of Latin America, the Mapuche people were never conquered by the Spaniards. After Chile's independence struggle against the Spanish Crown in 1810, the territory beneath the Bío Bío River remained in the hands of the Mapuches. In 1866, the Chilean state considered this unacceptable and, after 15 years of fighting, the Chilean army defeated the Mapuches in 1881 (Bengoa 2002 [1999]:45) in what has come to be known as the "Pacification of the Araucanía." The Chilean state seized Mapuche lands and forcibly transferred the Mapuche people to smaller properties called *reducciones* (reservations). The lands seized after the "pacification" were sold to immigrants from Europe, who engaged in intensive agriculture. In total, the reduced Mapuche lands constituted only 6.4 percent of their original territory (Richards 2010:62). The land title for these reservations was called a *título de merced*, a specific legal construction assigned solely to Mapuche communities. The sale of these titles was officially prohibited (Bengoa 2002 [1999]:164), but non-Mapuche farmers frequently obtained parts of such lands through fraudulent interpretations of the legal titles (2002:69) or plain threats and pressure (Barrera 1999:5). Since the Mapuche were forced into reservations, Mapuche activists have pressed for land reforms in Chile in various ways. Already, between the 1930s and 1970s, as well as in the 1980s, 1990s and 2010s, they tried using available legal avenues to pursue their land claims, but often to no avail. Mapuche communities have filed numerous civil lawsuits based on reservation land titles, but these lawsuits take many years and have frequently ended with negative results (Correa et al. 2005:63). Land reforms granted by Presidents Eduardo Frei (1964–70) and Salvador Allende (1970–73) were subsequently reversed by General Pinochet in the period of "counter-reform" (1973–89) (Correa et al. 2005).

After the 1989 referendum that ousted the dictator Pinochet, a new Indigenous Act and official mechanism for land reform led to high expectations of finally settling Mapuche communities' long-standing demands for the return of usurped lands. In the Indigenous Act, however, only reservations that had been granted to the Mapuches *after* the Pacification of the Araucanía and subsequently usurped were considered to be "indigenous" and up for redistribution (Richards 2010:68). Mapuche "ancestral lands" were explicitly excluded from the Fund for Land and Water, established to purchase land for Mapuche communities (Toledo 2007:260).[1] Complicating matters, the specialized government organ, CONADI (Corporación Nacional de Desarrollo Indígena or National Board for Indigenous Development), was only mandated to buy a piece of land for transfer to Mapuche communities if the owner agreed to sell. In addition to this catch, since its establishment CONADI has been notoriously underfunded and communities have criticized alternative substitute land parcels for not being of the same quality of the land taken from them. Mapuches expected real change from the new democratic governments, but were quickly disillusioned. For example, despite the new recognition for their land claims, in various

---

1   According to the Indigenous Act, the fund can buy lands for communities or individuals that do not own sufficient land (Art. 20a) or for communities that have a claim on land which is based on a *título de merced* or another state (judicial) decision that grants a land title to the indigenous community (Art. 20b).

court verdicts, laws on private property or electricity have been privileged over the rights in the Indigenous Act (Orellana 2005).

In 2006, the Chilean Centro de Estudios Públicos (CEP, Center for Public Studies), inquired in a national survey: "If we look at the history, do you think that the country should offer compensation to the Mapuche?" The vast majority of participants – 91 percent of the Mapuches and 79 percent of non-Mapuches – answered "yes" (CEP 2006:48). Even prosecutors and landowners often recognize the legitimacy of their land claims. "The demands may be just, but they [Mapuche activists] have to do it through political channels. Violence is against the democracy," said one of the prosecutors (Interview 2003, C-11). "Many of them [Mapuche activists] are right in their claims," said also a lawyer who works for SOFO (La Sociedad de Fomento Agrícola y Ganadera de la Región de la Araucanía) the association of Chilean commercial farmers, "but that does not justify the means they use. If you open that Pandora's box, then even Bin Laden could become justified in sending those planes" (Interview 2009, C-42). In line with the liberal separation between ends and means, surveys in Chile demonstrate simultaneous support for the Mapuche claims *and* for harsher measures against activists (Richards 2010:77).

Since the first disappointments in the 1990s, Mapuche mobilized and their protests have ranged from symbolic land occupations to the use of arson as a tool to pressure landowners into selling their lands to CONADI. In some of the places where conflict has erupted, with land occupations and arson, government officials have engaged in negotiations with Mapuche communities, resulting in the communities achieving land restitution. Non-Mapuche landowners have been quick to point out that, by granting lands to communities that were able to make media headlines, the state has made violence effective (Interview 2003, C-17). In response to a perceived lack of state protection for their properties, forestry companies operating on lands contested by Mapuche activists have employed private security companies to guard their plantations. Private landowners, however, often live on their property and have claimed they suffer from daily harassment. One farmer family has been living with constant police protection, who take the children to school and pick them up again. The children have been threatened and harassed and their father and grandfather were called "murderers" in graffiti in the village (Interview 2009, C-43).

In 1999, the forestry council CORMA (Corporación Chilena de la Madera) warned the government that private estate owners "can find themselves obliged to employ the means that they esteem convenient"

(CORMA 1999b). Indeed, in 2001, the major daily Chilean newspaper *El Mercurio* reported that private landowners had shot at Mapuches, warning the authorities who were considered to be too passive that "it's a miracle that no indigenous person has died yet." Private landowners were also reported to have claimed their readiness to defend their estates by any means necessary. With references to the Agrarian Reform in the early 1970s, a landowner said that "they [Mapuche] know that we defend ourselves well. If they want to verify [this], then they will find out" (Barria 2001). On 11 June 2005, the foundation of a paramilitary group was announced in an anonymous phone call to a local newspaper in Temuco:

> We are ready to start a reprisal against the indigenous gentlemen, in defense of the farmers, the forestry companies and the hydro-electric companies ... [g]iven that the Government has done absolutely nothing to stop the violent community members nor guaranteed the security of the farmers [...] Because of this, we communicate our foundation, to go in support of those that are trampled upon, we have the means and the people in the 8th and 9th Region and won't hesitate to get even with the Mapuche terrorists, and Chileans and foreigners who support this subversion. (Anonymous caller, cited in Cayuqueo 2005a:7)

Private landowners in Chile complained that the state failed to deliver the security and protection promised to them in the social contract. Simultaneously, Mapuche activists argued that the state used its monopoly on the use of force to arbitrarily repress Mapuches.

In 2016, the Chilean government called for an official dialogue with a number of civil society actors to make a diagnosis of the conflict. The leader of Mapuche organization CAM rejected the offer for dialogue, arguing that the framework was not right. Instead, he expressed willingness to negotiate if there was the possibility of a real political agreement, such as in the colonial era, when the Spanish Crown signed treaties with the Mapuche people. In a newspaper interview, he openly defended the use of violence in the Mapuche struggle for autonomy on the basis of a revolutionary ethics, targeting only the forestry industry and hydroelectrics, while denying that individual landowning farmers would be direct enemies. He addressed the government: "I invite the government to dialogue before the conflict escalates even more in confrontation" (Cayuqueo 2016). Earlier that year, a television channel was allowed to film CAM and its armed cells for the first time since its foundation in

1998, showing the capacity and willingness of its *guerreros* to continue acts of sabotage and occupations to reclaim territory and disputing the state's definition of such actions as violence or crimes (Informe Especial 2016). At the same time as CAM was escalating its demand for more autonomy, a 2016 survey by the CEP showed that 70–75 percent of Mapuches want to integrate more into Chilean society, whereas only 21–26 percent of those interviewed want more autonomy.[2]

Constant protest and discursive mobilization in the criminal justice arena related to the "Mapuche conflict" has created a challenging environment for prosecutors in Chile. They received letters from an international organization demanding that the indictments against Mapuches be dropped (WATU Acción Indigena 1997), while an advertisement in the newspaper *El Mercurio* (see Toledo 2007:282) called for anti-terrorism legislation to be applied. Prosecutors have also had difficulty finding witnesses willing to testify and learned that even if they secure convictions in a particular case against Mapuche activists, broader Mapuche mobilization efforts will continue undeterred. Conviction rates regarding incursions into disputed estates have typically remained low, engendering harsh criticism from current landowners. Discontent with the performance of the criminal justice system even led a right-wing senator to file an official complaint in 2006, requesting the removal of the regional prosecutor of Araucanía. At the same time, Mapuche defendants have continued to claim they are treated unjustly and are "political prisoners." Landowners who want attacks on their property to stop have claimed that the rule of law obliges the state to protect them, while also criticizing the rule of law for providing defendants with too many rights that ultimately hamper convictions. Mapuche activists, conversely, have challenged the rule of law by insisting on the legitimacy of older Spanish–Mapuche treaties and rejecting Chilean legal jurisdiction and land titles, as well as through their active support for prisoners and fugitives, refusing to adopt the condemnatory attitude that the state and its criminal prosecutions prescribe.

Environmental and animal rights protest in the United States

Moderate claims for animal welfare and nature conservation have long enjoyed widespread popular support within American society. Conservationism was given a big boost early on by President Theodore Roosevelt,

---

2   See: www.cepchile.cl/cep/site/edic/base/port/encuestacep.html

who introduced the national park system at the beginning of the 1900s. By the late 1970s, however, a growing group of environmental activists began to reject the prevailing model of conservation for its prioritization of human activities like recreation, tourism and hunting over animal rights and wilderness. In their view, wilderness should not be reduced to scenery, animals to meat, or minerals to resources. For most of the American population, though, such views are considered radical and pose a potential threat to the American way of life as they fundamentally overturn the accepted relationship between humans and nature. Radical environmental activists' claim that animals and nature deserve a voice in political decision-making also challenges American democracy. The notion of "animal rights" remains highly controversial as it is at odds with the ideological basis of liberal doctrine which presumes a distinction between humans and animals (speciesism).

Protest actions by environmental and animal rights activists in the United States challenge the daily practices of individuals, companies and organizations that use animals and the earth for human purposes and profit. In their campaigns, radical activists target a wide range of entities, including pharmaceutical companies, logging firms, biomedical researchers, animal-testing facilities, agribusinesses, the meat industry, sport hunters, circuses, ski resorts, SUV (sport utility vehicle) car dealerships and fur farms, among others. The list is long. These targets, in turn, generally defend the legitimacy of their activities as in the best interests of society. For example, according to a scientist, "[r]esponsible use of animals in research aimed at improving the health and welfare of the mentally ill is the right thing to do, and we will continue because we have a moral responsibility to society to use our skills for the betterment of the world" (*Daily Mail* Reporter 2010). In contrast, self-proclaimed "eco-warrior" and founder of the organization Earth First! Dave Foreman wrote:

> The ecologist Raymond Dasmann says that World War III has already begun, and that it is the war of industrial humans against the Earth. He is correct. All of us are warriors on one side or another in this war; there are no sidelines, there are no civilians. Ours is the last generation that will have the choice of wilderness, clean air, abundant wildlife, and expansive forests. The crisis *is* severe. (1991)

In defense of animals and nature, activists have made use of lawsuits, asked for court injunctions and engaged in undercover investigations to reveal violations of the law in places like laboratories or mink farms. Where the law fails to protect nature or animals, activists have attempted to influence public opinion by leafleting and demonstrating, as well as offensive messaging, such as yelling "puppy killer" or using red spray-paint – to signify the blood of animals – on fur clothing retailers and butcher shops. On other occasions, activists have engaged in direct action such as road blockades or sabotage. Sometimes they have smashed laboratory equipment used by vivisectionists, rammed whaling vessels or spiked trees, a process of driving nails into tree trunks to prevent them from being cut. For example, in 1989, activists broke into a vivisection lab at Texas Tech University to release animals, arguing that there was no point in alerting the authorities to the "cruelty" ongoing during the experiments, because the federal Animal Welfare Act did not cover animals during experiments; there was not even a requirement to use anesthesia (Scarce 2006:124–5).

Radical environmental activists' emphasis on urgent action, rejection of compromises, and conviction that trees and the lives of animals should be placed above prevailing US laws and the current wish of the majority of the population challenges the functioning of American democracy. One activist argued in his defense that "the people would want this [actions of animal liberation] if they knew," and criticized the lack of transparency in the meat industry and the fact that slaughterhouses and laboratories are always and purposefully hidden in buildings without windows (Interview US-15). Another activist told of her frustration with democratic avenues for addressing her concerns when a state governor vetoed a decision to save a piece of nature that had been passed by the majority of the state's Congress, using the argument that the impact would be economically crippling. He thus annulled the democratic victory fought for by the activists (Interview US-16).

Taking their ethical guidance from philosophy on animal rights and the environment, radical US eco-activists construe their own rules to guide their decisions. They openly challenge the legal system by questioning the premise that they should strictly obey existing laws they consider to be unjust. They defend their actions, including property damage, as civil disobedience in the American liberal democratic tradition, citing quintessential American examples like the Boston Tea Party and the anti-slavery Underground Railroad (Cook 2006; Scarce 2006:74). Activists emphasize, however, that law-breaking for their political goals is not just a carte blanche to do anything that would be most effective. For example, the

Animal Liberation Front (ALF) has formulated guidelines to which everyone who wants to claim an action in its name must abide:

1. TO liberate animals from places of abuse, i.e. laboratories, factory farms, fur farms, etc, and place them in good homes where they may live out their natural lives, free from suffering.
2. TO inflict economic damage to those who profit from the misery and exploitation of animals.
3. TO reveal the horror and atrocities committed against animals behind locked doors, by performing non-violent direct actions and liberations.
4. TO take all necessary precautions against harming any animal, human and non-human.
5. TO analyze the ramifications of all proposed actions, and never apply generalizations when specific information is available. (ALF 2011a)

Within the environmental movement, there tends to be widespread popular support for "compromising" goals, such as improving animal welfare and basic nature conservation, whereas there is far less public support for "radical" goals, such as demanding animal rights and the desire to de-develop lands back to wilderness. In 2009, the Humane Society, an animal welfare charity, claimed to be backed by 11 million Americans, while the Sierra Club, a non-profit organization dedicated to protecting the environment, had more than 3 million members in 2018 (Humane Society 2009; Sierra Club 2018). In comparison to these mainstream organizations, ALF and the Earth Liberation Front (ELF) do not have members and, though public support is hard to measure, it is generally assumed that the number of their supporters is comparatively small. Thus, while the general public seems to oppose the cruel treatment of animals, they continue to approve of eating meat and using animals to develop and test medication for human use. Similarly, while most people in the United States tend to support some nature conservation efforts, particularly for recreational purposes, they associate wilderness with loss of jobs and a way of life.

Mainstream organizations actively resist the tendency by the press to lump all environmental and animal rights organizations together. In a press release in 2003, the Sierra Club publicly distanced itself from ELF and complained that the group's actions hurt the entire environmental movement (Sierra Club 2003). In an earlier statement, Sandy Bahr, a legislative liaison for Arizona's Sierra Club chapter, said that "[t]hey make it more of a challenge for us because, unfortunately, we all get lumped together in the eyes of the public" (Vanderpool 2001). Such boundary drawing can also be seen in a statement by Caryl Terrell, a Sierra Club legislative coordinator in Madison, Wisconsin: "I walk in to a meeting of the Natural Resources Committee and they say 'Oh, you're with those extremists!' So I have to take time explaining that the Sierra Club isn't part of this and doesn't support these actions" (citation from Shepard Express Metro: in Sierra Club 2003). Similar press releases have been sent out by the Humane Society in reaction to actions by ALF. The day after a hearing before the US Senate Committee on Environment and Public Works on 18 May 2005, the Humane Society sent a letter to US Senator Inhofe in which it complained that witness David Martosko of the Center for Consumer Freedom:

> purported to show in his testimony how "mainstream animal charities" are funding criminal activities of the Animal Liberation Front (ALF) and the Earth Liberation Front (ELF). [...] This information is severely distorted and the suggestion that the HSUS [Humane Society US] supports any illegal action, or that it has ties to groups like the ALF and ELF that it has repeatedly denounced, is patently false and outrageous. (Humane Society 2005)

In 1986, the California Attorney General declared ALF a terrorist organization. Despite this symbolic warning, for a long time, hardly any of the activists who organized laboratory break-ins were detained or convicted. Prosecutors faced a committed group of activists with goals that were, at least in part, shared by a significant segment of society. For example, ALF had a support group of 10,000 paying members selling t-shirts boasting about its break-ins (Jasper and Nelkin 1992:34).

In an interview in 2007, a prosecutor admitted that charging people for "stealing seven beagles" would not be a "viable prosecution" because jurors would not be moved by that (Interview US-13). At the same time, scientists as well as mink farmers complained of the lack of attention they received from law enforcement agencies, pushing prosecutors to take up their cases. An alliance of "animal enterprises" strongly demanded protection of employees at, for example, animal-testing companies against incursions by protesters. Thus, there was a clear demand to establish order in the face of law-breaking by activists, while at the same time, the activists' concerns with animal cruelty and the loss of pristine nature easily appealed to a large audience. By 2004, the FBI warned of a new willingness among environmental activists to abandon the code of nonviolence, thus increasing pressure on prosecutors to take actions seriously and prevent escalation. In the same year, the FBI officially announced a proactive approach in its investigations to more effectively prevent what it labeled as "eco-terrorism."

Prosecutions on the edge of escalation

In each of these contentious episodes, though to varying degrees, the ability of the state to ensure both order and legitimacy was weakened by the willingness of significant groups of challengers as well as (at least in Spain and Chile) defenders of the status quo to take justice into their own hands. Some established alternative rules and sources of authority, undermining the legitimacy of the state's monopoly on the use of force in the eyes of both those who felt the state failed to use its power adequately to protect them and those who felt the state abused its power for unjust ends. As the episodes demonstrate, criminal prosecutions in these situations can be highly sensitive and the stakes in such contexts are high. Criminal prosecutions may indeed halt violence in the short run, but may also radicalize the defendants and their supporters in the long run. A lack of prosecutorial intervention against protesters can similarly lead to escalating violence. In the absence of state protection, those who feel victimized by contentious actions may take their defense into their own hands.

Those propagating a harsh penal response tend to think imprisonment is an effective way to deal with inconvenient groups and tactics. For example, in a conversation in 2005, a Chilean forestry manager was convinced that the decrease in arson attacks on plantations was the result of the arrest and conviction of prominent Mapuche activists in 2001 and 2002. Given the widespread anger that those criminal prosecutions had evoked among Mapuche students, activists and communities, it was not surprising that the situation did not remain as quiet as it was perceived to be in 2005. It turned out it took only a few years before renewed mobilizations led to even more attacks, backed up by a radicalized ideology propagated by CAM leaders. After 2008, the number of criminal complaints related to the Mapuche conflict increased from 49 in 2008 to 300 in 2012 (Baeza Palavecino 2013).

Balbus (1973:3) has framed this dilemma as the competition between the "immediate interest in order" and the "long-run interest in maximizing legitimacy." Prosecutors not only want to ensure that their proceedings lead to punishment of the perpetrators of crimes, they also like – and need – their trials to be viewed as legitimate. For example, a US prosecutor emphasized that it is good for the "public" when defendants admit what they have done (Interview US-1). He viewed it as the best demonstration that a prosecution was correct and legitimate. In a trial in which co-defendants had entered a plea bargain and testified against an indicted environmental activist, the prosecutor emphasized that the plea bargain of co-defendants has symbolic leverage for the prosecutor. This is so not only because co-defendants are witnesses at the trial, but also because it means that defendants acknowledge prosecutorial authority, the basis of the charges and punishment.

The courtroom is a mechanism of the liberal state to create order while maintaining legitimacy. According to Fletcher (2000 [1978]: xix), the central question of criminal law "is justifying the use of the state's coercive power against free and autonomous persons." Law and its social imaginary as "just" and "neutral" are essential to achieve this legitimization, which is why the criminal process is portrayed as politically neutral: it "generates 'objective' determinations of fact and law" (McBarnet, in Lacey and Wells 1998:16). This imaginary, however, can be contested.

The capacity of criminal trials to have a counter-productive effect on the state's claim to legitimate order has also been recognized by scholars. For Christenson, "A just trial may bring the revenge cycle to a halt, but an unjust trial will encourage the wronged faction to 'get even' and 'right the balance,' next time in their favor" (Christenson 1999:4). Even seemingly just decisions can be interpreted as manipulation by the state. This was the case when, halfway through a 2008 trial against a Basque prisoner support group, the prosecutor dropped the charges against two of the defendants. One of the other 27 defendants suspected that this was only done to make it seem as though prosecutors were proceeding on the basis of available evidence. He argued that the guilty verdict for the rest of the defendants had already been written even before the trial began (Interview S-5).

In cases of contentious criminalization, the government runs the risk that groups may identify prosecutors and judges with particular political interests and no longer see them as neutral representatives of legitimate authority enforcing the rule of law for the common good. To maintain control, a democratic government must address and send the right messages to different audiences in order to uphold the rule of law without alienating important sectors of society. Thus, it matters whether challenges to state legitimacy come from a minority or a substantial part of the population. Machiavelli noted long ago that minorities can be neutralized without causing much resentment. However, faced by opposition from a majority, he recommended trying "to win the allegiance of the populace" (Machiavelli 1994:122). When challengers of the status quo successfully convince the public at large of the justice of their cause, they undermine the state's legitimacy in punishing the protesters. For instance, the widely recognized legitimacy of Mapuche land claims, both domestically and internationally, put pressure on the Chilean authorities not to be perceived as overly repressive.

In the United States, the jury system explicitly brings in an element of public approval. For example, in the early 1980s, four Earth First! activists were summoned to report to the police for removing signs that had been placed on the mountain of Little Granite Creek to mark the planned route of a new road. Referring explicitly to widespread local opposition to the road, a local lawyer told them, "there ain't a jury in Teton County that will convict you" (Scarce 2006:65). Dynamics of such popular support are relevant for the state, among other things, because law enforcement agencies often depend on citizen cooperation. For example, disapproval of violent tactics has led some Mapuche community members to give police prior warning of upcoming arson actions (Case *Lonkos* of Traiguén, Declaration before the police 2002).

The lack of citizen cooperation in criminal prosecutions can indicate a loss of state control. This has been clearly visible in the Basque Country, where, especially during the early years of ETA's existence, it enjoyed substantial popular support for its armed struggle. For a long time, "*algo habrá hecho*" (s/he must have done something) was a common saying among ETA supporters after assassinations, conveying the extent of trust people felt in the fact that ETA had justifiable reasons for using force and its choice of targets. The assumption behind this phrase was that ETA victims somehow "deserved" to die. In this sense, public allegiance to ETA took on features usually reserved for allegiance to a sovereign. Instead of supporting law enforcement efforts, sympathizers often assisted ETA militants in hiding from Spanish authorities. Apart from genuine support for ETA, fear of cooperating with law enforcement also posed a problem for prosecutors. In 1979, the Spanish Attorney General reported that citizens "don't file complaints, report or communicate crimes or suspicions, they flee away from giving testimony, they hesitate in acts of recognition and identification of aggressors, and, in general, they prefer to avoid intervening, fearing to seek complications" (MA 1979:73). The fear of testifying in trials was reiterated by the Attorney General in 1989, as he noted that witnesses hesitated to identify perpetrators (MA 1989:214).

Threat assessment

Whether prosecutors get involved in prosecuting protest activity at all also depends on threat assessments – of the public and the government. Social reaction to a threat is always about what a threat represents. Scholars have coined the idea of "images" (Hall 1978) or "typical crime images" (Sudnow 1965) to indicate the role that these symbolic perceptions play in people's "definition of a situation" (Vold et al. 1998:221), the accompanying threat assessment and the decision as to how to deal with it. A state's definition of a situation determines and legitimizes the state's response. Publicly claiming the need to protect "victims" or to defend "national security" not only indicates, but also legitimizes a certain response. If the proposed definition of a situation is accepted by the public, the resulting response will be perceived as natural and taken for granted.

Defining a situation means that a government decides in which "box" it puts a perceived threat as well as what the best response is. In Spain, the government shifted from understanding the fight against ETA as a "war" to favoring a "criminal justice" approach in dealing with ETA and its supporters. In Chile, the government vacillated between a "political" approach and a "criminal justice" response to disruptive Mapuche protests for land restitution. In the United States, the government settled for a proactive approach to dealing with "eco-terrorist attacks" through criminal prosecutions. Clearly, a lot is at stake in the government's definition of a situation, as criminal prosecutions both rely on such definitions and reproduce them in charging narratives and decisions. Unsurprisingly, both challengers and defenders of the status quo attempt to influence them to their advantage through discursive mobilization in the criminal justice arena.

In Spain, state agents struggled to find an appropriate framework to deal with ETA's armed attacks. During the 1970s and 1980s, the challenge was mainly framed in military terms, while throughout the 1990s and 2000s, a criminal justice perspective prevailed. While assessing threats to the public generally falls within the purview of state agents, society also participates. For example, in 2008, an editorial in the Basque newspaper *El Correo* claimed ETA posed an increased threat because it had expanded its actions to include murders in France, urban attacks *inside* the Basque Country, and the targeting of press members and politicians even *after* they left office. Contrary to ETA's previous practice of always providing advance warning of attacks on civilian buildings, it cited an attack on a newspaper building *without* prior notification. The newspaper's conclusion was clear: "almost anyone can now be a potential target of ETA" (Barriusa 2008).

While state and public opinion eventually shifted closer together in Spain to condemn ETA's violence, the Chilean state's threat assessment of unlawful Mapuche protest vacillated between images of minor isolated disputes between private parties and full-blown terrorist attacks threatening national security. At times, narratives of escalating violence dominated state discourse on Mapuche activism, while at other times, officials downplayed claims that Mapuche protests posed any real danger to the public at all. In 1999, for example, a Chilean official asserted that "there is no Chiapas, no revolution or Mapuche uprising" (Barrera 1999:68). Yet, in 2003, justifying the terrorism charges against Mapuche defendants, a prosecutor claimed that protests were escalating from a narrow focus on forestry companies to the targeting of small and mid-size farmers (field notes, Case *Lonkos* of Traiguén, April 2003). In 2006, the arson of a private farmer's home spurred arguments that Mapuche protest constituted a threat to farmers lives, and in 2008 prosecutors researched supposed links between the FARC (Revolutionary Armed Forces of Colombia) in Colombia and CAM. Then, in 2009, Minister Secretary General of the Presidency Viera-Gallo again dismissed the notion that Mapuche protest posed a significant public threat. "We are not talking about an Al Qaeda in the Araucanía region," he emphasized, "We have to accept that this problem exists and treat it seriously, but we must never exaggerate it" (EFE 2009).

In the United States, government officials began speaking about a trend of violence by environmental and animal rights activists from the late 1980s onward. In response, Congress passed the Animal Enterprise Protection Act in 1992 and congressional references to the "growing threat" of animal rights "extremists" and "eco-terrorists" increased throughout the 1990s and 2000s. FBI testimonies referred to an "escalation in violent rhetoric and tactics" during this period (Senate Report 2006), while prosecutors increasingly painted an image of dangerous anarchist ideologues manipulating and inciting young animal rights and environmental activists into breaking the law. Prosecutors sought to deter such youngsters by asking for high sentences in key exemplary cases.

In sum, in each of the contentious episodes, significant groups challenged the status quo and legitimized transgressions of the law to advance their cause. Targets of such contentious actions appealed to the state for protection, while often initiating efforts to protect or retaliate themselves as well. They organized armed self-defense groups in Chile, created so-called anti-terrorist groups in Spain and formed lobby groups in the United States. Whether prosecutors get involved in prosecuting actions of challengers or defenders of the socio-political status quo depends primarily on their understanding of such conduct as criminal. In turn, once prosecutors get involved, their framing and charging choices create a powerful narrative about events, groups and motives. Under scrutiny and criticism for either not delivering enough convictions or for unduly criminalizing legitimate conduct, it is not surprising that prosecutors choose to retreat behind their mandate to "just apply the law" to justify their decisions. At the same time, though, the development of prosecutorial narratives reveals how prosecutors attempt to counter these challenges. The following chapter introduces the concept of prosecutorial narrative in more depth.

3

The Prosecutorial Narrative and the Double Bind of Liberal Legalism

Criminal prosecutions as social constructions of reality

In March 2008, politician Isaías Carrasco from Mondragón in the Basque Country was killed by ETA. Just two weeks later it was *Semana Santa* in Spain, the "Holy Week" of celebration leading up to Easter Sunday during which many people go on holiday. Every year, the infamous traffic jams of *Semana Santa* unfortunately result in many deaths. In that year, the death toll reached 63. The same number of deaths from holiday traffic in that one week in 2008 equaled approximately the same number of people killed by ETA over the last ten years, between 1998 and 2008. Clearly, ETA is considered a major threat in Spain not solely because of the number of deaths it causes. Carrasco had been a local councilor for a Spanish political party and his assassination was understood as a continuing threat to other politicians. More importantly, perhaps, was the small but significant number of people shrugged upon hearing the news of his death and said, "He must have done something wrong," legitimizing ETA's decision to kill. At the end of the day, traffic accidents are perceived to be a different kind of threat from that posed by the existence of an armed political organization like ETA. Criminal prosecutions also reflect these differences.

Associations of victims of ETA violence have criticized Spanish prosecutors for being more lenient during government truces with ETA, such as during the 14-month truce in 1998–99. The chief prosecutor of the Audiencia Nacional confirmed and justified this trend, noting that some conduct is simply evaluated differently during a truce: "The application of the law depends a lot on the context and circumstances of each case. That is a legal criterion and within the rule of law" (Interview S-21). He admitted that the prosecutors were more flexible during the truce, particularly regarding actions by individuals and organizations regarded as being associated with ETA but not part of its military structures. While such leniency was criticized by associations of victims of ETA, he defended this approach as only logical, arguing that meetings and demonstrations by these groups during a truce, when ETA had stopped its use of violence, were legal when their goal was to support the peace process. However, when ETA broke the truce and returned to killing and extortion, then such meetings and demonstrations, when they supported the methods and strategies of ETA, had an illegal goal:

> Therefore, the application of the law cannot be the same in one circumstance or the other. [...] The laws are applied according to the social reality and the context in which they are applied. You cannot pretend [to have] a rigorous application of the law when the circumstances do not warrant that rigor, but a more flexible application. (Interview S-21)

At the same time, the chief prosecutor emphasized that all criminal proceedings for "clear" crimes of terrorism continued. In cases of attacks, property destruction, arson and collaboration with ETA (for example, providing housing to militants), indictments continued to be formulated and people were convicted. "Clear crimes don't change," he said (Interview S-21).

This chapter focuses on how prosecutors across the three contentious episodes react as different interest groups mobilize in the criminal justice arena. The focus on discursive mobilization assumes that crime is a socially constructed category and that the response to crime is "shaped by particular and contingent interpretations of reality" (Wiener 1990:7). After establishing criminal prosecutions as social constructions of reality couched in the logic and vocabulary of criminal law, the chapter introduces the concept of prosecutorial narrative as a key methodological tool for studying how prosecutors legitimize their proceedings. Criminal law applies key liberal values in its role of protecting individuals against arbitrary state violence. Within liberal legalism, a decontextualized narrative is the default in assessing the criminality of certain conduct on the basis of general norms. However, pressure from determined victim alliances or defendant support groups can effectively lead prosecutors to adopt different narratives that recontextualize conduct in a way deemed necessary to understand and adequately prosecute the crimes alleged. In addition to having real impact on convictions and sentencing, the chosen prosecutorial narrative also contributes to the institutionalization of certain truths about the assessed situation.

When a prosecutor receives a criminal complaint, she has to define the situation to decide whether, how and against whom to build a criminal case. What information is deemed relevant to define the nature of the event? What information is excluded from consideration? What kinds of questions are asked to determine what happened? Judicial verdicts, in this approach, are discursive products that can not only send someone to prison, but also institutionalize "truths" and "marginalize other ways of looking at the world" (Lacey and Wells 1998:10). Many scholars have emphasized this truth-producing character of criminal proceedings (Bennet and Feldman 1981; Abel and Marsh 1994:38; Brass 1996). The approach used in this book follows Garland in viewing criminal prosecutions as forms of communication:

> [Penality] communicates meaning not just about crime and punishment but also about power, authority, legitimacy, normality, morality, personhood, social relations, and a host of other tangential matters. Penal signs and symbols are one part of an authoritative, institutional discourse which seeks to organize our moral and political understanding and to educate our sentiments and sensibilities. They provide a continuous, repetitive set of instructions as to how we should think about good and evil, normal and pathological, legitimate and illegitimate, order and disorder. Through their judgments, condemnations and classifications, they teach us (and persuade us) how to judge, what to condemn, and how to classify, and they supply a set of languages, idioms, and vocabularies with which to do so. These signifying practices also tell us where to locate social authority, how to preserve order and community, where to look for social dangers, and how to feel about these matters ... In short, the practices, institutions and discourses all *signify* ... Penality is ... a cultural text – or perhaps, better, a cultural performance – which communicates with a variety of social audiences and conveys an extended range of meanings. (Garland 1990:252–3)

Anthropologist Clifford Geertz (1983:173) writes that law is "not a bounded set of norms, rules, principles, values, or whatever from which jural responses to distilled events can be drawn, but part of a distinctive manner of imagining the real." The law and the courtroom can thus be studied as a discursive arena (Silbey and Ewick 1998; Foucault 2001). Foucault describes discourses as that which can be said about certain issues and is deemed acceptable, legitimate or truthful. Law is constitutive of discourses. According to law professor and literary critic James Boyd White, "[t]he law, of which legal punishment is a part, is a system of meaning; it is a language and should be evaluated as such" (in Wiener 1990:9, fn 26).

In criminal proceedings, the social construction of reality is constituted and constrained by the logic and language of criminal law. This system creates classifying concepts and categories of crimes as well as principles and rules, such as the presumption of innocence and rules about proper evidence (cf. De Roos 1987:4). Criminal prosecutions can be studied as operations of translation from everyday reality into the specific reality of criminal law (cf. Berger and Luckmann 1967). In his book *Reconstruction of a Criminal in England*, Wiener (1990) mentions a number of relevant elements that play a role in the process of constructing a crime and the criminal: one's understanding of the nature and meaning of crime; whether focus is put on the act performed or on the character of the offender; what the theory is that guides one's understanding of where crime comes from and what it causes; and what one's judgment is of which cases are "equal" or "unequal" (same versus difference).

Criminal law as the practical application of liberalism

Criminal law can be viewed as the practical application of a liberal political philosophy based on the values of rationality, legality, formality and individual justice (Norrie 1993:12–14). This ideology originated in the Enlightenment period, when it became the basis for liberal democracies and the rule of law as a means to guard against arbitrary government repression. Weber stressed the distinction between formal procedures and substantive justice ("formal rationality") as an important feature for allowing the state to maintain both order and legitimacy (Balbus 1973:13). Criminal law can thus be understood as the specific system developed to justify and legitimize the coercive power of the state, making the struggle to interpret violence important for governance. Paul Brass (1996:45) introduces scholars to this possibility of studying "the struggle to interpret violence, the attempts to govern society or a country through gaining not a monopoly on the legitimate use of violence but to gain control over the interpretation of violence." Prosecutors play a key role in establishing control over the interpretation of violence. "Law converts violence into an act of state. That which would otherwise be seen as a form of defensive self-help [as the state's punishment] acquires the mantle of legitimacy. The rest of the community not only condones the use of violence against aggressors; they think it is right" (Fletcher 2007 [1978]:23).

As the main characteristics of liberal legalism to legitimize legal outcomes, Nonet and Selznick emphasize the separation between law and politics, the importance of rules and procedure, and strict obedience to positive law (2005:54). Procedural fairness is a core value; formal equality before the law is one of the devices that make a criminal prosecution seemingly impartial and unrelated to structural societal differences. Hence the famous quip by Anatole France about "the majestic equality of the French law, which forbids both rich and poor alike from sleeping under the bridges of the Seine" (Balbus 1973:5). These values are reflected in the self-understanding of prosecutors in each of the contentious episodes under examination in Spain, Chile and the United States. For example, after the transition to an electoral democracy in Spain, the Attorney General described the role of the prosecutor as the "defense of the juridical order and the prevention and punishment of crime" while emphasizing the importance of "objectivity" and "impartiality" (MA 1978:87–8).

The French Enlightenment philosopher Montesquieu argued that democratic states are also open to the abuse of power and that the antidote to power is power. In this vein, he proposed that a state should have three powers – legislative, executive and judiciary – subordinated to each other. He postulated that having the lawmaker judged by the judiciary on its own laws would give a strong incentive for fair laws, just as in the custom that the person cutting the cake should be the last to choose a piece. Every branch of these powers requires legitimacy. The judiciary, for example, needs legitimacy because it lacks the force to execute its own verdicts.

The presumption of innocence in liberal legal frameworks is meant to safeguard individuals from state repression. At the same time, as Feeley (1979) describes, there actually is a working presumption of guilt among state agents as they move cases through investigations and proceedings. After all, a person is arrested for being suspected of committing a crime. In this regard, Packer (1964) talks about the need to establish "legal guilt," in the sense that a person who is arrested is not so much presumed innocent factually as they are presumed innocent in terms of the legal guilt still yet to be proven. The working presumption of guilt among state agents at the trial stage is an expression of confidence in the working of the system and the fact-finding capabilities and trustworthiness of the activities by other state agents in earlier stages. This confidence is (generally) also present on the part of prosecutors, judges, and even defense attorneys.

Differentiation in society in the form of a distinction between persons and roles is another important component of a professionalized liberal criminal justice system (Weber 1972:124–8; Elias 1982). Police and judges wear uniforms designed to mask their individuality and are supposed to perform their tasks based on their role rather than personal motives. These roles are no longer the "property" of a person, but are (often temporarily) assigned (Weber 1972). Formally, police and prosecutors represent the nation and the public interest. In prosecutors' offices, courtrooms and prisons, this is symbolized by the national flag and pictures of the head of state, reflecting the unity of these organs and their role as representatives of the state. In the adversarial system of the United States, the prosecutor represents the government. In trial transcripts, the prosecutor is literally referred to as "the government," presenting criminal cases "on behalf of the United States." As prosecutors perform their representational role, the outcome of a criminal prosecution does not impact them like it does defendants. According to one US attorney, "whether we win or lose, we walk out through the same door" (Interview US-2).

According to liberal ideology, people should not be punished for their ideas. In liberal legalist frameworks, the subjective element of a crime is reduced to the abstract notion of intent: "Only abstract human characteristics such as intentionality, 'factual' recklessness, voluntariness and rationality [can] be relied upon in the courtroom. Personal circumstances, and characteristics linked to circumstances such as motive, were closely confined" (Norrie 1993:83). A prosecutor in the US expressed that: "as a general rule and one I certainly practiced in this case, I do not look at the political motivations of defendants. I look to their intent (not to be confused with motive) and their actions" (personal communication with author).

Criminal law has a crucial function in relation to all other areas of the law as an arena of last resort for problems or conflicts originating elsewhere. As the Criminal Law Commissioners in the United Kingdom expressed already in 1843, the "paramount importance of the Criminal Law consists in this consideration, that upon its due operation the enforcement of every other branch of the law ... depends" (in Norrie 1993:17). That criminal law is seen as the ultimate guardian of the entire legal system is also visible in the arguments brought into the courtrooms in the

contentious episodes discussed in this book. For example, the US prosecutor in the case against activists of the "Stop Huntingdon Animal Cruelty"
(SHAC) campaign pointed out that, in testing drugs and other products on
animals, the research lab Huntingdon Life Sciences is engaged in lawful
practices that are actually "mandated by the Food and Drug Administration" (Case SHAC 7, trial transcripts, 7 February 2006). Similarly in
Chile, landowners justified their call for a penal response to attacks on
their lands by pointing out that they possess legally acquired and recognized land titles for the estates contested by Mapuche communities. The
laws under which they acquired their estates are thus presented as the
set-in-stone referent to be relied upon in the criminal justice framework.

Criminalization: a mixture of a technical and political process

Criminalization in legislation is the act of isolating a generally defined
conduct and labeling this conduct as criminal. This, in turn, opens up
the possibility for public (and sometimes private) prosecution, enabling
the use of coercive mechanisms under state authority against individuals
for the purpose of finding them guilty of criminal conduct and imposing
a sentence, such as a monetary fine or time in prison. Criminalization,
as such, is a technical and descriptive concept and refers to typical state
behavior based on its punitive power. Primary criminalization occurs
through prohibition in legislation, and secondary criminalization through
criminal investigation, indictment, trial and sentencing.

In addition to the technical act of criminalization described above, criminalization can also be pursued as a strategy in a political dispute – by the
state as well as other groups in society. If contested, such criminalization
becomes contentious. It often begins with the rhetorical stigmatization of
political opponents, through speeches, documents and the media, seeking
to define their activities as criminal. It can escalate to using the criminal
law apparatus in an effort to enforce this definition by initiating charges
against and potentially detaining an opponent with the aim of further
stigmatizing or sanctioning them or their conduct. If successful, the
organization (and its activities) targeted by the actor strategically using
criminalization as a means to advance its position in a political dispute
will come to be primarily viewed by the broader public in terms of their
(allegedly) violent, illegal or terrorist means, instead of their political
goals. This is what Kirchheimer (1961) calls "political justice." Authorities
can also target challengers of the status quo for unrelated legal infractions
like traffic or administrative offenses, or they can order inflated bail. The

authorities can raise these obstacles while still adhering to the formal due process requirements of criminal law. Even when these proceedings end in acquittals or when charges are dropped halfway, activists and social movements may still suffer consequences detrimental to their political activities, such as having spent time in preventive detention.

Using criminalization as a political strategy is believed to be at odds with the basic principles of criminal law in the framework of liberal legalism, which strives to be a politically neutral instrument of conduct regulation. At the same time, such processes are part and parcel of liberal legalism as interest group lobbying and the inherently political process of the social construction and definition of crimes, as well as the application of the criminal law apparatus, make such deliberate and strategic criminalization unavoidable to a certain degree. A key feature of the contentious episodes and criminal cases presented here is that a significant part of the pressure on prosecutors to adopt and advance a certain viewpoint does not stem from arm-twisting by higher-ups in the government or corruption, as is characteristic of legal outcomes in many authoritarian countries. Instead, discursive mobilization and lobbying by interest groups in the criminal justice arena, a characteristic feature of liberal democracies, is highlighted as a major factor putting pressure on prosecutors to take particular conceptions of "public interest" into account. The upcoming chapters show that in each episode, some groups manage to muster far more access and power to influence prosecutor's perceptions of the public interest than others.

Prosecutorial narrative

Although formal legal rationality suggests that prosecutors simply "apply" the law, they actually have many *choices* along the way that matter in terms of who gets prosecuted and for which offense. As De Roos writes, "The definition of conduct as criminally relevant is never an automatism, but always a conscious human decision" (1987:18). Prosecutors are important professional "characters" responsible for moving cases toward criminal proceedings. The prosecutorial narrative, or the narrative that drives the prosecution in a case as it describes the crime and allots criminal responsibility, can draw upon discourses in society, subsequently reproducing, institutionalizing or providing them with new input. The prosecutorial narrative's status as narrating "facts" has important implications. To initiate a criminal case and decide upon the appropriate charge, a prosecutor has to decide whether or not specific conduct falls within the boundaries of generally indicated crime categories described by the lawmaker. This requires a translation from the general to the specific, reducing a complex situation to a specific selection of legally relevant facts, which can be more or less contested. The prosecutorial narrative guides the entire process of investigating, charging, prosecuting and accusing a defendant by building a case and constructing a narrative of harm and the responsibility for it. As such, it is never only the narrative of a single prosecutor, but a construction with many authors. In Spain, the investigative judge is an important shaper of the prosecutorial narrative, whereas the FBI plays an important role in the United States. In both Chile and Spain, private and popular accusers frequently participate in the construction of the prosecutorial narrative.

In the research for this book, tracing Spanish prosecutorial narrative in relation to ETA and the Basque left-nationalist movement was fairly easy, as terrorism prosecutions are the exclusive domain of the Audiencia Nacional in Madrid. In Chile, almost all prosecutions in relation to the "Mapuche conflict" were carried out in the southern offices in Temuco and Concepción. However, this type of geographical clustering was not present in the United States, where contentious criminalization of environmentalist and animal rights actions occurred across the country. Still, there was substantial effort by US federal agents of the FBI and different attorney offices to coordinate activities and ensure cooperation, for example in the Joint Terrorism Task Force. While coordination thus took place, US attorneys claimed their independence from the executive government. For example, the US attorney in Oregon explicitly stated "we would be seeking the same [terrorism] enhancement if this case had been prosecuted under the previous administration. This is not a political prosecution" (Case Operation Backfire, Terrorism Enhancement Hearing, 2007: 19).

Criminal prosecutions tend to be long. Trials can last days and even several weeks. Criminal investigations can last years. Prosecutions are often detailed excursions into the lives of specific people, such as when defendant Cayupe in Chile testified on trial about how he cared for his mother who suffered from Parkinson's disease and was tied to her bed during the last years of her life (Case Cayupe, 16 April 2009). Just two months after her death, he was detained and spent four months in jail awaiting his trial. During the oral hearing in 2009, Cayupe expanded on his obligations toward his mother, whereas the interrogating prosecutor pushed the defendant to come to the point in relation to the crime with which he was charged. This push to "come to the point" is related to a broader notion of "legally relevant facts," which may be at odds with the perception of defendants. Such on-trial conversations between the prosecutor and the defendant take place within the specific meta-discursive practices (Briggs 1996:19) of the courtroom and the playing field offered by liberal rules. The defendant is allowed to be silent, according to the principle by which no one can be forced to incriminate oneself. The prosecutor can ask questions, but is held in check by the defense lawyer who scrutinizes questions and objects when the questions are leading, repetitive or "unrelated" to the charges. It is within this strictly orchestrated setting that evidence is presented, a prosecutorial narrative built, images evoked or contested, and judges or juries decide on the guilt of the defendants.

The elements of a prosecutor's narrative have to be framed, classified, and ordered in such a way that it becomes a convincing criminal case. Criminal liability subsequently forms the justification for the application of a coercive measure against the defendant. Criminal liability is the key concept of criminal doctrine: "By legal doctrine we mean the story told (and assumptions made) by judges and legal commentators about both the general structure of, and the rationale for, criminal liability" (Lacey and Wells 1998:31). McConville et al. describe the process in which a case is constructed, from the moment the suspect becomes an object of police suspicion:

> It must be emphasized that at each point of the criminal justice process "what happened" is the subject of interpretation, addition, subtraction, selection and reformulation. [...] It involves not simply the selection and interpretation of evidence but its *creation*. Understanding the selections made and the decisions taken requires, therefore, analysis of the motivations of the actors, their value systems and ideologies. (McConville et al. 1991:12, emphasis in original)

The construction of prosecutorial narratives in the research for this book was based on analysis of prosecutorial statements in verdicts; attendance or oral recordings of trials; police transcripts, including witness declarations; as well as interviews with prosecutors, police and investigative judges. Sometimes, I had access to databases and digital records. At other times, I had to visit courthouses for hard-copy transcripts. This study of prosecutorial narratives in processes of contentious criminalization is "semiotic" (Barthes 1977) in the sense that criminal law is studied as a language that communicates and has a standard grammar and local slang. Criminal law and the social practice of criminal prosecutions constitute a system of signification. Understanding the prosecutorial narrative as a semiological phenomenon means asking how the signs receive their meaning and what they signify. In the analysis, the prosecutorial narrative could loosely be viewed in relation to criminal law as "*parole*" stands to "*langue*" à la Saussure (Barthes 1977:13–17), that is, the criminal law is that which is codified and not used, whereas the prosecutorial narrative is the application and use of that language. As such, the chosen medium of criminal law and criminal proceedings contributes to the message it sends. Linguistic categories and images have material consequences when, for example, terrorism enhancements and special security prisons turn activists, defendants and prisoners into "terrorists," which can deeply affect sentence length, in-prison treatment, and even life after release.

Decontextualization and de-politicization: the liberal default

Prosecutorial narratives in line with the core values of liberal legalism are generally expected to be "de-politicizing" (Balbus 1973; Nonet and Selznick 2005:58; Melossi 2008). De-politicization can be defined as arbitrarily treating an issue as if it is not a proper subject of politics (Held 1996:130). It is a way to legitimate judicial proceedings as it denies politically motivated defendants exactly what they most seek: political legitimacy (Shapiro 2007:10–15). In Mertz's analysis of the process in which lawyers learn to translate a story into the relevant legal framework and legal categories, she emphasized that lawyers "operate in a world where social context and identity have become invisible" (Mertz 2008 [2000]:110). According to Mertz (2008 [2000]:104), this peculiar aspect of the way the law works, is both good and bad. While this approach pretends to select legally relevant facts and otherwise exclude the social context, there is no such thing as "no context." Indeed, the context chosen by a prosecutor is a very particular one that is then claimed to be politically neutral.

For example, during one trial in Chile, the prosecutor argued that "the Public Ministry does not prosecute ideologies or convictions, and certainly does not pretend to adjudicate social conflicts" (Case CAM, audio proceedings, 23 June 2005). Instead, the prosecutor called upon the "*estado de derecho*" (rule of law) and argued that the "legal and constitutional mandate" of the prosecutors was to "investigate facts that constitute crimes." In doing so, the prosecutor reproduced the legalist image of simple "facts that constitute crimes," which can presumably be found, observed, investigated and adjudicated in an objective manner. He thus denied the significance of the multitude of voices engaged in constructing narratives about those "facts."

Nonet and Selznick (2005:58) argue that in the modality of what they call "autonomous law" (I understand this as synonymous to liberal legalism), the courts have the specific function of de-politicizing issues. So, "each major attribute of autonomous law can be understood as a strategy of legitimation" (Nonet and Selznick 2005:55). Rules are a potent resource for legitimating power: an orientation to rules tends to limit the responsibility of the (actors in the) legal system. Autonomous law suggests that one can solve particular cases with general rules. It thus adheres to the paradigm of mechanical justice. In this way, autonomous law is closely related to bureaucracy; everything boils down to procedural fairness. In this framework, substantive justice is the "hoped-for by-product of impeccable method" (Nonet and Selznick 2005:67). This is part of a historical bargain, according to Nonet and Selznick: "legal institutions purchase procedural autonomy at the price of substantive subordination" (2005:58). In the same vein, courts demand obedience of citizens at all time. If you do not agree with a law, protesting through legal means is allowed, but one must obey the law. In turn, administrators can be held accountable if they violate the law. Criminal laws not only enable penal interventions and the consequent use of force, but also put the required constraints on the government's use of force against its citizens.

De-politicization means that courts move away from the substantive issue at hand to formal (understood as neutral) rules, making a strict distinction between ends and means. Instead of dealing with the dispute of political claims, the focus of a criminal prosecution is on the appropriateness and legality of *means* used by defendants to pursue their ends, make their claims or defend themselves. Debates about the legitimacy of the underlying political claims are deliberately excluded from the trial, whether this is done silently or explicitly. De-politicization is further achieved by creating generally formulated legal definitions that make a seemingly objective and de-politicized division in behavior, categorizing certain conduct as deviant or wrong and other conduct as acceptable (Lacey and Wells 1998:12). Beetham makes the same point when he writes:

[T]here are features inherent in most legal systems that serve not only to encourage respect for the law in general, but to put the particular content of existing law beyond question, and make it difficult to challenge. [...] What are these features? Most deeply embedded are those terms used in everyday language which serve to distinguish the lawful from the unlawful in the achievement and exercise of power, and which demarcate, for example, theft, violence and murder from legally permitted forms of acquisition, compulsion and deprivation of life or livelihood. (Beetham 1991:67)

While building a criminal case in the spirit of liberal legalism, a prosecutor thus decontextualizes, individualizes, chooses legally relevant facts, and applies appropriate legal labels. This process of narrative formulation relies on specific doctrinal tools and choices of criminal policy, such as the choice of a narrow time-frame, the focus on individual perpetrators and the exclusion of a political motive. Thus, a US prosecutor insisted in the courtroom that "this [case] is not about animal rights," although he privately acknowledged later that the defendants' allegations of animal abuse in the animal-testing company may indeed be true. "But then they have to go to Congress," he noted (Interview US-13). This approach assumes a society in consensus, where dissent can be solved in parliament or civil lawsuits, disrupted only by a few criminals who are motivated by self-interest, such as financial gain or desire for adventure.

Each of the three contentious political episodes discussed in this book included prosecutions that followed the decontextualized mode. For example, in various cases against Mapuche activists in Chile, their Mapuche identity and claims based on this identity were ignored. Protest actions in which many people took part led to the prosecution of a specific few, without taking into account the collective nature or political motivation of the action. For years, the Chilean government chose to view "the Mapuche conflict" as a collection of isolated cases of private disputes between particular communities on the one hand and specific landowners on the other (Barrera 1999). Criminal incidents were framed within the context of these private disputes. Government officials typically maintained that criminal prosecutions were not only appropriate and necessary, but also sufficient to deal with the crimes and disorder related to these private disputes. In 2003, the mayor of Collipulli, a village in the middle of the area at the center of struggle for land redistribution, commented that after the incarceration of one of the main Mapuche leaders in the region, everything was quiet. His comment reinforced the image that the social conflicts were caused by a few "bad apples," who lacked broader social support, suggesting that to maintain or re-establish order and stop illegal actions, state prosecution of selected individuals was effective (Interview C-19). In an interview, a functionary of one of the bigger forestry companies adhered to this narrative: "our policy is to deal with these actions as ordinary thefts and crimes" (Interview C-34).

Challengers of the status quo often criticize decontextualized prosecutorial narratives as problematic because their political grievances and claims are not taken into account. Activists tend to criticize the strict distinction between means and ends that enables prosecutors to condemn the use of illegal protest tactics and instead refer activists to the parliamentary route as the appropriate (legal) avenue for change, while leaving structural inequalities unaddressed. Mapuche activists ask, in response to allegations of arson in plantations on contested lands: "What about the trees, which suck up all the water making it impossible for the Mapuche residents on the adjacent lands to get water from their wells?" (Interview C-46). They perceive such induced erosion to be more "violent" than any of their protest actions, while only the latter are prosecuted as crimes.

Attempts by protesters to discuss their grievances during a criminal proceeding are often blocked. This was the case, for example, in the trial against the US climate change activist Tim DeChristopher, who, in December 2008, had participated as a bidder in an auction and increased the bids on 22,000 acres of land in Utah national parks. In addition, he acquired parcels worth $1.7 million. While he later raised money for the first payment for those parcels, he was charged with interference in the bidding process. DeChristopher wanted to argue that his actions were necessary because, at the time of the auction, several investigations had revealed the level of corruption and bribery ongoing in the preparations of such auctions (Case DeChristopher, statement at sentencing hearing, 26 July 2011). This so-called "necessity defense" and context was excluded from the trial.

The criminal justice systems in Spain, Chile and the United States are based on a liberal ideology that asserts formal equality of autonomous individuals and the assumption that fair proceedings will generally also lead to substantive justice. In order to legitimize criminal proceedings, political issues are generally excluded from criminal justice questions, as political goals are to be attained through dialogue and political lobbying. The next section outlines a different prosecutorial strategy, used to regain legitimacy in the face of pressure to secure convictions by forceful alliances of interest groups united by claims of victimhood.

Putting crimes in context: politicization

Typically, prosecutors attempt to extract "criminal behavior" from a blurry and complicated range of events. Committed to the ideology of liberal legalism, they tend to work in a decontextualizing manner, selecting specific events and individual perpetrators, and charging them with narrowly framed offenses. Present-day landowners in Chile, animal enterprises in the United States, and associations of victims of ETA violence in Spain have criticized existing decontextualized prosecutorial narratives for their perceived failure to secure convictions. These alliances of "victim groups" have criticized, for example, how, in the absence of convincing evidence or witnesses prepared to testify, criminal prosecutions have led to acquittals. In other instances, those mobilizing as victims deemed sentences for isolated actions of vandalism insufficiently severe. Commercial farmers and forestry companies in Chile effectively pushed the government to change its perspective and to view incidents of arson in plantations and theft of wood not as isolated events but within the context of the so-called "Mapuche conflict." Although decontextualization is the default way in which criminal proceedings obtain legitimacy, in the cases selected in this book, prosecutors sought an alternative basis for legitimacy when that claim appeared to fail, by resorting to varying degrees of recontextualization.

For example, animal releases from labs and fur farms in the United States were previously prosecuted as property destruction and later recontextualized as terrorism. In a case against activists who ran a mobilizing website against animal abuse in the US, a prosecutor explained having shifted his focus from the "foot soldiers" of such actions to the "generals." Similarly, village ceremonies celebrating the return of former ETA prisoners in the Basque Country were once viewed as protected speech and only later reformulated as the glorification of terrorism. In Chile, prosecutors spent large portions of trials debating whether defendants actually represented a Mapuche constituency or not. A Chilean prosecutor chose to shift the legal interest when she claimed that the burning of a plantation on contested land was not only harming someone's "property," but also a threat to "democracy" more broadly (Interview C-10). These examples show how criminal law can be stretched to fit complex narratives about "terrorist" organizations or links between speech and violence. Calling an act "terrorism" can move it up the priority list of incidents to be investigated and prosecuted as crimes. At the same time, these constructions can also lead to a loss of the benefits of contextualization as a legitimating approach.

In analyzing the variety of modalities of criminal justice proceedings, the approach taken here builds and draws on existing models, such as those put forward by Herbert Packer (1964), who devised two ideal typical models of criminal process (crime control and due process); or that of Jakobs and Cancio Meliá (2006), who distinguished between *Feindstrafrecht* (enemy penology) and ordinary citizen penology; and that of Nonet and Selznick (1978), who propose a sequence model of repressive and autonomous law. These theories all posit some form of "ordinary" justice, while highlighting a particular type of "special case scenario" specific to each author that then precipitates deviations from the "normal." These models touch on what kind of conditions would lead to the alternative modality posited, and describe what it would look like in action. Instead of adopting any of these models wholesale, the approach taken here is informed by the observations made by these authors on the different criminal dogmatic devices that constitute alternative modalities. This book does not ask whether any of these ideal types were found exactly as such in practice, but instead contributes to existing analyses by showing the role that narratives play in shaping and informing the adoption of such devices, such as the move toward proactive investigation or the adoption of a broader time-frame. The key to these narrative changes is the role played by context in providing the lens for interpretation.

Contextualized narratives mobilize different legal dogmatic devices, such as a change in the legal interest, kind of criminal liability, or time-frame relevant for constituting a crime. In the context of time and place, for example, Kelman (1981) asks: How far back in time does one go to look for legally relevant information about a defendant or situation? How wide a scope does one consider for the place where actions occurred? It is clear that such assessments are not only based on abstract law, but also on commonly shared understandings of what is going on. Narrative changes may also include changing the audience that is addressed or the image of the perpetrator that is painted. In a contextualized narrative, the context chosen by the prosecutor is portrayed as the relevant or even "natural" context that should be taken into account. The basic description of this context, which is often considered "background" information, can color or influence the interpretation of everything else. The chosen "background" can be responsible for filters and selective recognition of relevant elements, actors, or events that determine what "really" happened.

Prosecutors often present contextualized narratives as an inevitable representation of criminal events, while in truth there can be no single determinate narrative.

The shift to define an act as terrorism invokes a broader legal interest as more people are supposedly affected by terrorist offenses. In Spain, this process of identification with the victims of ETA attacks was obvious, for example, when a magazine headline declared *"todos somos Isaías."* According to the magazine, the victim was not just the politician Isaías Carrasco or his family. His death was not only the murder of an individual, but "everyone" (*todos*) was assumed to be affected. In Chile, the prosecutorial narrative moved to interpret a threat to plantations in the south as a threat to the national economy and national security. At the same time, in the episodes from Spain, Chile and the United States presented here, there was no grand shift in which the decontextualized strategy for legitimization was entirely abandoned by prosecutors once and for all. Rather, there was often a "back-and-forth" consisting of partial shifts that included some elements of de- and re-contextualization – especially in those instances where judges refused to accept the novel prosecutorial narratives.

In a contextualized prosecutorial narrative, a criminal case becomes categorized as a "kind of" case – in the chosen episodes an "eco-terrorism case," "ETA case" or "Mapuche conflict case." In the United States, while environmentalist activists pleaded for their actions to be viewed in the context of a dying earth and abuse of animals, animal enterprises and lab scientists advocated for viewing the protests as "eco-terrorism." The classification of conduct as a "case of" eco-terrorism initiated a series of choices in criminal proceedings that would not be possible without this classification. For instance, it allowed defendants' bail amount to be increased and enabled courts to order that a defendant sever contact with fellow activists and publicly denounce violence. It also enabled charges on the basis of the Animal Enterprise Terrorism Act and allowed the application of terrorism enhancements for harsher sentences.

The double bind of liberal legalism

The concept of a double bind comes from theories on contradictory communication (Bateson 2000:206). This chapter refers to the double bind of liberal legalism to highlight the conflicting message the prosecutorial narrative is inevitably emitting as – despite claims to the contrary – its decontextualized narrative is not contextually neutral and a contextualized representation of reality is inherently political. In a process of contentious criminalization, social groups pick up on these contradictions and push or criticize the prosecutor to amend the narrative while the preferred narrative of one group is not acceptable to another and vice versa.

For the subjects of criminal proceedings, prosecutions in the contextualized mode are not necessarily better or worse than the decontextualized mode. Decontextualized prosecution can be just as damaging to a social movement or individual as any other kind of criminalization. Indeed, without resorting to any context references, governments can easily imprison "inconvenient" protesters on bogus or pretext charges, such as traffic or administrative offenses. While contextualized prosecutions may be particularly prone to violations of the liberal legalist rulebook, decontextualized prosecutions can also lead to the imprisonment of innocent men or women, introduce illegal evidence, or otherwise violate due process requirements. In any case, the power that criminal justice measures have to negatively impact social movements is huge. For example, in Spain, suspending a Basque-language newspaper for allegedly being part of the ETA network effectively put the newspaper out of business, even though the defendants were ultimately acquitted and a new newspaper was founded.

Facing an incriminating contextualized narrative, activists and social movements have three options. They can propose a different context and argue for a *different* definition of the crime (for example, rejecting the terrorism label, while accepting prosecution for property destruction). Defendants and their supporters can also reject the contextualization, emphasize liberal legalist values, and call for a decontextualized manner of prosecution. Finally, they can choose to resist criminalization altogether and keep pushing back the boundaries of the criminal justice arena by emphasizing that the proper arena for dealing with their demands and tactics is the political. Often, their response is a mixture of these three approaches. Determining who is responsible for politicizing a trial can also be contested. A foreign lawyer who attended a trial against the Basque prisoner support group Gestoras pro Amnistía to show solidarity with the defendants commented on the ambiguous meaning of politics: "they [the prosecutors] say that the defendants try to make it a political trial, and then they talk politics for hours. If they talk, it is legal, if we talk, it is political" (field notes, June 2008, Madrid).

The representation of reality by the prosecutor in the courtroom is always a reconstruction and, as such, always partial and selective. Prosecutorial narrative is enabled and constrained by the vocabulary and logic of criminal law. Prosecutorial choices, like the selection of defendants, the criminal offense(s) they are charged with, and the arguments used for guilt and sentencing are thus an inherent part of the representation of reality. While the decontextualized approach of liberal legalism can be a powerful tool to process complicated events in a non-contentious manner, the perceived need to contextualize the conduct in question that gave rise to the charge can change the way people think about what is going on in the courtroom. In particular, supporters of the defendants on trial can come to view prosecutors, inevitably political actors, as politicized.

Discursive mobilization inside and outside the courtroom

In contested socio-political terrain in liberal democracies, discursive mobilization by interest groups aims to advance or combat particular narratives regarding harm, crime and public interest, both inside and outside the courtroom. Those mobilizing in the name of victimhood appeal to the state to use its criminal justice system to punish alleged perpetrators as a means of seeking remedy for harms incurred and protection from future injury through deterrence. Those mobilizing as supporters of those charged with crimes for contentious protest actions, in turn, refute the state's definition of conduct as criminal, show solidarity with the accused, and challenge the legitimacy of the state's prosecution. Such discursive mobilization can take many forms: street demonstrations criticizing a court's decision to convict a defendant in Spain, newspaper advertisements in Chile demanding the application of anti-terrorist legislation to Mapuche activists, or online communiqués defending the release of animals as a legitimate response to unethical testing practices in the United States. Actions by vying interest groups can appeal directly to prosecutors to take up or drop cases, challenging them to accept or dismiss a particular narrative of events and define conduct as criminal or not. At the same time, such actions also appeal to a broader audience to support a particular definition of a situation, in an attempt to sway public opinion one way or the other and put pressure on the state.

Prosecutors often portray the "public interest" they seek to represent as a stable category rather than one subject to contestation and change over time. The chief prosecutor of Spain's Audiencia Nacional, for example, referred to "the" Spanish society and "the" public interest to justify prosecutorial decisions in relation to ETA (Interview S-21). Yet, historical examples demonstrate that public perceptions of certain conduct as criminal frequently change over time. Perspectives on rape, for instance, have changed considerably throughout the past century. After deliberate mobilization to have non-consensual sex within marriage considered as rape, many countries today recognize marital rape as a criminal offense, though notable exceptions persist. In Spain, Chile and the United States, discursive shifts occurred in relation to the characterization of actions like releasing animals from factory farms, honoring ETA prisoners in homecoming ceremonies, and peacefully occupying disputed private land. These actions gradually became criminalized due to the discursive mobilization of different interest groups and the transfer of these political disputes into the criminal justice arena, with its particular scripts (victim/perpetrator) and ability to lend legitimacy (via exercise of force/authority) to a political cause.

Chapter 4 traces how those targeted by contentious protest action from animal rights campaigners, ETA militants and sympathizers, and Mapuche activists asserting land claims managed to create alliances, mobilize as victims and push their narrative in order to obtain leverage in the criminal justice arena. The successful discursive mobilization of animal enterprises in the United States, sufferers of ETA violence in Spain, and owners of disputed land in Chile led their narratives to be "honored" (Scott and Lyman 1968) in court cases in which they figured as the officially recognized "victims" of alleged criminal conduct. Their narrative was also bolstered by political interest groups without a direct claim to victimhood, such as the anti-separatism platform Manos Limpias in Spain, which filed criminal complaints against those financially contributing to ETA, and the Center for the Defense of Free Enterprise in the United States, which pushed for the classification of protest actions as "eco-terrorism."

In chapter 5, the spotlight is on those challenging the state's legitimacy in carrying out criminal proceedings. It shows efforts by defendants, prisoners and those in sympathy with them to respond by forming support groups, critiquing the state's performance, and presenting counter-narratives of their contentious protest actions and criminalized conduct. In Spain, Chile and the United States, this so-called "prisoner support" mobilization generally started with the creation of a prisoner support group and call for solidarity. Many of the prisoners in the selected cases identified as "political" prisoners, leading to discursive mobilization for their recognition as such, as a way to challenge the general aims of criminal prosecution: to incapacitate, deter, rehabilitate and/or retaliate against individuals and the movement.

4
Mobilizing the Power of Victimhood

Victim mobilization – appealing to the state for protection

The episodes in this book show that what I call "victim mobilization" can be a key factor in driving processes of criminalization, because crime is not a fixed category. Following Hulsman's (1986) understanding of criminalization as a social construction, the world is full of potentially "criminalizable events." When actors mobilize as victims, they set the process of criminalization in motion by actively translating their grievances into an appeal for state protection. The claim to victimhood is a reference to the logic of criminal law and the institution of a criminal trial in which the victim has a specific place, role and significance. Victimhood is more likely to be honored by prosecutors if the actors are able to present a narrative palatable to the criminal law framework. Whereas a political conflict is always more complicated than a simplistic division into victims and perpetrators can convey, guilt and innocence are supposed to be clear-cut in criminal justice: is the conduct a crime and did the defendant do it (Hulsman 1986)? Examples will follow in which the mobilization of victimhood claims led to the criminalization of conduct that was previously not regarded as criminal, or to the elevation of criminal conduct to a more serious crime with harsher penalties (for example, from property destruction to terrorism).

In their accounts of decisions taken in the criminal justice system, many scholars mention the relevance of "interest" groups, "pressure" groups or "moral entrepreneurs" (Becker in van Swaaningen 1999:204; see also Quinney 1964; Chambliss and Seidman 1982; de Roos 1987; Vold 1998). Those who feel victimized and are frustrated by the impunity accorded to those who attack them set out to change this. While processes of victim mobilization are common and legitimate in liberal democracies, not all who attempt to be recognized as victims are equally heard – with consequences for the conduct of state officials in the criminal justice arena. For example, Waddington suggests that police officials change their routine behavior when potential victims are "important people" like ambassadors or royalty, who can cause significant "in-the-job trouble." He defines effective "troublemakers" as those who occupy institutionalized positions of power (Waddington 1998:127). Similarly, prosecutors are more receptive to some victimhood narratives than to others. In recognition of differing abilities of groups in society to put a government under pressure, Dickson points out that there are "cases and investigations that do *not have to be* initiated and that *could be* ignored with little or no serious consequences" (cited in Holden Jr. 2006:19).

Examples in this chapter show how groups in each of the contentious episodes in the US, Spain and Chile have claimed the victim label and taken steps toward creating institutionalized positions of power in order not to be ignored. Common elements across the contentious episodes include the self-identification of particular groups as victims, the forging of alliances, declaration of a common problem, demanding protection from the state, and the creation of a narrative that translates grievances into the language and logic of criminal law. While in liberal democracies defendants are at the center of criminal proceedings – with a set of rules and measures to protect individuals against arbitrary or politically motivated prosecutions – there are institutionalized ways for victims to mobilize and make their interests heard as well. For example, the legal systems of Spain and Chile allow victims to play an official role at the side of the prosecutor. In Spain, judges are also allowed to weigh in the effects of social "alarm" (that is, concern and fear) when deciding on preventive detention.[1] Beyond such judicial venues for mobilization, victim groups in Spain, Chile and the United States have issued press releases, organized demonstrations and lobbied politicians in order to convince the state of its duty to provide protection and intervene on their behalf.

Targets of animal rights activism in the United States: the alliance of animal enterprises

Common targets of environmental and animal rights protest – pharmaceutical companies, animal researchers, logging companies, the meat

---

1   See for example the Spanish Organic Law 7/1983 of 23 April 1983, Art. 504 sub 2.

industry and others – have successfully allied in the United States to appeal for government protection against such protest. The members of these alliances are, at times, strange bedfellows, such as sport hunters and veterinarians. Industry associations such as the National Association for Biomedical Research (NABR) and the Fur Commission have also played a key role in pushing the FBI and prosecutors to take protests targeting lab scientists and fur farmers more seriously, successfully redefining the release of animals by activists as terrorism. In 1992, NABR played an important role in getting the Animal Enterprise Protection Act (AEPA) through Congress. With its enactment, the concept of an "animal enterprise" became a legal reality. The conceptualization of such different entities into a coherent category is a prime example of mobilizing the power of victimhood to appeal for state protection in processes of contentious criminalization.

In 2000, the National Animal Interest Alliance (NAIA) sponsored a petition requesting that the Senate Judiciary Committee convene hearings on the subject of animal rights terrorism. Calling himself a "victim of animal rights terrorism," Edward Walsh, a member of the NAIA advisory board as well as a lab director and professor in biomedical sciences, criticized the sheer inactivity on the part of prosecutors and the fact that there had been no prosecutions to date under AEPA:

> [N]o one seemed to care very much about the Act [AEPA] that offered such hope for so many just seven years ago. I immediately picked up the phone and began calling colleagues who I knew could help me understand how this potentially important piece of legislation, written to protect honest users of animals from animal rights terrorists, had suffered such undignified rejection at the hands of the federal prosecutors it was designed to energize. I was then stunned to learn that no one has been prosecuted under the provisions of the Act. (Walsh 2000)

He pointed out that this inaction could not be explained by a lack of animal rights activity. "On the contrary," he noted, "[n]umerous laboratory break-ins have occurred during this time-frame, violence and vandalism at fur farms are on the rise, as are animal releases from research and animal husbandry facilities around the world" (Walsh 2000). He strongly appealed to the authorities to take animal rights protests more seriously:

If an animal rights terrorist violates my right to privacy by protesting in front of my home, then punches me in the nose when I answer the doorbell and terrifies my five-year-old son in the process – all for the explicit purpose of either making a spectacle of me for the benefit of public relations, or to intimidate me into submission – the action constitutes something worse and far more dangerous to society than a simple punch in the nose. I claim that the act is actually a smack in the nose of all of us – to society – and thereby constitutes a significantly larger offense, one that warrants a proportionally larger penalty. (Walsh 2000)

Walsh successfully influenced prosecutorial narrative. In 2004, six activists were indicted on the basis of AEPA for organizing the kind of protests in front of lab scientists' homes that Walsh described (see chapter 11 for more on this case). In an interview with one of the prosecutors in the case, he drew upon the narrative proposed by Walsh and other industry associations when he told me that people were victimized and frustrated, that they felt nobody was out there for them (Interview US-13). During the trial, the prosecutor even adopted the image of "foot soldiers," a phrase previously used by Walsh when he wrote that "animal rights leaders continue to egg on their foot soldiers with inflammatory talk of revolution" (2000).

Animal releases (or "animal liberation" for activists) are another concern for "animal enterprises." In March 1979, for the first time, activists broke into a lab at the New York University Medical Center and released two dogs, two guinea pigs, and a cat in name of the ALF (Jasper and Nelkin 1992:33; ALF 2011b). Since then, activists have conducted similar "animal liberation" raids at fur farms, laboratories, and factory farms throughout the United States. After years of such actions, labs have increasingly been built and designed to defend against them. Today, research laboratories using animals are all equipped with security cameras and other surveillance and security measures (Scarce 2006:215). Victim mobilization, though, goes beyond such individual protective measures. When Peter Young raided six mink farms in the American Midwest in 1997, he released between 8,000 and 12,000 mink, causing two of the fur farms to go out of business. Fur farmers reported that "1997 was a dark time for U.S. fur farmers as eco-terrorists struck repeatedly" and lamented the lack of government attention to their plight (Fur Commission 2009). Teresa Platt, director of the Fur Commission that has represented mink farmers since

1994, said: "We need to evaluate how big it is and put it into perspective. [...] I don't think the government took it seriously or acted as quickly as they should have" (Hollenbeck 1999).

Indeed, during the 1980s, prosecutors and the FBI did not yet label such releases as terrorism. One activist, for example, was prosecuted for burglary, although the charges were later dismissed (Flies on the Wall 2007). Platt described how they proceeded to "engag[e] political will" (Platt 1999). In 1998, on a tour in Europe, the Director of the FBI Louis Freeh said that "[e]co- and animal rights terrorism [...] was not an issue, not a priority and not on the agency's 'radar screen'" (Platt 1999:1). The fur farmers were outraged by this lack of serious attention to the raids they experienced. When the FBI publicly announced a year later that animal rights and environmental activists pose a threat, the Fur Commission proudly announced having played a key role in influencing the FBI's priorities:

In talking to FBI agents, the redirection of FBI manpower to include eco- and animal rights terrorism entailed a bottom-up educational process. Fur America's *Fur Netwatch*, an Internet info distribution system, has been a vital component in that process. Over the last year, the people of the fur trade have been key players with other animal- and resource-based industries in a concerted effort to push eco- and animal rights terrorism up the government's priority pole. These efforts have resulted in a strong statement of commitment from the FBI. (Platt 1999:2)

In order to successfully present fur farmers as victims worthy of government protection, the Fur Commission referred to them as "those who make their living in concert with the Earth" and "resource caretakers" (Platt 1999:2). In its public communication, the Fur Commission emphasized the "vital role we play in helping clothe this planet's 6 billion people, with a product that is not only practical and beautiful, but is also natural, sustainable and environment-friendly" (Fur Commission 1998). Similarly, Walsh explicitly wanted to remind politicians "just how many of us there are" by counting "the scientists, the farmers, the cattlemen, the rodeo and circus and motion picture entrepreneurs, the furriers, the hunters and fishermen, the physicians, the conservationists." He argued that together these groups "constitute the vast majority of Americans" (Walsh 2000).

Another way animal enterprises drew attention from the government was to calculate the economic costs of break-ins and animal releases. The Fur Commission and the NABR estimated that their respective industries lost more than $45 million dollars due to actions claimed by ALF during the 1990s. Thanks to their outreach efforts, this number later found its way into the testimony of domestic terrorism section chief Jarboe before the House Resources Committee (Jarboe 2002).

US animal rights activists have also employed victimhood terminology to describe their grievances, for instance, when claiming that meat is murder and that owners of animal-testing companies are assassins. They have not, though, made serious efforts – let alone undertaken a consistent campaign – to translate such slogans into a palatable criminal justice narrative to be taken up by a prosecutor. As their challenge to the status quo regarding the use of animals and the earth (for example, the concept of animal rights) is already outside of the accepted legal framework, this is not surprising. A few lawsuits initiated by the US Department of Agriculture have alleged "animal cruelty" in a number of industries, but these have rarely taken place in the criminal justice arena, as most were civil lawsuits. In contrast, alliances of industry associations have actively entered the criminal justice arena and played a key role in pushing the narrative that animal enterprises are victims of a category of crimes by animal rights protesters (for example, animal releases) that the government should take more seriously. This narrative has indeed been taken up in criminal prosecutions. By 2009, the release of animals had transformed into a terrorist offense. In that year, two activists were convicted and sentenced to 21 and 24 months respectively under the newly enacted Animal Enterprise Terrorist Act (AETA) for the 2008 release of 650 mink from a fur farm in Utah ("AETA 2 case"). Thus, the victimhood narrative centered on animal enterprises became accepted in the criminal justice arena and materialized in prosecutions against animal rights activists, whereas the slogan "puppy killer" by animal rights activists did not lead to criminal prosecutions against animal-testing companies.

Victims of ETA violence in Spain: from "mere statistical fact" to driving force

While in the United States a varied alliance of highly different groups advocated on behalf of "animal enterprises," in Spain over the course of the past four decades a number of different associations were founded to represent the interests of victims of ETA in Spain and in the Basque Country (Alonso 2016). For some, though by no means all of these organizations, a key part of their strategy was to engage in the criminal justice arena. The organization Dignidad y Justicia was founded in 2005 to advocate for the stringent application of the Spanish criminal justice system against ETA. During my fieldwork in the Basque Country in 2008, I met a member of the organization in a café. Due to her activity with the group, she was threatened by ETA and therefore usually accompanied by bodyguards everywhere she went. On this particular day, however, we met alone. Her anxiety was evident, though, as she asked me to change places with her when we sat down, so as not to sit with her back to the door (Interview S-17). Her request was a small reminder of the constant vigilance and concern faced by those people who opposed ETA or criticized demands for Basque independence. They had bodyguards, parked their cars in unexpected places, and checked for bombs before driving (field notes, April–May 2008). In the Basque Country at the time, more than a thousand people employed daily bodyguards out of fear of ETA's violence. Collectively, they were known as "the threatened" (los amenazados) (Santos 2008:21).

Dignidad y Justicia is just one of at least a dozen associations across Spain created by people impacted by ETA's violence, all with different emphases and political leanings. The first such group, the Asociación de Víctimas de Terrorismo (AVT), was formed in 1981. Originally comprised mostly of widows and parents of Guardia Civil killed by ETA, the AVT expanded in the 1990s – along with the breadth of ETA's targets – to include the family members of right-wing politicians and journalists. From its inception, the AVT advocated for better treatment as victims of ETA's violence, who felt "abandoned and marginalized by the state and many sectors of Spanish society" (AVT 2008). One complaint, for example, was that family members were not even notified of the date for the trial concerning the killing of their loved one (Interview S-16). Later, other victim organizations were founded as well, as not all victims of ETA attacks wished to be connected with the highly politicized, right-wing AVT. Some of these organizations were more reconciliatory than others, with notable differences between those in Madrid and those based in the Basque Country. Controversies also existed within and between groups over who qualified as victims of ETA (for example, did "the threatened" also count as victims?) (Águeda 2013).

Against these victimhood narratives, ETA and its supporters maintained that their targets, particularly the Guardia Civil, constituted legitimate military targets in a war of independence, who actively defended the status quo of the unitary Spanish state. Yet, in some of their attacks on Guardia Civil barracks, ETA also killed or wounded the guards' children or other family members. Similarly, when ETA targeted politicians, it also occasionally killed their bodyguards or random bystanders, such as the young boy who happened to lose a leg and an eye due to a bomb-package by ETA in 1982 that exploded later than planned (Barrio 2017). For a long time, ETA's supporters justified such deaths as collateral damage in a conflict in which violence came from two sides.

Family members of Basque left-nationalists killed during the 1980s by right-wing paramilitary groups, such as the Grupos Antiterroristas de Liberación (GAL), also formed victim associations demanding recognition as victims of state violence. Furthermore, non-governmental organizations monitoring human rights violations have published numerous testimonies of detainees suspected of ETA membership or *kale borroka* (street struggle/ violence) alleging abuse by the state. In the 1990s, Spanish Investigative Judge Garzón from the Audiencia Nacional successfully prosecuted a number of state agents for the killing of alleged ETA members during the Dirty War. These criminal cases produced official records on an otherwise hidden episode. In other cases, torture allegations led to criminal proceedings against Spanish police. Yet, unlike the narratives pushed by the AVT and Dignidad y Justicia, the victimhood narratives of Basque left-nationalist associations did not become as dominant in the criminal justice arena. The fact that significant parts of Spanish and Basque society did not believe the torture allegations by suspected ETA members could explain this lack of take-up, while the silence by prosecutors also reinforced the belief that prisoners lied about being tortured (Terwindt 2011). Since 2010, however, (former) prisoners suspected of belonging to ETA who filed torture complaints managed to get their cases heard by the European Court of Human Rights, resulting in seven convictions of Spain for not sufficiently investigating the torture allegations (Nicolas and Camps 2018) as well as a conviction for violating Article 3 of the European Convention on Human Rights which prohibits inhuman and degrading treatment (Case Portu and Sarasola, 2018).

Not all associations of victims of ETA have actively pushed for specific narratives in the criminal justice arena. In concerted discursive mobilization efforts, particularly the AVT and Dignidad y Justicia made it a priority to push Spanish prosecutors to use criminal proceedings to cut off ETA's funding, curb its social support, and hamper its recruitment efforts. Notably, their narrative denied the existence of a political conflict with two sides and analogies with the conflict in Northern Ireland. Instead, they advanced a binary narrative of guilty perpetrators and innocent victims, and emphasized the criminal justice framework as the only context within which to view ETA's violence. They also shunned the idea of negotiations between ETA and the Spanish state, which they viewed as sacrificing the victims of ETA in exchange for a flawed peace. They refused to view ETA prisoners and their families as victims of state oppression.

While the narrative of a conflict with two sides was dominant during the 1980s, societal opinion shifted significantly over time. By the late 2000s, the criminal justice narrative had become the dominant framework for dealing with ETA and its supporters. Individuals, organizations and state officials also began to express solidarity with victims of ETA violence in honoring ceremonies, demonstrations and publications. For example, after an ETA attack in 2008, the organization Gesto por la Paz issued a press release explicitly to say: "We want the family of Uria Mendizábal to know that the majority of this society is with them, shares their pain and rejects those who today have swept them into the tragedy" (Gesto por la Paz 2008). Similarly, when ETA killed Isaías Carrasco, a former local councillor for the Socialist Party in a village in the Basque Country, the magazine of another victim organization bore the title "*Todos Somos Isaías*" (We Are All Isaías). This increased identification with victims of ETA went hand in hand with the perception that "almost anyone can now be a potential target of ETA," as a Basque newspaper put it, commenting on ETA's broadening of its targets beyond the Guardia Civil (Barriuso 2008). The mobilization of victims of ETA violence even resulted in their becoming a significant force in electoral politics. A critique by the son of an assassinated Guardia Civil, "first we didn't have a voice, now we can influence the vote" (in Díaz Lombardo 2007:37).

The institutional rise of victims of ETA violence in the 2000s also coincided with a shift in orientation toward victims at the Audiencia Nacional, spearheaded by Investigative Judge Garzón.[2] In 2005, Garzón

---

2   As a continental legal system, Spanish prosecutors work in cooperation with investigative judges. As investigative judges prepare a case and take crucial decisions regarding who is charged with what, they play an important role in the creation of "the prosecutorial narrative." Only when the investigative phase is closed and the case goes to trial does the prosecutor take over.

wrote that during the 1980s and early 1990s "the victims were a mere statistical fact when it came down to terrorist acts" and declared that going forward "victims had to form part of the anti-terrorist actions" (2006:160–1). He blamed the prevailing impunity for ETA's crimes on the "indifferent ones" and their "silence" and "passivity" (2006:170). Due to mobilization by victim organizations, however, this changed. In Spain, victims have two formal ways in which they can represent themselves as a prosecuting force in a criminal trial together with the state prosecutors. They can choose between private accusation and popular accusation. A victim can be a private accuser as the specific and direct victim in the case (for example, kidnapping or assassination), or popular accusation can be used when an organization represents a class of victims relevant in the case at hand. Since the beginning of the 1990s, the two organizations AVT and Dignidad y Justicia have frequently employed popular accusation to promote their interests.

Time and again since the 1990s, these victim organizations successfully lobbied the criminal justice system with concrete demands. For example, a spokesperson for the AVT was confident that the groups' lobbying efforts were responsible for well-known ETA militant Iñaki de Juana being tried under new charges and sentenced again to prison (Interview S-16). In other instances, their lobbying efforts went beyond a single case. In Spain, sentences were previously capped at a maximum of 30 years. As prisoners could be released after they had fulfilled two-thirds of their sentence, a convicted ETA member could be back on the streets after 18 years of prison, even if their formal sentence ran up to 1,000 years for cumulative crimes. Victim organizations found this unacceptable and advocated for the "full completion" of sentences (of ETA members as well as other convicts). Concretely, they wanted the two-thirds rule to be applied to the entire sentence, not to the thirty-year sentence cap. They succeeded in court and the new interpretation became known as the "*doctrina Parot*," in reference to ETA commando-member Henri Parot, who had been detained in 1990 and accused of involvement in 82 assassinations. This 2006 Supreme Court decision was highly controversial among Basque left-nationalists, who spoke about "hidden life sentences." While the influence of victim groups had been successful at the domestic level, in 2013, the European Court of Human Rights overturned the Parot doctrine for violating the right to no punishment without law.

Discursive mobilization by interest groups other than victim organizations also pushed the Spanish state to take on ETA's support network in the criminal justice arena. Anti-corruption and anti-separatist organization Manos Limpias filed criminal complaints to tackle the issue of the so-called "revolutionary tax" levied by ETA, whereby it threatened businesses in the Basque Country and beyond with violence if they did not make regular monetary payments to the group. During the 1970s and 1980s, such payments were estimated to comprise up to €6 million per year (Urquia 2017). Explaining the lawsuits, the spokesperson of Manos Limpias argued that "when the money is finished, ETA is finished" (Interview S-20).

Initiatives to push prosecutors to take up certain cases were not always successful. For example, for a short while victims of ETA attempted to shift the discourse around ETA's use of violence to one of "ethnic cleansing." Although Investigative Judge Garzón made one attempt to get this charge against the political party Batasuna accepted by the court, he did not succeed. Another attempt by victim lobby groups aimed to shift the qualification of ETA's use of violence from terrorism to "crimes against humanity" in order to overcome the statute of limitations on certain crimes, which denied victims the possibility of ever knowing who carried out the violence and why (Unzalu 2008:15).

Although not all proposals were taken up by prosecutors, organized victims of ETA were able to significantly transform the common discourse around ETA's use of violence and increasingly shift the locus of this contentious political struggle to the criminal justice arena. While in the past ETA enjoyed some amount of legitimacy in its resistance and struggle for self-determination, by the 2000s, victim associations had effectively lifted the plight of victims of ETA violence into the spotlight. Their interests had firmly become part of the public interest, to be taken into account by prosecutors as well as state negotiators.

Multiple victimhood narratives in Chile

In each of the contentious episodes, there are multiple victimhood narratives. Sometimes, challengers of the status quo did not seriously translate their grievances into a criminal justice narrative to be taken up by the prosecutor (for example, animal rights activists shouting "puppy killer" in front of the house of the chief executive officers [CEOs] of an animal-testing company). In other cases, there was such concerted mobilization, as in the Basque Country where lawyers and (former) prisoners drew attention to alleged incidents of torture during incommunicado detention. This section devotes more attention to these simultaneous victim mobilization efforts by political opponents. In Chile, both Mapuche activists as well as present-day private owners of contested indigenous lands have mobilized as victims in the criminal justice arena. Commercial landowners have drawn attention to illegal incursions on their property by Mapuche activists carrying out protest actions, while Mapuche activists have rallied against police violence and threats by landowners.

In articulating their victimhood narratives, both groups have frequently drawn on and inverted concepts from the competing narrative. Examples include when Mapuche claim to be the "real" landowners, or when commercial landowners suddenly appeal to human rights, thus adopting a register previously monopolized by the Mapuche movement. The few prosecutions against Chilean police officers scarcely took account of the narrative proposed by the Mapuche movement. Although the discursive mobilization of private landowners has been more successful in terms of influencing prosecutorial narrative, it has not always led to the desired results. Since the early 1990s, conviction rates and the severity of sentences for Mapuche activists vacillated between harshness and leniency, reflecting the contentious nature of criminalizing Mapuche protest in the absence of a political resolution to their long-standing, legitimate land claims.

Present-day commercial landowners cast themselves as victims

In a newspaper interview in 2003, private landowner Juan Agustín Figueroa referred to the rural Araucanía region of central Chile as the "Far West." As a prestigious lawyer and member of the Constitutional Court, his words carried significant weight when he said: "In a society, citizens renounce their right to self-defense, because they hand it over to the State … But when [the state] does not lend me its support and leaves me in a situation of defenselessness, I am indirectly invited to take justice into my own hands" (cited in Cayuqueo 2003). Together with other landowners, commercial farmers and forestry companies, he claimed to be a victim of harassment by Mapuche communities and activists connected to historic claims to their estates. The manager of a large forestry company similarly invoked the social contract in demanding state protection from Mapuche protest actions on contested land: "We comply with all the labor and environmental laws. The state has to guarantee us the right to private property" (Interview 2003, C-34).

Unlike the AVT in Spain, Chilean landowners have long recognized the so-called "Mapuche conflict" as a political conflict and have even acknowledged the general legitimacy of some Mapuche grievances. They are also aware that Mapuche demands for land restitution are viewed sympathetically by a large portion of the Chilean population. However, as the current private owners of disputed lands, they reject any blame and portray themselves exclusively as victims of the situation. Forestry companies emphasize that the problems forming the basis of Mapuche grievances predated their arrival in the region during the 1970s. Using the vocabulary of "human rights," they resist the idea that the human rights of some would be privileged over the human rights of others (Villegas 2008). For example, when in 2009 the United Nations Special Rapporteur on the rights of indigenous peoples visited Chile, a coalition of landowners sent him a report in which they listed the violations of their human rights as they perceived his focus on the Mapuches to be one-sided (Interview C-43). In this narrative, even legitimate demands do not justify law-breaking. For instance, after Mapuche communities entered, occupied, and started to log the plantation on the Santa Rosa de Colpi estate, the company Forestal Mininco wrote:

> We call for the public opinion to not be confused by false and tendentious versions and images about what has happened, which pretend to legitimize actions of violence and terrorism. The grave social problems that exist among the inhabitants of this region date very much from before the presence of the forestry companies in the region. The historical claims to lands or the social problems, however serious they are, cannot justify the use of illegal and violent means of pressure, if we want to live in a civilized and democratic society. (Mininco 1999)

In establishing their victimhood, landowners have often emphasized that attacks on their properties should not be viewed as isolated incidents, but part of a broader "Mapuche conflict." As a witness for the prosecutor in a 2003 trial, the executive vice-president of the Chilean forestry association, CORMA, Juan Correa Bulnes, testified:

> There was the idea that the crimes were separate facts. Now, we raise the alarm to say that there were 600 of those crimes. And now we have described them in detail, so that the government can see how many

crimes there are. We want attention for the truth, to enable unified action. (field notes, Case *Lonkos* of Traiguén, April 2003)

Another red thread in the victim narrative was the emphasis on their innocence. For example, during a session in a parliamentary commission, the landowning family members expressed: "We haven't damaged anyone, not nature, not anyone. [...] What have we done to the people that are attacking us?" (Comisión Seguridad Ciudadana 2009). Furthermore, while portraying big forestry companies as victims was not always persuasive to the larger public, the victimhood narrative regarding the dangers posed by arson attacks tended to focus on the danger to security personnel patrolling the plantations and the commercial farmers and their families living on the estates.

Victim alliances and the mutual recognition of victimhood among landowners and corporations have not been a given in Chile, but were created. For instance, following two attacks on private landowner Jorge Luchsinger, associations of commercial farmers organized in solidarity. In response to the 2005 attack in which Mr. Luchsinger and his wife were assaulted and their house burnt down, the Consorcio Agrícola del Sur (Agricultural Consortium of the South) offered compensation to any person who could find the perpetrators (Cayuqueo 2005b). This also triggered several members of the farmer's association Sociedad de Fomento Agricola de Temuco (Society for the Promotion of Agriculture, in short SOFO, founded in 1918) to support each other by setting up a solidarity fund for legal assistance. The director of SOFO explained that there was a fear among landowners that "I could be the next" (Interview 2009, C-55).

Despite efforts to unite under the common banner of victimhood, collective mobilization by Chilean landowners has alternated with individualized efforts by some to emphasize the differences between various kinds of landowners. Some private landowners have highlighted that they have always had good relations with adjacent Mapuche communities, in contrast to the major forestry companies. In turn, smaller forestry companies have underscored that they are not the same as big transnational companies. There have also been inter-industry divisions. A forestry engineer claimed, "This is a problem of the last 50 years with *agriculture*. It is not a problem of forestry" (Interview 2003, C-34). Moreover, not all private landowners have supported the use of criminal proceedings to combat contentious action by Mapuche activists.

In the early 2000s, the manager of CORMA in Chile's 9th Region was convinced of the efficacy of the penal approach, as he observed less arson and attributed this to the use of harsher laws (Interview 2003, C-35). In the belief that detentions worked, some landowners actively assisted prosecutors and the police in the investigation of events, and also participated as "private accusers" during trials. Forestal Mininco has also provided assistance in fact-finding and judicial investigation. One of the duties of the company's private security personnel, for example, was to take pictures and videos during occupations or incidents and provide witness testimony (Interview C-18). In 2001, SOFO distributed a manual among farmers that gave instructions on how to act in the situation of a land occupation or another threat by Mapuche protests. It included information about how to file a criminal complaint, listed names and directions of prosecutors, and gave information about the rights of victims and the possibility of asking for police protection (Barria 2001).

Despite these efforts to initiate and support criminal prosecutions, landowners became frustrated over the lack of convictions achieved. A senior lawyer for Forestal Mininco estimated that at least 80 percent of the complaints that he filed were simply archived without obtaining convictions (Interview 2009, C-44). He did not, however, see this as a huge failure. For him, it was important to keep the "system functioning." For Forestal Mininco, it was not just the possibility of punishment that was important, but rather the process of labeling incidents. A lawyer for SOFO who filed criminal complaints on behalf of farmers noted: "The solution is not in the court rooms. The Mapuche problem is a socio-political problem. But while the state is not solving it, we have to continue reacting" (Interview 2009, C-42).

While some private landowners and big forestry companies clearly pushed for strong state intervention, others actually made the conscious decision *not* to speak about crimes in public or file complaints. Sometimes to avoid an escalation of events or due to fear of reprisals, or simply to avoid any unwanted (negative) publicity or being perceived as over-reacting, private landowners decided not to pursue any prosecutions in response to incursions on their property by Mapuche communities disputing their land titles. Some forestry companies preferred to put their efforts into special "good neighbor" (*buen vecindad*) programs. Others have simply been too disillusioned with conviction rates in such cases to bother. "I am tired of filing criminal complaints" said the owner of several plantations in 2009 (Interview C-54). Thus, not all landowners strategically cast themselves as victims to push for criminal prosecutions against Mapuche activists. The only reason he kept filing complaints was that the insurance company required him to do so.

The move into the criminal justice arena was often explained by a perception of escalation. According to a Chilean public defender, theft and usurpation were often only prosecuted if they were perceived to be a prelude toward worse actions (Interview 2009, C-47). Agreeing with that observation, the SOFO director explained that many instances of small theft were generally perceived to be customary practice in their region, characteristic of the relations between rural neighbors and, more specifically, relations between business farmers and their workers, who often came from Mapuche communities. According to the "laws of the countryside" (Interview C-55), it used to be common for Mapuches from rural communities to enter other properties to look for firewood or graze their animals. The SOFO director said that workers for private business farmers commonly took small amounts of grain or fertilizer, in a practice he compared to employees using copy machines for their own purposes or taking home small office supplies, such as pens. Explaining the landowners' mobilization in the criminal justice arena, he noted that, to a certain degree, such private usage of company materials was part of an unspoken agreement, but not, he emphasized, when it involved the theft of "forty or sixty animals in two months; that is not like a single pen any more" (Interview C-55).

The mobilization to draw attention to more severe transgressions of the law succeeded when, in March 1999, a parliamentary commission was installed to assess the threat due to the growing number of incidents of arson in the 6th, 7th, 8th and 9th Regions, with a special focus on the influence of the "property conflict between indigenous communities and private parties." The report emphasized the importance of the forestry sector for the country and the economy, as the sector provided 120,000 jobs and represented US $2 billion per year in exports (Comisión Especial 2000). It also framed arson as a grave threat to Chile's national identity as a "*país forestal*" (forestry country). In the 9th Region, about 90 percent of forestry fires were deemed intentional, often intended to damage forestry companies. The report also confirmed the lack of prosecutions that landowners criticized. In 95 percent of the cases, the perpetrators were not found, and in less than 1 percent was there an actual legal sanction (Comisión Especial 2000:25).

Through effective discursive mobilization in the criminal justice arena, landowners were able to push for the application of anti-terrorist legislation in response to arson incidents. On 10 March 2002, corporate associations published a two-page advertisement in Chile's major newspaper *El Mercurio* claiming that "terrorism is expanding in the sectors in the Araucanía region" and demanding state intervention using the Law on State Security and the Anti-terrorism Law (Toledo 2007:282). Between 2002 and 2003, provincial governors and regional governors in Chile's 8th and 9th Regions responded to their appeals by officially intervening in criminal prosecutions to request the use of the Anti-terrorism Law on 12 occasions (Comisión de Constitución 2003:76). The possibility of direct intervention by government actors through filing criminal complaints is a key feature of Chilean prosecutorial politics.[3] The lawyer filing such complaints for the Governor of Malleco said he filed them whenever there was "public commotion." For example, in cases where a truck had been ambushed on the highway, he argued, it was impossible for the governor *not* to file such a complaint. Acknowledging the pressure from corporations in these cases, he said that, otherwise, the criticism in the media would be obvious: "the government does not take responsibility!" (Interview 2009, C-56).

Thus, while not all non-Mapuche landowners and companies favored a criminal justice solution, some made it a key part of their strategy to file complaints and support prosecutors in evidence collection and prosecution. Despite succeeding in obtaining governmental attention and the application of anti-terrorism legislation in the early 2000s, private landowners continued to experience what they called impunity. In October 2008, a coalition of professional associations reiterated in a public declaration that "this is a theme of the country, not only of one region" (Confederación de la Producción y el Comercio 2008). In a parliamentary commission in 2009, a private landowner complained that when he visited the local governors, they belittled the problem, saying it concerned ordinary criminals and isolated cases. He experienced 25 instances of theft and arson with no arrests made in response (Comisión Seguridad Ciudadana 2009). According to the SOFO director, some farmers even paid the police for fuel for their cars to come and protect

---

3   Between 2001 and 2003, regional governors and the Ministry for Internal Affairs filed more than 80 complaints in relation to the Mapuche conflict, many for arson, but also for theft, damages, injuries, public disorder and usurpation (Comisión de Constitución 2003:78).

them. Yet, even those farmers with 24/7 protection still suffered attacks (Interview 2009, C-55).

Mapuche activists as victims of police violence and threats by landowners

In response to their narrative of historical injustice and protest activities, Mapuche activists have faced threats by landowners as well as efforts by law enforcement authorities to break up their protests or police their communities in response to landowner appeals for protection. Their key grievance of usurpation by non-Mapuche landowners was never taken up by prosecutors. As with the slogan "meat is murder" by US animal rights activists, the framing of non-Mapuche landowners as criminal usurpers probably too radically challenges the status quo to be taken up by prosecutors. Somewhat more successfully, Mapuche activists urged prosecutors to take up cases of police violence against protesters and Mapuche communities. Between 2002 and 2010, the Mapuche movement mobilized around the victimhood of three young Mapuche activists killed by police violence. They disputed the government's finding that their killings were "accidental deaths" in "confrontations" with the police, and instead claimed that they were deliberately assassinated. In a narrative that resonated with the experiences of other Mapuche activists in Chile, one activist expressed that "the police are out there to kill" (Interview 2009, C-57).

As the cases involved police officers supervised by the Ministry of Defense, the trials did not take place in ordinary courts, but in military tribunals. In the case of Alex Lemún who was killed in 2002, the proceedings ended with the dismissal of the charges, leaving the family and the entire Mapuche movement disillusioned. When Mapuche activist Matías Catrileo was killed by police in 2008, the activists' lack of confidence in fair legal proceedings led them to keep Matías's body hidden from the government during the first few days after his death. They deeply distrusted the state's forensic investigators and wanted to protect the body against police tampering. Matías's death garnered immediate solidarity from a wide variety of people who all came to Temuco to attend his funeral. Demonstrations were organized to condemn his death and call for the investigation and punishment of the responsible police officer. Graffiti in Temuco called the policeman a "murderer" (*asesino*) and decried "state terrorism" (field notes, April 2009).

In June 2009, the police officer whose bullet killed Matías was tried in military court. For a long time, the police argued that they had been defending themselves when Matías was killed. They claimed that he was shot in a confrontation with activists who had burnt haystacks on the estate of a private landowner. However, evidence revealed that the bullet had hit him in the back, disproving the police version of events and vindicating his friends, who long held that he was shot while running away. The prosecutors charged the police officer with "unnecessary violence resulting in death" and asked for 10 years' imprisonment, but upon conviction he was only sentenced to two years on probation (*La Tercera* 2010). The tribunal argued that the police officer had acted in "legitimate defense." The sentence was a disappointment for the friends and family of Matías and a radio host declared: "Here is a message for the police: kill tranquilly by shooting in the back, because they will apply mitigations and you will be able to go home and sleep soundly while a family has their child assassinated" (Radio Cooperativa, quoted in *La Tercera* 2010). Incidents of disproportionate police violence against Mapuche communities and activists continue. In 2016, a young Mapuche was shot in the back and severely injured as a result. The trial of the police officer started in January 2019. In November 2018, a Mapuche from one of the CAM-affiliated communities demanding land redistribution was killed by the police. In response, CAM claimed it had carried out the destruction of machines belonging to the Forestal Arauco company (CAM 2018).

Mapuche activists have also attempted to be recognized as victims in the criminal justice arena in relation to threats from landowners. In 2002, Mapuche leaders filed criminal complaints related to death threats by a retaliation commando group (Toledo 2007:283), which a prosecutor reportedly investigated (*Austral* 2002; Palma 2002). Mapuche claims to victimhood in this context were thus honored by prosecutors initiating investigations, though no indictments ever followed. A few years later, in 2009, Mapuche activists filed complaints alleging "genocide" and "ethnic cleansing" after a spokesman of one such retaliation commando group was reported to have said that "the main Mapuche leaders will disappear from the world, due to two sticks of dynamite which we will place in their belts if they continue with their demands for lands" (P.A.S. 2009). The governor of Chile's 9th Region ordered an investigation, which was initiated, but led to no further proceedings.

These cases represent rare instances in which Mapuche activists have officially taken on the role of victims in criminal proceedings – though hardly with the results demanded by the Mapuche movement. Otherwise, criminal cases related to the "Mapuche conflict" have typically involved

Mapuche activists as defendants, with estate owners of contested indigenous lands occupying the institutionally recognized role as "victims." Despite differences in approach between private landowners and industry associations in crafting their victimhood narratives, they succeeded in putting the "Mapuche conflict" on the agenda of the central government in Santiago, and at times convincing prosecutors to apply Chile's Anti-terrorism Law to contentious Mapuche protest activities. At the same time, the fact that Mapuche protests have predominantly been dealt with in the context of the criminal justice system – while the issue of land redistribution remains unresolved – continues to be controversial. The resulting ambivalence in criminal prosecutions and the back and forth between leniency and the application of terrorism legislation are discussed in more depth in subsequent chapters.

Mobilization and discursive action in the criminal justice arena

As these contentious episodes demonstrate, once groups are effective in establishing their capacity to act as "troublemakers" (Waddington 1998), the state comes under pressure to re-establish confidence in the criminal justice system. For example, threats by landowners to "take justice into their own hands" put pressure on the Chilean state. In the process of becoming effective troublemakers, defenders of the status quo frequently entered into alliances on the basis of a shared narrative of victimhood. State authorities perceived the need to reassure the public that the police and judicial system work for the citizens and are capable of punishing criminals. As Nieburg points out, "all state systems must integrate into their power structure at least the groups which are self-conscious, organized, interested, and able to exercise private power in the streets if barred from the magic circle [of government decision-making]" (1968:19). To the extent that they are listened to, "victims" can propose an alternative narrative and transform the way the prosecutor constructs a criminal case.

The examples above show that interest groups mobilizing in the name of victimhood generally seek broad societal sympathy for and identification with their plight as victims, for example, by emphasizing their innocence. Further, these groups tend to seek strength by building organizations and coalitions. Once unified as a group, victim organizations or alliances can declare a common problem: the lack of protection by the state and dangerous implications of continuing impunity. In turn, they lobby government agencies, file criminal complaints, and influence discourses, crime "images" (Sudnow 1965) and the definition of the situation.

In line with liberal ideology as sketched by Nonet and Selznick (2005:54), the "victims" and their advocates in the three contentious contexts outlined above generally requested "legal security" and a strict obedience to positive law. Defenders of the status quo invariably would take individual measures to protect their property by hiring private security guards or installing surveillance cameras. In addition, they tended to point to state obligations as understood in the social contract paradigm. In their appeals, they invoked the rule of law as a guarantor against crime and the source of their right to protection. At the same time, they also tended to view the law, and "rule of law" more broadly, as a serious obstacle in the struggle against crime or terrorism, as they perceived it as providing too many benefits to defendants, making effective police and prosecution work very difficult. Some victim advocates thus viewed rights as a zero-sum game: the granting of certain rights to defendants meant the negation of victims' rights (cf. Jakobs and Cancio Meliá 2006). The rule of law's function to protect citizens against arbitrary state repression is thus portrayed as being in tension with its role in helping states to protect citizens against crime.

As Beetham (1991:67) points out, it is not surprising that powerful defenders of the socio-political status quo are particularly likely to appeal to the rule of law for their protection:

> The much readier access of the powerful to the law, and the fact that it provides both the source and protection of their power, makes appeal to the law as the ground of legitimacy a particularly favored strategy for dominant groups. Indeed, respect for the law is insisted on as the first duty of the subordinate, and legal validity is made to appear not only as the necessary, but as the sufficient, condition of legitimacy: its ultimate, rather than merely its proximate, source. (Beetham 1991:67)

While powerful defenders of the status quo may be most inclined to seek a strict application of the law to bolster their position as victims, other groups can and have done so as well. Typically, such mobilization has emphasized that the state must be subject to its own rules in relation to the exercise of violence by police or prison personnel, as when Basque defendants sought redress for torture or Mapuche activists pursued criminal complaints for police raids in their communities. As such, claims to victimhood in relation to the state's criminal justice agents are closely linked to the logic of prisoner support mobilization. These efforts to challenge the state's criminal justice proceedings are analyzed in more depth in the next chapter.

Challengers of the status quo were generally not heard in the translation of their grievances about the history and consequences of that status quo into the language of criminal justice. The less compatible victimhood narratives are with the status quo, the less likely they were to be successfully translated into prosecutorial narratives. Mapuche activists failed in their efforts to claim victimhood when they accused the current legal owners of contested lands of "usurpation." No criminal prosecution against non-Mapuche landowners was opened on that charge. They were also unable to translate their complaint that commercial eucalyptus tree plantations sucked up all of the groundwater, thus emptying their wells, into a recognized crime. Similarly, environmental and animal rights activists in the United States were not successful in having their victimhood claims – that the earth and animals are the "real" victims – honored in criminal prosecutions. Such claims challenge the ideal of a clear separation between humans and animals on which liberal legal discourse is premised. The notion of the earth and animals having interests is alien to the anthropocentric structure of the criminal law, which only takes damage to the earth and animals into account if this impinges on the interests of a human being. Basque left-nationalists did not translate their claim to independence into a criminal justice narrative. More successful, some Basque victims of the state-sponsored torture and killings in the Dirty War were recognized as such in criminal prosecutions against Spanish state agents – just as in some cases Mapuche victims of police violence were recognized in prosecutions. As the chapters in Part II will show, the extent to which groups have been able to claim victimhood and influence the prosecutorial narrative in the contentious episodes in Spain, Chile and the United States have varied and also changed over time. But before that, the next chapter explores the narratives of those put on trial and their supporters, that aim to counter the prosecutorial narratives that criminalize their actions.

5
Challenging the State's Crime Definition

Prisoner support: condemning the state's definition of the situation

While the previous chapter looked at those groups that claim victimhood and successfully manage to influence prosecutorial narrative, this chapter turns to those who identify with the defendant in a criminal case. The upcoming examples describe how groups in the three contentious episodes in Spain, Chile and the United States rejected the state's crime definitions and called the legitimacy of the courts into question. In his seminal study, subtitled *Black Rebels before American Courts*, Balbus credited the smooth processing of the criminal cases that followed the mid-1960s riots in Detroit, Chicago, and Los Angeles to the lack of a consistent challenge to "the very logic of the court authority effort – their very definition of the situation" (Balbus 1973:258–9). Contrary to this observation, in many of the prosecutions discussed in this book, the defendants and their sympathizers actively challenged the state's definition of the situation.

A letter written by two Mapuche activists to the President of the Court of Appeal in Temuco to ask for parole (*"libertad condicional"*) demonstrates this well:

> Finally, we manifest that for us it is not valid to consider parole as a way to prove that we have been corrected and are rehabilitated to rejoin social life, instead that it would be a small political signal to recognize on behalf of the state the political-judicial error that was made in our imprisonment, and that it is your obligation to take responsibility for the violation of our rights. (Signed by Juan Patricio and Jaime Marileo Saravia, "Mapuche Political Prisoners," 9 April 2009)

In rejecting the common meaning of parole as a signal of "correction" and "rehabilitation," the prisoners instead asked the state to adopt an alternative reading of "parole" as a signal of the state's "political-judicial error."

Criminal prosecutions for contentious protest activity often cause defendants and their supporters to redirect some of their time and money away from their usual political activities to address issues related to the prosecution itself. Attention to criminal justice issues can complement activists' original political aims or even come to replace or overshadow them (Starr et al. 2008:265), which some claim is the objective of such prosecutions. Support groups form, for instance, to organize the money needed for a defense lawyer and look after the practical needs of a prisoner who is locked up. In each episode discussed in this book, prisoner support groups have also coordinated protest actions related to prosecutions. As a case drags on, and of course also during an activist's time in prison, there are many occasions for outcry and rallying to their support. Prisoner support groups have distributed information about trial dates and the treatment of prisoners, as well as demonstrated in front of prisons, organized homecoming ceremonies for prisoners, and publicized or even participated in hunger strikes for better prison conditions. Activists engaged in prisoner support invariably emphasize the need to act in solidarity. As one Mapuche activist put it, "their repression is our repression" (Interview C-67).

Prisoner support narratives can be differentiated depending on the political commitment of the supporters. Irrespective of the political cause, family and friends usually offer "personal support" intended to alleviate the suffering of the defendant or convicted prisoner. This type of support does not directly challenge a prosecution's legitimacy. Another type of support focuses on whether a state adheres to its own rules, but remains limited to "formal" support in relation to the legal case rather than "substantive" support in relation to the defendant or prisoner's political cause. For example, human rights organizations often monitor and advocate against state abuses like torture, excessive periods of preventive detention, disproportionate sentences or the lack of due process. This type of "formal" prisoner support de-legitimizes a state by criticizing its performance in accordance with the rule of law without necessarily disputing whether the contentious conduct in question constitutes a crime. Finally, a third kind of support criticizes the state's definition of the criminalized conduct more fundamentally, by offering an alternative account of the contentious action and claiming the defendant or prisoner as a political prisoner. Such support typically comes from fellow movement activists. Frequently, different types of prisoner support overlap. In each of the episodes, family members and friends often, though not always, supported prisoners' political demands in addition to providing personal support. Some support groups occasionally chose to focus on "formal" liberal arguments against the state for strategic reasons, but "substantively" challenged the very criminalization of contentious events in other instances.

Prisoner support groups in the episodes under examination often attempted to convince a broader public that the state was overreacting to the contentious protest activity. Social movement scholars Della Porta and Reiter concluded that "[w]hen the police are perceived as 'overreacting,' a process of 'solidarization' is set in motion between those who are the direct target of repression and larger – often more moderate – forces" (1998:18). To that end, prisoner support groups in each of the episodes often kept detailed track of legal irregularities and published lists with the number of "political" prisoners in jail as a way to denounce state repression. In different ways, they framed their messages to encourage the larger public to identify with the prisoners, suggesting that illegitimate repression might also victimize *them* at some point. When prisoner support groups succeed in de-legitimizing the validity of state evidence or the prosecutorial narrative, they can lead people to doubt charges and convictions, thus disrupting the prevalent belief (or even foundational myth) in liberal democracies that everyone in prison deserves to be there.

Critics of prosecutions of Mapuche activists in Chile, for example, argued (along "formal" liberal reasoning) that the sentences were too high and disproportionate to the damage done. Five years in prison for an alleged "terrorist" threat of a landowner in Chile, where an actual murder can also yield a 5-year sentence, they argued, violates the principle of proportionality essential to ensuring legitimacy through the rule of law. Similarly, a US activist pointed out that a man who killed a woman while driving drunk received a 10-year jail sentence, whereas environmental activist Jeffrey Luers was sentenced to 22 years and 8 months for causing several thousand dollars of damage after setting some SUVs on fire (Harper 2002).

In analyzing the claims prisoner support groups make, it can be useful to distinguish between competing truth claims and competing moral claims (Rehg, in Habermas 1998:xv). Truth claims dispute the course of events as such. Competing truth claims may exist, for example, when Mapuche activists deny responsibility for or even the existence of an incident of arson, whereas a landowner attributes responsibility to them. Often, however, there is no disagreement about "what happened." Instead, the moral valuation of what happened differs. Thus, for example, both animal rights activists and fur farmers can agree upon the basic facts of a case in which 2,000 mink were released. Yet they offer different moral claims as they either defend or condemn the action. In these cases, "political" prisoners and their supporters choose to respond to charges by openly disputing the label the state gives to the criminalized conduct, claiming responsibility for their actions and usually widely publicizing, explaining, justifying, and defending them. For example, a CAM member denied that theft of wood is a crime, because the territory belongs to the Mapuche (Informe Especial 2016). In each of the contentious episodes, this type of moral claim was usually made during the trial, or earlier, at the time of the action, for instance in a communiqué published claiming responsibility. In the United States, for example, specific people calling themselves "Press Officers" for the Animal Liberation Front and the Earth Liberation Front wrote and published communiqués to explain actions done in the fronts' names.

Liberal juridical institutions exist only because people give them legitimacy and play the roles that they require. These institutions can also be challenged when people refuse to interact according to the scripts that run the institutions. As Gargarella describes:

some people listening to the discourse of the law are no longer able to identify their voice at all [...]. What they hear instead is another voice, one that is illegitimate, foreign, incomprehensible, and distant. This strange voice, however, is backed by state force, which enables it to impose its will on those who do not understand it, do not adhere to it, or directly reject it. (2011:24)

Those who reject the law's voice backed by state force may thus decide to support the defendants on trial or under investigation, as well as prisoners. People in Spain and the Basque Country defied the state's definition of criminal acts most radically when they collaborated with commandos of the armed organization ETA and, for example, provided housing for fugitives. In each of the contentious episodes, defendants at times decided to evade proceedings and become fugitives. The act of providing support for them, while often practical in nature, can simultaneously be read as a challenge to the legitimacy of the prevailing legal order that criminalized them in the first place. It can be understood as an attempt to redefine the meaning of the acts in question in relation to the law and broader socio-political status quo. Regarding the struggle against slavery in the United States, Cover argued that "[r]escuing fugitives, and aiding and abetting them or their rescuers, were at once practical acts and symbolic ones" (1983:35). Such efforts thus aim to thwart the state's attempt to take control and assert its criminal justice response as legitimate.

Balbus (1973) emphasizes that in fundamentally challenging the logic of the court, protesters sacrifice their short-term interest (in acquittal or a lenient sentence) in the name of the consciousness of a broader, longer term interest. This requires strong identification with a larger collective and is both a condition for and goal of prisoner support. Self-identification as a "political" prisoner may advance a prisoner's political cause but prejudice their criminal case. Self-identified ETA militants have tradition-ally refused to recognize the state's jurisdiction. For this reason, they never defended themselves in court, refusing to play along with the expected script. They would routinely limit their trial participation to the words "I am a member of ETA and I ask my lawyer not to defend me here."

ETA prisoners were supported in their defiant position by their orga-nization in the Collective of Basque Political Prisoners (EPPK), which represented their interests, while prioritizing the long-term interests of the independence movement over individual benefits. As EPPK members, prisoners were not supposed to negotiate with the state at all. This meant that they were always kept in "Grade 3" conditions, the worst possible, whereas they could have been transferred to "Grade 2" conditions if they agreed to cooperate with the state. They were further obliged to take a lawyer from the group's associated lawyer collective and commit them-selves to a "political solution" instead of seeking lenience in their individual case. ETA strictly enforced this commitment, as it showed when in 1986 it assassinated former ETA militant Yoyes for negotiating with the state. While proud ETA militants rejected a juridical defense in the courtroom, ETA publicly claimed their actions and provided an alternative reading of the situation by explaining and defending them in public declarations and interviews. Such communiqués allowed ETA's sympathizers to understand the group's actions and facilitated the continued provision of support to ETA militants facing prosecution in defiance of the state's intention to isolate convicts.

Many prisoner support activities aim to reverse the stigmatizing function of criminal proceedings that seek to create a distance between the "ordinary citizen" and those imprisoned. Garfinkel (1956) likened this stigmatizing process in criminal procedure to a "status degradation ceremony". As a consequence of prisoner support actions, prisoners can be transformed into heroes, which can turn the usual cost of repression into a benefit for the movement and its members (Opp and Roehl 1990). I observed this type of admiration for prisoners, for example, in the regular prison visits undertaken by some Mapuche students to learn from "political" prisoners. It was their way to educate themselves about the conflict and the movement's leaders from the people who directly experienced it. They viewed the prisoners as experts, as people with intimate knowledge of what was going on (field notes, April 2009). This attitude was not necessarily shared, though, among all Mapuche communities. One Mapuche activist complained about the attitude he found among his community after returning from prison, observing, "They have all adopted the governmental discourse against violence. They have all accepted the image portrayed by the government that any act of resistance is terrorism" (Interview C-62).

Prisoner (or defendant) support mobilization thus provides a counter-narrative to the account proposed by the prosecution in relation to criminality and public interest. The practical aspects of prisoner support – the need for material support for the detained person as well as his or her family – are interwoven with the communicative aspects – the desire to present a counter-narrative for internal and external consumption. As recognized by other scholars, mobilization to support prisoners and challenge the state's narrative and crime definition can even become "a social movement activity in its own right" (Zwerman and Steinhoff 2005:96).

In what follows, key characteristics of the different trajectories of mobilization in support of defendants and prisoners in Spain, Chile and the United States are discussed, highlighting issues such as the cooperation of some defendants with law enforcement, and the controversy this arouses. Some of the mobilization strategies took place in the courtroom, such as in speeches by defendants. Other strategies challenged crime definitions in very different venues, such as in public demonstrations or newspaper communiqués. Common elements across the three episodes are the creation of prisoner support groups and calls for solidarity; critiques of state abuse for a human rights-oriented audience; identification of defendants and convicts as political prisoners, thus changing the impact of criminal prosecutions; and attempts to persuade the public of a different definition of the criminalized event.

"State of exception" in the Basque Country

Even after Spain's transition to democratic structures, many Basque left-nationalists maintained a "state of exception" discourse to justify ETA's continued use of violence in its campaign for Basque independence. This refers to the situation in which a government resorts to unusually repressive measures in response to extreme internal conflicts, suspending the ordinary rule of law (see also Agamben 2005). They reasoned that as long as Spain's Constitution precluded democratic means to pursue Basque independence, the armed struggle remained justified as a defense against oppression. This analysis was fueled by the fact that, particularly early on, the Spanish state often responded to ETA attacks by declaring generalized states of emergency in the Basque Country. Indiscriminate police violence further contributed to the perception of illegitimate state repression (Woodworth 2017). Declaring the political party Batasuna illegal in 2002 provided left-nationalists with further arguments to maintain that all political means to fight for their political project were blocked. Comments justifying the use of violence were expressed openly, as for example when a 28-year-old Basque left-nationalist activist claimed that his generation had not lived one year without political and judicial harassment:

> They are educating us in violence. If they don't give the youth the necessary instruments, then our reaction will be the only method they leave us, which is violence. It is a reaction to what we receive, and we respond in kind. The state imposes this on us. It is our right to confront the violence. What we do is politics, and our goal is to overcome the violence. (Interview 2008, S-24)

Whereas organizations identifying as victims of ETA violence pushed the state to address what they perceived as impunity and asked the state to ensure that ETA militants and their supporters were imprisoned, defendants and their support organizations contested the prosecutions and challenged the legitimacy of the proceedings. In 1980, the Attorney General of Spain noted in his Annual Report that the audience attending trial sessions against ETA militants came with the "decided intention to disturb them" (MA 1980:150). A year earlier, the Attorney General commented that the location where such trials were held was inadequate given the specific audience attending the trials:

The hearings have converted into tumults and interventions of the defendants continually cause disrespectful disorder, taking the courts as a useful platform for their propaganda. The lack of the most minimal possibility for control and security creates an inevitable situation of tension for the court and the prosecutors, incompatible with the necessary intellectual freedom and peace proper to its function. (MA 1979:59)

Graffiti in a village in the Basque Country in 2008 called for an end to the perceived *estado de excepción* (state of exception) (see Photo 2). This discourse and the resulting belief that the Spanish state represses supporters of Basque independence just for their beliefs has been persistent in the left-nationalist movement. Concretely this meant that criminal trials and convictions of ETA militants as well as left-nationalist activists were not viewed as legitimate by a significant portion of the population in the Basque Country. Many recognized the prisoners as "Basque political prisoners." In line with a particular political analysis of ETA's actions, the prisoner support group Gestoras pro Amnistía was founded in 1977 to demand amnesty for ETA convicts. By 2009, the collective of "Basque political prisoners" counted more than 700 prisoners (Gara 2009). Over the years, widespread attention to the rights of "political" prisoners in

Photo 2   Photo taken by the author, Basque Country 2008.

the Basque Country turned their interests into one of the major issues discussed in negotiations between ETA and the Spanish state.

It is not only cases involving alleged ETA militants or alleged ETA supporters from the left-nationalist movement that have attracted such support, though. For example, the former president of the Basque parliament, Atutxa, who is a member of the moderate Partido Nacionalista Vasco (PNV, Basque Nationalist Party), was prosecuted for disobeying a judicial decision to dissolve the political party that succeeded the Basque left-nationalist Batasuna party after it was declared illegal. The trial was initiated as a consequence of a formal complaint filed by the organization Manos Limpias. His conviction in January 2008 (later overturned by the European Court of Human Rights) led to a massive demonstration in Bilbao, with more than 50,000 people in the streets (Europa Press 2008).

Contentious criminalization and challenges to the legitimacy of the Spanish state's criminal prosecutions have not been limited to supporters of Basque independence. The conviction in 2000 of former Spanish police official Enrique Rodríguez Galindo, sentenced to 75 years' imprisonment for the illegal detention and murder of two Basque youth, both allegedly members of ETA, drew significant solidarity from different types of prisoner supporters. In 2006, journalist Jesús María Zuloaga wrote the prologue for Galindo's memoirs *My Life against ETA: The Antiterrorism Struggle from the Inchaurrondo Quarters* (Galindo 2006). Despite Galindo's judicial conviction, Zuloaga described him as a "frontline servant of Spain." He also called the criminal proceedings against Galindo a "media circus with clear political goals" and expressed the belief that time would prove Galindo's innocence (in Galindo 2006:ii–iii). During Galindo's stay in prison, his family presented a petition for a pardon with 100,000 signatures. Indeed, even former president González affirmed his belief in Galindo's innocence a decade after his conviction (Millás 2010). While thus recognizing that multiple groups engage in discursive mobilization to challenge the state's crime definitions, the remainder of this section focuses on discursive and practical challenges related to the prosecution and imprisonment of alleged ETA militants and their supporters.

Throughout the years, various prisoner support groups in the Basque Country actively tried to bring the plight and suffering of "their" prisoners to the attention of the general public. Professionalized organizations were responsible for solidarity with those prisoners that the left-nationalist movement identified as "Basque political prisoners" as well as fugitives. An organization of family members of prisoners coordinated visits to far-away prisons, while another group organized solidarity for prisoners of *kale borroka*, the term for street struggle carried out by Basque youth. They created websites with information about "political" prisoners and ongoing trials, as well as websites explaining how to react in case of arrest. In addition, a lawyer's collective formed to provide defense lawyers for ETA militants and other left-nationalist defendants.

Some prisoner support groups articulated criticisms of the Spanish state's criminal policy vis-à-vis ETA militants using a "formal" rule of law approach shared by human rights organizations and even UN representatives. For example, critics questioned the legitimacy of using the Audiencia Nacional to try ETA militants, as it was founded in 1977 by an executive decision, neatly replacing the Tribunal of Public Order used by Franco to detain political opponents. For many years, appeals were only possible in a limited review at the Supreme Court. Only after the UN Human Rights Committee deemed this insufficient was a law adopted in 2003 to create an Appeals Chamber (HRW 2005:17), which did not become operational until 2017. Another recurring point of critique was the Spanish state's so-called "dispersion policy." In 1989, due to suspicion that ETA was conducting meetings and organizing attacks from prison, the Spanish state decided to separate ETA prisoners by distributing them among different jails all over Spain. In addition, ETA prisoners had to change prisons every few years. The state claimed the policy was necessary in order to split "hardliners" from "soft liners." Prisoner supporters demanded that the state "bring the prisoners home" to the Basque Country, citing international legal standards such as Principle 20 of United Nations (UN) General Assembly Resolution 43/173 (9 December 1988) prescribing that a prisoner be allowed to stay in a detention facility "reasonably near his usual place of residence" (Template Petition to the Juzgado de Vigilancia Penitenciaria, 1 October 1997).

For many left-nationalist activists in the Basque Country, prisoners, trials and repression play an enormous role in daily life. One interviewee noted that not only had he and his older brother been convicted of terrorism, but his younger brother had been convicted of spray-painting *"Gora ETA"* (Long live ETA) in the street. The continued experience of repression against their children turned his parents from moderate PNV voters into supporters of the left-nationalist party Batasuna (Interview S-23). Every year, professional posters identifying all of the "Basque political prisoners" were published as an annual census of sorts and displayed in bars and other establishments throughout the Basque Country. In 2008, this poster contained pictures of each of the 700 prisoners identified as "political" prisoners, in addition to several empty spaces meant to represent fugitives. Through such efforts and others, left-nationalists have successfully turned "their" prisoners into a political issue. For a long time, public debate in Spain related to the Basque struggle has engaged with demands such as amnesty, reintegration and dispersion. In interviews in 2008, it became clear that many left-nationalists identified with the prisoners, who they felt were suffering for the same thing that every Basque left-nationalist fights for: a free and socialist Basque Country. Many left-nationalist activists believed that they could easily have been or still could be imprisoned for belonging to the left-nationalist movement.

Since the late 1970s, prisoner support organizations in the left-nationalist movement have provided a narrative of support for ETA, its militants and its actions – challenging the state's narrative about its transition to a liberal democracy. This narrative was shared among a significant portion of the Basque population, thus challenging the state's criminal definition of ETA's actions. The narrative defended ETA's action according to a logic of war, justifying the group's designation of military targets for attack. Meanwhile, other supporters and human rights organizations highlighted "formal" deficiencies in criminal prosecutions, leading many in the left-nationalist movement and beyond to opine that the Spanish state was repressing the Basque people for seeking independence. For example, they pointed to allegations of systematic torture of incommunicado defendants and the lack of an appeals chamber at the Audiencia Nacional as evidence of the state's failure to adhere to its own rules when trying Basque activists. Mobilization of supporters also ensured that trials were often accompanied by street demonstrations and that the interests of prisoners were represented in many venues, which was not easily ignored by the state and its prosecutors.

The (alleged) torture of prisoners suspected of militancy with ETA or of involvement in *kale borroka* severely damaged the state's credibility and legitimacy among a substantial portion of the population. Already in 1984, the Spanish Attorney General noted the "Kafkaesque" situation that torture allegations produced. The Audiencia Nacional would investigate a crime based on a declaration made at a police station, while this same declaration was simultaneously subject to a criminal investigation in a local court that could end up disqualifying the declaration and thus the principal procedure. The Attorney General called it "dysfunctional" (MA 1984:138). Instead of a basic trust in the state's evidence and convictions by judges, the assumption among many in the Basque Country was that evidence was fabricated and guilty judgments based upon confessions extracted through torture. A family member of an ETA prisoner expressed no doubts that torture existed: "You have seen the pictures; do you think they do that themselves? And why else would they confess?" He thought that the Spanish trials were just theater and was by no means the only one who believed that many innocent Basque youth were unjustly imprisoned (Interview S-28).

Thus, ETA and its sympathizers in the left-nationalist movement organized to spread the "state of exception" narrative, made the interests of the prisoners a central concern for the movement, and effectively challenged prosecutors in their efforts to make the trials a display of legitimate use of force by the state. From the mid-2000s onward, though, the tight Collective of Basque Political Prisoners began to show signs of dissent. Older, important ETA members were thrown out of the EPPK in 2008 as the collective accused them of collaborating with the Spanish government. After ETA's dissolution in 2010, the EPPK continued to represent prisoners' interests, but by 2017 the collective had decided to allow its members to accept individual benefits (Guenaga 2017).

"Criminalization of social protest" of the Mapuche movement

The voice of victimized landowners in Chile pushed the state to take their experiences and fear of escalation seriously and respond with a "*mano dura*" (iron fist) to attacks on their property. This voice was countered, however, by supporters of Mapuche defendants and prisoners, who proposed an alternative reading of the criminalized events. In response to criminal prosecutions of Mapuche activists, their supporters challenged the state's definition of the situation, assisted defendants in the practicalities of standing trial, and raised awareness among the larger public about the claimed political nature of the criminal proceedings. Despite the relative disorganization of Mapuche prisoner support efforts, they successfully established a counter-narrative in which the Chilean state unjustly criminalizes legitimate social protest through exaggerating the threat posed by Mapuche activists, prosecuting them under trumped-up charges, and exerting excessive police violence during raids on Mapuche communities.

Prisoner support mobilization has garnered significant domestic and international attention to the state's questionable use of military tribunals and anti-terrorism legislation to try Mapuche protesters, as well as disproportionate sentences and long periods of pre-trial detention (for example, FIDH 2006:52). A lawyer representing the office of the UN High Commissioner for Human Rights for Latin America and the Caribbean attended the trial against the CAM as an observer and commented: "Here, for threats or burning a field they want to apply the same criteria with which they act against those that put bombs in London. The disproportionateness couldn't be bigger" (cited in Cayuqueo 2005c). The Chilean government also had to account for its use of anti-terrorist legislation before the Human Rights Commission of the UN during the 2009 proceedings of the Universal Periodic Exam, a mechanism to examine the human rights performance of UN member states (Univisión 2009). International human rights organizations like Amnesty International and Human Rights Watch, as well as the UN Special Rapporteur on the rights of indigenous peoples and the Inter-American Commission on Human Rights have all criticized the way in which the Chilean state has conducted such proceedings.

Many Mapuche activists have claimed their prisoners to be "political" prisoners. The Mapuche organization Meli Witran Mapu explains that:

> For our organization, a Mapuche Political Prisoner is any Mapuche whose liberty is taken away, or is in that process, as a product of his/ her participation in actions that lead to the reconstruction of the *Pueblo-Nación Mapuche* [People-Nation Mapuche], understanding as such the processes of recuperation of lands and/or executing Territorial Control over recuperated lands, actions of resistance against police repression, as well as mobilizations that lead to the recuperation of Political Rights of the Mapuche People. [...] With the aforementioned criteria, clearly our brothers are not common prisoners or criminals, as the oppressive state has treated them. (Meli Witran Mapu 2011)

Contrary to such claims by activists, the Chilean state has categorically rejected the notion that it holds any "political" prisoners. In her visit to the Netherlands in 2009, Chilean President Michelle Bachelet officially declared that there were no Mapuche political prisoners in Chile: "No one is imprisoned because of a specific ideology or because of belonging to an original ethnic group [*etnia*]" (cited in Silva 2009). Notably, Mapuche activists were able to exert enough pressure that the president felt the need to take a public stance on the issue.

In the 1990s and the early 2000s, Mapuche prisoners and their supporters seldom challenged the state's crime definitions directly when identifying Mapuche activists as political prisoners. Instead, their narratives often focused on the trajectory of state repression. The seizure of potential evidentiary material by the police, for example, was often perceived by activists as deliberate "theft" in order to weaken the movement. Indeed, many Mapuche activists claimed that searches and arrests were meant to disturb and intimidate, more so than to obtain convictions. Mapuche activists saw themselves as continuing the struggle of their well-known ancestors Lautaro and Caupolicán, who defended their lands against Spanish conquest in the 16th century. As such, the battle itself was viewed worthwhile and repression an accepted part it. For Mapuche activists, the individual cost of repression was thus mitigated by the myth of martyrdom and heroism, and the knowledge of being part of the *pueblo* and its struggle against oppression. A former CAM member reported that within his organization, prison became an essential part of the "education" of a true nationalist Mapuche (Interview 2003, C-28). Instead of the simple criminal justice premise that imprisoning "rotten apples" would stop mobilizations, Mapuche activists believed in *Marrichiweu!* – the old Mapuche battle cry meaning that for every fallen person, ten others will arise.

Mapuche activists thus interpreted criminal prosecutions of fellow activists and police raids in communities as continued repression in the context of the historical and continuous dispossession of and violence against the Mapuche people. They quickly jumped from hearing about a single confrontation between police and a particular Mapuche community to speaking about police violence against the Mapuche "people." Similarly, they interpreted a specific fight for land in a specific area as a struggle about "the" Mapuche territory. The suffering of those in prison was felt as personal suffering. "They [the prosecutors and judges] apply the law to *us* [Mapuches]," said one activist about ongoing criminal proceedings, who herself was not being prosecuted (field notes April 2009). Another young activist told me that he visits his "brothers" in prison, meaning his fellow Mapuches rather than siblings in the biological sense: "At times I get up at five in the morning to walk two hours and catch the bus to [the city] Angol to visit my imprisoned brothers. It is a sacrifice, but for me it is enriching. I am supporting my brothers," he said with tears in his eyes (Interview 2009, C-67).

In response to the allegations that Mapuche activists committed arson, for a long time the Mapuche movement denied that Mapuches would do that as a protest tactic. They thus leveled an alternative "truth claim" instead of a "moral claim." Only at the end of the 2000s did Mapuche activists actually start claiming and justifying incidents of arson in public communiqués (for example, CAM 2009; *Cooperativa* 2018). Until then, they routinely argued that criminal prosecutions against them for alleged arson were the result of fabricated charges and evidence. They believed that the state and corporations set them up, either by orchestrating the crime itself and then imputing it to them, or by tampering with the evidence and making them seem guilty. Activists also suggested that the summer heat caused the forestry fires (field notes March 2003) or that landowners committed arson on their own properties to gain insurance money (for example, Asamblea Mapuche de Izquierda 2008). Indeed, in 1999, a worker at a forestry company reported that he had been pressured by his superiors to commit arson and blame it on Ancalaf, a well-known Mapuche leader (*Cooperativa* 2006a; Villegas 2008:99–100). This confirmed the widespread notion among Mapuche activists that Mapuches did not actually commit the arson incidents for which they were prosecuted.

Thus the Mapuche movement successfully created a counter-narrative that the prosecution of their activists meant the criminalization of legitimate social protest, which obtained recognition from a number of high-ranking institutions. In relation to arson attacks, this narrative was largely based on "formal" rule-of-law arguments such as proportionality, while Mapuche activists have always defended their position that entering an estate to recuperate it is not violent, arguing instead that the continuation of usurpation by forestry companies and commercial farmers is violence (for example, Informe Especial 2016). In addition, the narrative contextualized contemporary incidents of police violence or prosecution in the longer heroic history of the Mapuche struggle against colonization. It thus discredited the criminal justice response of the Chilean state while making the Mapuche struggle appealing for activists, despite possible penal consequences. By 2016, CAM openly countered the state's definitions of its actions with its own narrative (Informe Especial 2016).

The "Green Scare" in the United States

In October 1997 Peter Young raided six mink farms in the Midwest in the name of animal rights. He was arrested after seven years of living as a fugitive. When he spoke with his lawyer, his counsel said: "It is incredible; it seems that the prosecutors are more interested in your friends than in the issues in the indictment. They are making a master list with the names of your friends" (cited in Interview US-15). This represents what activists have dubbed the "Green Scare." In the words of journalist Will Potter, who is credited with coining the term, the Green Scare refers to the "disproportionate, heavy-handed government crackdown on the animal rights and environmental movements, and the reckless use of the word 'terrorism'" (Potter 2011a). Mobilization by animal enterprises and lobby groups like the Center for the Defense of Free Enterprise had led to increasing criminal investigations and prosecutions of environmental and animal rights protest activities as "eco-terrorism." In response, defendant and prisoner support groups mobilized to spread the term "Green Scare" as a challenge to the state's definition of the situation.

Liberal juridical institutions only function because people give them legitimacy and play the roles that they require. In a public call for events in solidarity with environmental and animal rights activists accused of "eco-terrorism" in the US, prisoner supporters flipped the script prescribed by the courts by calling on people to "Honor the Fallen, Remember the Snitches, Resist the Greenscare!" (Potomac Earth First! 2007). Throughout the 1990s and 2000s, US environmental and animal rights activists challenged the legitimacy of "eco-terrorism" proceedings by rejecting the validity of prosecutorial claims and refusing to take them seriously or to comply with judicial demands. Their refusal was expressed through basic activities condemning the state response, such as communicating with prisoners, providing practical support for fugitives and vocal support for protest actions.

Prisoner support groups in relation to environmental and animal rights activism in the United States have typically been organized around specific defendants, with family members and close friends playing an important role. As a result, their efforts have been rather fragmented and decentralized. This section describes how supporters have attempted to mobilize sufficient solidarity to cover legal expenses and mobilize a broader sustained challenge to the state's criminalization of their actions. Attempts to dissuade fellow activists from cooperating with law enforcement agencies have been particularly notable among their efforts. They have also visited and written to prisoners, attended hearings, organized benefit concerts, and published information on blogs and websites. An example of practical defendant support can be seen in the following call to raise money for the gas needed to travel to prison for visits:

> [Prisoner's name] is currently being held in [location], CA – which is almost 7 hours from where I live. Renting a car and paying for gas is incredibly expensive, and it's a cost I just can't carry on my own. The support [prisoner's name] has received from all of you over the last four years has been amazing, and we are more than thankful for all you have done. [Prisoner's name] has shown a steadfast, unwavering commitment to do the right thing and fight the outrageous charges against him, despite facing severe repercussions for that decision. Please consider making a donation to support him, however small. Every tiny bit helps. (Email on a listserv on 24 February 2010)

Such requests for support are often directed at an imagined collective of fellow activists and sympathizers, as exemplified by appeals like: "[e]very conspiracy case directed against radicals sets a precedent for more of the same; defending one of us is literally defending all of us" (Conspiracy 2011).

Apart from practical support like money for transportation costs, prisoner support of environmental and animal rights activists in the US has also been more substantive. For example, when the FBI accused forest activists Judi Bari and Darryl Cherney of having themselves fabricated the bomb that exploded in their car and injured them, Greenpeace hired a private detective to find the real perpetrators (Scarce 2006:85). In other cases, defendants and their supporters have not offered a competing truth claim, but actively questioned the prosecutor's criminal qualification of their actions. For example, when Peter Young was on trial for releasing mink from a fur farm, he openly defied the court's legitimacy:

> I don't wish to validate this proceeding by begging for mercy or appealing to the conscience of the court, because I know if this system had a conscience I would not be here, and in my place would be all the butchers, vivisectors, and fur farmers of the world. [...] It is to those animals I answer to, not you or this court. (Young 2005a)

He received support from a broader community sympathetic to his goals and activism. Upon his release from prison, Young wrote that he received donations ranging from food delivery to his home to skateboards and other products provided by companies such as Alternative Outfitters, Vegan Essentials, New Eden Records and Vans (Support Peter 2007). Others showed a rather different kind of solidarity when, on 29 April 2006, activists identifying with the Animal Liberation Front raided a Minnesota fur farm and dedicated their release of animals to the imprisoned "mink liberator" Peter Young. These solidarity actions – the material donations as well as the raid and dedication to Young – openly defied the state's criminal definition of animal releases.

For moderate environmental and animal welfare activist organizations in the US, criminal proceedings have often meant needing to "choose sides." The Sierra Club, for example, "does not condone any acts of violence," which it emphasizes, "is not a new position" (Sierra Club 2003). As a consequence of this position, the Sierra Club has at times actively supported law enforcement in cases related to environmental activism. While the Sierra Club actively assisted law enforcement, the Department of Homeland Security (DHS) suspected various animal rights groups of assisting those it labeled "eco-terrorists":

PETA [People for the Ethical Treatment of Animals], the Fund for Animals, In Defense of Animals, the New Jersey Animal Rights Alliance, and certain individuals within the HSUS [Humane Society of the United States] are known or suspected of having financial ties to individuals and groups associated with ecoterrorism. In addition to financial ties to ecomilitancy, both HSUS and PETA, or at least individuals within those organizations, have an established record of supporting individuals and/or groups commonly associated with ecoterrorism. (Department of Homeland Security 2008:9)

In the same year that this DHS report came out, and in a clear effort to distance itself from the tactics employed by other animal rights activists, the Humane Society offered a $2,500 reward for information that could help resolve the case of a car bombing in California that had targeted an animal researcher (Brown 2008). On 18 February 2010, a notification on the Humane Society website stated that the DHS had changed its assessment regarding HSUS and the Fund for Animals.

Thus, US-based activists competed with or against law enforcement officers for the "hearts and minds" of the public, persuading people to comply or not comply with criminal investigations. As opposed to moderate groups, more radical environmental and animal rights activists have tried to dissuade fellow activists from "falling for" government cooperation, often by severely condemning "snitching" and cutting off contact with those who do cooperate. Several activists have managed to successfully resist Grand Juries, even accepting time in jail for refusing to testify. Grand Juries can issue subpoenas that force people to testify, even without the presence of a lawyer. They can also hold people in contempt for refusing to share information that may be "in the public interest to enforce the criminal laws of the United States." In a few instances, environmental and animal rights activists were prosecuted for making false declarations before a Grand Jury and were imprisoned as punishment for their refusal to cooperate. Animal rights activist Kevin Kjonaas has called Grand Juries "one of the best things that ever happens to animal rights movements" as in his view it made people active (Case SHAC 7, trial exhibits, vol. V:2196). Former US prisoner Peter Young openly called for a "demystification" of the prison experience, arguing that it is not as bad as one might fear. He reasoned that if activists lose their fear of prison, they may be bolder in their activism (Young 2008).

In the case of one activist sought by law enforcement for "eco-terrorism," the FBI asked the public for their cooperation. On its website, the FBI announced: "You can help. Have you seen Daniel Andreas San Diego, an animal rights activist wanted for his alleged involvement in two bombings in California in 2003? If so, contact us" (FBI 2005). At the same time, animal rights activist Peter Young called upon fellow activists to reflect on their response to the search for Daniel Andreas:

> It is impossible to know where Andres [sic] San Diego is hiding, but please ask yourself what you would do if he showed up at your door tonight, asking for help. San Diego faces a potential life sentence if arrested, and is out there somewhere right now literally running for his life. (Young 2011)

Prisoner and defendant support mobilization for environmental and animal rights activists in the United States has predominantly been on the defensive. Attempts to strengthen loyalty among activists have not always been successful in protecting activists against detentions and prosecutions. Increasingly since the mid-2000s, activists have cooperated with law enforcement agencies by agreeing to be informants or by taking plea deals in exchange for providing testimony against their fellow activists. One of the defense lawyers attributed this trend to the high sentences involved, suggesting that "Those federal sentences finally cranked them down," as "They are kids" (Interview US-3). The proposed counter-narrative of the Green Scare was well received within certain activist circles, but not picked up by mainstream organizations such as the Sierra Club and the Humane Society. This lack of discursive and practical support further weakened their efforts to convince the larger public of their definition of the situation.

Discursive mobilization and contentious criminalization

In each of the contentious episodes in Spain, Chile and the United States, groups mobilized support for those put on trial and imprisoned for their (alleged) role in protest actions done in the name of a shared cause. Their discursive mobilization with narratives of repression questioned the crime definitions put forward by prosecutors, sometimes by disputing the facts ("truth claims") in a case, but often by rejecting the "moral claims" in the prosecutorial narrative and advocating an alternative definition of the situation. The particulars of the narratives and the logistical organization of prisoner support mobilization were highly context specific, not just across episodes, but also across cases. For example, the professionalization of prisoner support in the Basque Country and the kind of loyalty demanded by ETA in its rejection of the state as a legitimate counterpart were not present among prisoner support groups in Chile and the United States. Further, while some defendants put up a detailed legal defense, others refused to defend themselves at all, rejecting state legitimacy and jurisdiction. Despite their differences, each contentious episode featured prisoners who self-identified as political prisoners, with support for that definition from a significant portion of the population. Also, each episode included accusations of activists suspected of having assisted law enforcement as snitches or traitors. The counter-narratives of repression also sought to persuade fellow activists and even the public at large to refuse cooperation with law enforcement agencies.

As chapter 4 shows, in each contentious episode groups mobilized to claim their role as victims in what they perceived to be crimes, asking the state to punish the other side accordingly. Once a group's victimhood was recognized by a larger public constituency, whether domestically or even internationally, these groups obtained leverage in the criminal justice arena. Prosecutors were forced to respond to their claims by honoring or refusing to honor them in criminal prosecutions. Successful claims to victimhood provided actors with the possibility to mobilize the prosecutorial narrative on their behalf. If accepted by a judge, this also established the narratives' definition of the situation as the "truth." Thus, mobilization gave victim groups a chance to have their narratives honored, but it didn't guarantee results, which the Mapuche convictions demonstrate well – they frequently received low sentences and/or got favorable land restitution deals afterwards.

Thus, in each episode, an enormous amount of discursive mobilization occurred in and around the criminal justice arena by actors demanding recognition of their victimhood or rallying in support of defendants and convicts criminalized in connection with activities challenging or defending the status quo. The narratives developed by these actors sought to persuade prosecutors either to initiate criminal prosecutions or drop charges. At the same time, the mobilization efforts of prisoner support groups targeted broader audiences to de-legitimize the state and its prosecutions while redeeming defendants. The following chapters in Part II focus on the influence on and changes in prosecutorial narrative in interaction with discursive mobilization of "victim" alliances and prisoner supporters in the criminal justice arena. By highlighting themes and tracing shifts in prosecutorial narrative over time in each episode, Part II explores how prosecutors respond to the discursive challenges and attempt to maintain or restore state legitimacy to interpret and enforce the rule of law.

PART II

WHEN PROSECUTORS RESPOND: NARRATIVES IN ACTION

In this second part, prosecutors engage with the narratives of powerful victim alliances and challenges to these narratives from prisoner supporters. As they navigate their duty to represent the public interest, they generally portray their criminal cases as the strict application of the law, thus casting their narrative – the prosecutorial narrative – as legitimate. In each of the episodes, actors mobilizing in the name of victimhood appealed to the state for protection, criticized impunity, and called upon prosecutors to obtain convictions. Dissatisfaction with the performance of the criminal justice system characterized the narratives of animal enterprises in the United States, victims of ETA in Spain, and landowners in Chile. In turn, criminal proceedings against Basque left-nationalists, Mapuche activists and US animal rights and environmental activists led to mobilization by prisoner support groups, who countered prosecutorial narratives, challenged crime definitions, and questioned the legitimacy of the prosecutions.

In establishing prosecutorial narratives, prosecutors make a number of choices in terms of how they select relevant facts and describe actors and events. For example, they often draw upon and reproduce social identities of defendants and victims. Given that people always have multiple identities, the prosecutor can choose to prioritize and emphasize certain identity aspects over others, such as political affiliation, gender, or ethnicity. Prosecutorial narratives can also differentiate between leaders and followers, and distinguish between direct perpetrators, collaborators, or those who give instructions or inspiration for the acts under examination. Prosecutorial narratives further choose the legal interest at stake. This can be specific and refer to a piece of property or a physical injury, or it can be more abstract, such as the constitution, democracy, legal security, public peace, or economic stability. The prosecutor can emphasize the alleged motive or dangerousness of the defendant and ask for high bail or a longer sentence. The prosecutor can also choose to narrow or broaden the circle of defendants. In order to argue the necessary causation of defendants less obviously linked to the action, prosecutorial narrative can draw connections between speech acts and subsequent crimes like property destruction. Prosecutors can also choose to intervene before actual harm has been done and criminalize preparatory activities. All of these choices can be revised and change over time, thus leading to discursive shifts in prosecutorial narrative. Finally, the prosecutorial narrative needs to present the credibility of evidence and make choices about maintaining anonymity of sources. All of the chapters in Part II highlight a particular example of prosecutorial narrative in action in each of the chosen episodes, underscoring the choices that prosecutors made as well as changes in those choices over time as a consequence of continued mobilization by victim alliances and prisoner supporters, thus demonstrating the interactive process of contentious criminalization in liberal democracies.

ETA CASES IN SPAIN

6

Casting the Net Wider by Calling the Armed Group a Network

In 1989, Baltasar Garzón took office as an investigative judge in the Audiencia Nacional, Spain's special court for money laundering and terrorist offenses in Madrid. As one of his first moves in his new role, he ordered police to collect all available documents whenever they arrested an ETA member (Garzón 2006). In 1992, an important police operation in Bidart, France, led to the detention of ETA leaders and the confiscation of an enormous trove of internal ETA documents. After analyzing these documents, Garzón determined that the prevailing prosecutorial understanding of ETA's military apparatus as an entity separate from broader left-nationalist efforts for Basque independence was mistaken. He concluded that "before anything, this organization was purely politics, even though its methods were violent, it sought political changes, according to its sovereign projections over a part of Spanish territory" (2006:290). He proposed that ETA should be viewed as a "network" (*entramado*) that included not only militant commandos, but also a political wing comprised of organizations belonging to the broader Basque left-nationalist movement, even including a Basque-language newspaper. In his assessment, these organizations constituted a subset of ETA's violent strategy, making them complicit in the military wing's crimes. For Garzón (2006:297), "a terrorist organization was something more complex than a mere collection of persons that kills, bombs, kidnaps and extorts to achieve its political objectives." In accordance with this assessment, Garzón instigated a shift in prosecutorial approach toward ETA with far-reaching consequences.

By redefining the military structure of ETA as a political organization, Garzón recontextualized the existence and activities of nearly all Basque left-nationalist organizations. Suddenly, prosecutors were able to charge members of social and political organizations that espoused support for Basque independence with "membership in a terrorist organization." This served to cast a wider net, allowing people to be indicted without their having been directly involved in terrorist acts. The criminalization of mere membership in an organization provided clear advantages for law enforcement officials, as it "permits the government to incarcerate persons based not on their involvement in past illegal conduct, and not even on their involvement in planning future crimes, but on the basis of their affiliation or association with others who have engaged in illegal conduct" (Cole 2008:233). This goes against the liberal premise of personal guilt. In addition, according to the principle of legality, individuals must be able to know whether they are a member of a prohibited organization or not and what personal conduct makes them a member of such an organization – especially if they are not personally involved in placing bombs. To overcome the allegation that these trials amounted to a simple "guilt by association," in their narrative, Spanish prosecutors emphasized the specific and personal contributions defendants made to the network's ability to conduct armed attacks. As prosecutorial narrative toward ETA changed in Spain, criminal proceedings increasingly became a site for dispute over what constitutes a terrorist organization.

This chapter traces the shift in Spanish prosecutorial narrative about the make-up of ETA as a terrorist organization. It broadly identifies a period of the 1970s and 1980s in which ETA, in combination with other armed and paramilitary organizations, posed a real threat to the Spanish state and its criminal justice apparatus. Popular support for ETA and its armed struggle also made it difficult for prosecutors to obtain citizen cooperation in their cases against ETA members. During the 1990s, however, things changed. The Spanish state increasingly favored a criminal justice approach in combating ETA, no longer viewing the organization as a military opponent, but as a political group guilty of criminal conduct. At the same time, public support for nationalist armed struggle in the Basque Country decreased. Prosecutors began to focus their efforts on indicting members of what they termed the "ETA network" (*el entramado de ETA*) for alleged ties to the group, rather than focusing more narrowly on prosecuting armed commando units for specific acts of violence. So-called "macro-trials" since the late 1990s have led to the conviction of many activists in Basque left-nationalist socio-political organizations for interacting with ETA or even espousing similar political ideas, which prosecutors equated with membership in a terrorist organization. Despite the new narrative in which lawyers for victim associations and prosecutors insisted that "you don't need a weapon to be a terrorist" (for example, Interview S-27), the image of ETA members as "*pistoleros*" (gunmen), which prosecutors had spent decades cultivating, proved hard to shake. The chapter shows how prosecutorial narrative serves to determine the scope of "eligible defendants" and how the narrative construction of a collective underpins criminal liability.

Shift from ETA as an enemy in a war to criminal prosecutions

In the 1970s, the Spanish state struggled to transition to democracy after decades of military dictatorship under Franco. This included efforts to reform many of the institutions of the old regime. The period from 1975 to 1985 was characterized by numerous legal reforms and attempts to bolster the state's judicial institutions in the face of continuing terrorist attacks carried out by ETA and other armed challengers of the status quo. In the early years of Spain's democratic transition, the annual reports published by the Attorney General's Office, which list ongoing or terminated criminal proceedings for the year along with crime rates and policy considerations, frequently highlighted the strain placed on the state's emergent democratic institutions by the overwhelming number of groups, both large and small, left-wing and right-wing, that employed violence to pressure the state.

In 1979, Spain's Attorney General feared further violent escalation from such groups. Pointing to a rising number of terrorist attacks in Spain, he wrote that "we find ourselves before a declared war against civilization" (MA 1979:65). He described the many violent organizations threatening the state as dangerous and professional, with international connections, technical expertise, and enormous financial means (MA 1979:69). While he called for additional funding to improve the state's crime-fighting performance, he also made clear that he did not view ordinary criminal prosecutions as an adequate way to deal with the prevailing threats:

> Any pretension to apply analogous norms to the ordinary delinquent and the terrorist is aberrant. It is not that we would declare him at the margin of the law, but if there is no specific substantive and procedural normative framework to deal with his criminal and psychic characteristics, and his fanaticism and pathological desperation, then the work of

the administration of justice will be impossible and will be shipwrecked between disillusion and indifference. (MA 1979:74)

The Attorney General also criticized other countries for their tendency to interpret terrorist actions, particularly those carried out by ETA, as "political crimes" precluding law enforcement cooperation and extradition (MA 1979:71). During the Franco regime, ETA members received refugee status in France (Harrison 1994:123–4). For years after his death, France was still viewed as a safe haven for ETA members, as it refused to extradite them to Spain. From the mid-1970s to the mid-1980s, the image of ETA as an opponent in a war guided the Spanish state in its fight against the group. Indeed, it later came to light that government officials waged an extra-legal "Dirty War" against ETA during the 1980s. Reporting by the newspaper *El Mundo* revealed that the Spanish government was deeply involved in facilitating the operations of the paramilitary group GAL (Grupos Antiterroristas de Liberación), which killed 27 suspected ETA members, including the head of the left-nationalist political party Herri Batasuna, and tortured several others.

In the criminal justice arena, prosecutors focused on highlighting the differences between ETA's "terrorism" and "ordinary crime" as a means of justifying special measures against the group. Until reform in 1978, terrorism crimes in Spain fell under the jurisdiction of military courts. That year, however, an executive decree made terrorist offenses the province of a new court, the Audiencia Nacional, which adjudicated according to terrorism legislation introduced through one-year provisions, renewed annually. What started out as an exceptional and temporary measure eventually became integrated as a permanent fixture in the ordinary legal system. In 1995, Spain's temporary terrorism provisions were integrated into the penal code, including the criminalization of membership in a terrorist organization. These terrorism provisions authorized special measures, such as incommunicado detention, and are examples of legal provisions in which the interest of order is temporarily prioritized over the state's interest in legitimacy. Such special measures were enabled by Article 55(2) of the Constitution, which allows that rights related to the length of detention, privacy of the home and secrecy of communications can be limited or suspended "in connection with investigations of the activities of armed organizations or terrorist groups." Thus, even though defendants in such cases have not been proven guilty yet, and the presumption of innocence still prevails, special measures allow for the suspension of certain constitutional rights. Also, the dispersion policy of spreading ETA prisoners out among different jails across Spain to prevent their contact behind bars was based on assumed differences between ETA prisoners and ordinary prisoners. The policy was also intended to facilitate dissidents within ETA (that is, those in favor of negotiations and giving up the armed struggle) to take distance from the hardliners among ETA prisoners. It was implemented in 1989 and is still in place.

After the scandalous experiences of the Dirty War, the prosecutorial narrative began to change in the late 1980s, along with the Spanish state's discourse, to reflect a strong determination to deal with ETA through the "rule of law" and criminal prosecutions. A crucial step that influenced the Spanish state's commitment in this regard was the French state's turn away from providing ETA fugitives with a safe haven. In 1984, France began cooperating with the Spanish state, by both arresting and extraditing ETA militants to Spain to stand trial (Garzón 2006). By 1989, the estimated threat posed by ETA had changed dramatically, as the organization's operational capacity and popular support waned. Prosecutors in Spain observed a downward trend in the number of attacks and a change in attitude among the general population that left them optimistic about the future (MA 1989:122). The prosecutor of San Sebastián, a city in the Basque Country, explicitly noted that the majority of the Basque people increasingly and openly rejected violence, opting instead for pacific and democratic solutions. He observed that the "democratic idea," in which everyone can voice his or her ideas, even extremist ideas, was taking root. He speculated that, in a short time, the image of a Basque Country tainted by "barbaric" acts of violence could be nothing more than "a sad and forgotten past" (MA 1989:123). Other legal tactics to combat ETA's violence included efforts like the passing of the 2002 Law on Political Parties that led to the Basque left-nationalist party Batasuna being declared illegal.

By 2008, the Chief Attorney at the Audiencia Nacional argued that, after 40 years of experience, Spain now knew that the rule of law and criminal prosecutions were "sufficient to respond effectively against terrorism" (Interview S-21). He advocated fighting the struggle against ETA's terrorism with "*all* the arms of the law, but also *only* the arms of the law." In an affirmation of the effectiveness of this shift in approach, Naty Rodríguez, a family member of several victims of ETA violence, felt able to declare in 2008 that "ETA is defeated, regardless of the suffering they will still be able to cause" (*Bake hitzak* 2008:55).

Thus, during the 1970s and 1980s, prosecutors described ETA as an "enemy" in a "war" and the criminal justice arena was not viewed as the primary or even adequate venue in which to address ETA violence. To this end, prosecutors highlighted the differences between "terrorism" and "ordinary crime." They expressed their hesitation to take on this challenge of adequately addressing ETA's killings in criminal prosecutions alone and feared an escalation of violence. This can be contrasted to later decades in which the "rule of law" was hailed for its effectiveness in dealing with ETA and its terrorist activities, which was treated as a particular mode of criminality. By the late 2000s, the debate in Spain was still ongoing as to whether acts of terrorism differ from ordinary crimes and, if so, how their characterization as such should influence the state's response (for example, Unzalu 2008:14).

With the decrease of popular support for ETA violence in the Basque Country and the increased dominance of the criminal justice arena as the appropriate site for dealing with ETA's killings, the mobilization as victims and prisoner supporters gained prominence in the interactions between different groups in the context of the Basque conflict, thus sidelining the conversation about the legitimacy of Basque self-determination. As described in chapter 4, family members of individuals assassinated or injured in attacks by ETA created a number of victim organizations that actively lobbied prosecutors to take up their cases. Those mobilizing as victims of ETA sought to translate events and demands into the language of criminal law, while those who were charged under the new prosecutorial narrative resisted attempts to do so. Defendants accused of belonging to the ETA network insisted on the legitimacy of their political claims and activities. Different views on the nature of ETA and its relation to activists and organizations in the left-nationalist movement underpinned their competing narratives.

Changing the image: from "pistoleros" to the ETA network

In May 2008, as I traveled by bus from Madrid to Bilbao, a young man sitting next to me explained, "*ETA es mucho más,*" a stock phrase that I had come to hear repeatedly during my time in Spain and the Basque Country. This phrase – "ETA is much more" – sounded like a refutation of something. "More than what?" I wondered. Pushing the notion to the extreme, a family member of someone killed by ETA suggested that the organization included all actors whose aims posed a nationalist challenge to the status quo of an indivisible Spain. "The Basque president also belongs to ETA," he told me, referring to Juan José Ibarretxe, a member of the moderately nationalist PNV (Basque Nationalist Party) political party (Interview S-16). In contrast to this sentiment, I often heard another stock phrase employed by Basque left-nationalists: "*nos sobreestiman*," meaning "they overestimate us" (Interview S-3). This phrase also served as a kind of refutation, but in a sense that expressed the view that ETA was not as highly organized as many made it out. It suggested that ETA accounted for no more than a handful of Basque left-nationalists and was definitely not the grand organization painted by prosecutors as capable of dictating the behavior of the entire left-nationalist movement.

From its founding, ETA's animating mission was Basque self-determination in a free and socialist Euskal Herria (Basque homeland). As a self-proclaimed people's army, it purported to represent the will of "the" Basque people. In 1968, for example, after an ETA attack on a member of the Guardia Civil known for torturing Basques, ETA described its action as the "execution of the verdict of the Basque people" (Alcedo 1996). By the late 2000s, many in the Basque left-nationalist movement no longer viewed ETA as the political and military vanguard organization that it had aimed to be since its inception.

As the Spanish state's fight against ETA increasingly shifted into the criminal justice arena, the question of "What is ETA?" took on new importance. In response to discursive mobilization by victim groups and judicial activism by an investigative judge at the Audiencia Nacional, the prosecutorial narrative began to expand the scope of who counted as members of ETA. The classic image of ETA members as gun-wielding "*pistoleros*" gave way to the broader concept of "the ETA network." In the 1980s and the beginning of the 1990s, Spain's prosecutors focused on investigating ETA commandos, their direct support structures, and the armed attacks they carried out. The list of crimes committed by ETA catalogued in the Attorney General's 1992 Annual Report contains only armed attacks (MA 1993:252). In 2008, the chief prosecutor confirmed that in the 1980s, the "vision regarding terrorism was much more limited" (Interview S-21). The annual reports from the Office of the Attorney General in those years described the dismantling of ETA commando units in various parts of Spain. An essential part of this dismantling included breaking down the "infrastructure" that directly supported ETA commandos in each city (MA 1993:250). People who arranged transport for and provided housing to members of ETA were prosecuted for "collaboration" with ETA. In those criminal proceedings, prosecutors thus constructed a narrative about ETA as an armed organization and its members (the defendants on trial) engaged primarily in armed attacks.

In 1991, the concept of the "milieu of ETA" (*entorno de ETA*) appeared for the first time in the Spanish Attorney General's Annual Report, loosely defined as those "political sectors with goals similar to the terrorist organization ETA" (MA 1991:197). A prosecutor in the Basque Country described how a large part of the "street violence" in the region was the responsibility of "what is generally called the milieu of ETA" (MA 1991:297). According to the Spanish Attorney General, demonstrations organized by prisoner support collective Gestoras pro Amnistía or the youth organization Jarrai against detentions of ETA activists or hunger strikes would often lead to disturbances of public order, causing damage to official buildings, banks, telephone cabins, and urban buses (MA 1993:147). It was generally assumed that ETA would recruit its future members from the pool of youth engaged in street violence. It was further assumed that ETA collaborators, such as those providing housing to fugitives, came from the "milieu of ETA." In reflecting on the term's meaning, the chief prosecutor of the Audiencia Nacional said, "If ETA's milieu didn't exist, terrorism would be much more marginal. It is the breeding ground" (Interview S-21). However, without a generally accepted definition of the broader social "milieu" associated with ETA, people had different views on who would be part of it and why. One right-wing interviewee maintained that anyone who did not condemn ETA attacks belonged to ETA's milieu (Interview S-13).

Over the course of the 1990s, the concept of the "milieu of ETA" was eliminated from prosecutors' conceptual toolbox. Instead, the notion of the "ETA network" (*entramado de ETA*) developed by Investigative Judge Garzón became central in prosecutions related to ETA. According to Garzón, police and judicial activity against ETA in the 1980s had been ineffective and uncoordinated because it followed the rules of the game as dictated by ETA. By accepting the existence of a strong division between the military wing and the political organization, law enforcement had limited its efforts to prosecuting the military wing. In response to what he saw as a failing, Garzón set out to design a new prosecutorial strategy that aimed to show the connections between them, or even more so, to show that there were no fundamental differences between them. In his view, it was all ETA. As the chief prosecutor of the Audiencia Nacional explained, "Terrorists are not only those who commit attacks, but also those that share the strategy and the methods of the terrorist organization, and in addition contribute materially to the development of that strategy and those methods, even if they don't use weapons" (Interview S-21). Similarly, on 21 February 2003, Spain's then-president Aznar was reported in newspaper *El Mundo* as saying, "terrorists are not only the commandos that kill, but the whole network of the organization that gives them shelter and helps them" (EFE 2003). This notion of the ETA network received significant support from many victim organizations (for example, Portero 2007a).

With the creation of the prosecutorial concept of the "ETA network," many people previously situated outside of ETA (though possibly as part of its "milieu") became viewed as "members" of ETA. In 1998, prosecutors and investigative judges initiated a series of so-called "macro-trials," in which the defendants were not suspected of being directly involved in armed attacks by ETA, but "related to" the group through their activities with socio-political organizations in the broader Basque left-nationalist movement. Within the criminal justice arena, members of these socio-political organizations became perceived, and prosecuted, as "members" of ETA. Prosecutors put movement activities such as prisoner support and newspaper publications in the context of the presumed "ETA network" by identifying alleged "functions" that these "members" fulfilled within the prosecutors' understanding of ETA's strategy. During trials against members of the "ETA network" in the 2000s, prosecutors also suddenly referred to early ETA refugees in Cuba as "reserves" of ETA, thus criminalizing contact with them. While defendants accused of building the infrastructural support for ETA attacks were generally prosecuted as *collaborators* in the 1980s, the novel conceptualization of the "ETA network" changed the charge. During the 2000s, those accused of belonging to the network in the macro-trials were prosecuted as *members* of the terrorist organization.[1]

---

1   The number of people prosecuted for collaboration with ETA commandos was high during the 1980s. In 1983, 131 of all criminal proceedings on crimes by armed organizations (mostly ETA) at the Audiencia Nacional were for collaboration with commandos, compared to just 22 proceedings involving assassinations (MA 1984: Table B6). In 1989, there were 825 charges of collaborating with terrorists at the Audiencia Nacional versus 10 charges of membership in an armed band (MA 1989:213). Apart from "collaboration," the Spanish law also defines a form of conduct called "necessary cooperation," which was used to prosecute someone who collected information for ETA that was necessary, for example, for the execution of an assassination or some other criminal act.

Criminal prosecutions based on the concept of the ETA network

In the series of macro-trials against the "ETA network" that began in Spain in 1998, prosecutors defined a terrorist organization as a complex network of cultural, political, economic, and armed parts working together toward a common goal in a coordinated structure. Within this narrative, they emphasized how different parts of the network could perform distinct but complementary "functions" in pursuit of the organization's ultimate goal. According to this rationale, the activities of many socio-political organizations within the broader Basque left-nationalist movement could be reconceptualized as fulfilling particular "functions" in the "ETA network." For example, prosecutors cited the complementarity of Spain-wide attacks by ETA's armed commandos and the smashing of windows (*kale borroka*) by disgruntled Basque youth groups, claiming that both performed different "functions" toward the common goal of Basque self-determination in a free and socialist Euskal Herria. On this basis, a wide range of entities including a newspaper, a prisoner support group, a youth organization, a language institution, and more than a hundred cafés and companies were rendered illegal or had their activities suspended, while many of their leaders, members and employees were indicted for "membership in a terrorist organization." Unlike earlier prosecutions of ETA's armed commandos, the macro-trials against the ETA network were not triggered by a specific violent event, such as an assassination. Instead, they were proactively initiated by prosecutors. By suddenly rendering what had been considered legal political activity illegal without preceding legislative reform, the liberal principal of legality was called into question, as people complained that they could not reasonably know whether their conduct constituted a violation of the law (for example, Behatokia 2003).

The macro-trial known as "18/98" involved 62 defendants from multiple organizations tried as part of the ETA network, distinguishing it as the trial with the highest number of people charged in a single terrorism case at the Audiencia Nacional. The trial lasted a total of 16 months and resulted in 47 convictions handed down by the Audiencia Nacional on 19 December 2007. It targeted businesses that were allegedly financing ETA, an Euskara (Basque) language institute (AEK), a cultural association (XAKI), an individual journalist (Pepe Rei), and various other Basque socio-political organizations including the Fundación Joxemi Zumalabe. The Fundación actively supported various Basque grassroots social movements, including a controversial project in which it proposed making Basque ID cards.

The prosecutor specifically cited this project during the trial as evidence of an alleged plan to conduct destabilizing acts of civil disobedience in coordination with ETA in conjunction with the fact that a document about such civil disobedience strategies had been found in the hands of ETA (military wing) leaders (Case Sumario 18/98, indictment:101). Eight members of the Fundación were convicted and sentenced to up to ten years' imprisonment. On 22 May 2009, the Supreme Court overturned the previous verdict and acquitted the Fundación members, while reducing the sentences for the other defendants.

Other macro-trials were initiated against the political party Batasuna, several left-nationalist cafés (*herriko tabernas*) and companies, an association of Basque municipal mayors and councilors, the prisoner support organization Gestoras pro Amnistía, the newspaper *Egunkaria*, and the youth organization Jarrai. Significantly, and unlike trials against typical members of ETA's armed commando units, the defendants in these macro-trials, except the Gestoras defendants, all recognized the jurisdiction of the court, or at least did not make a point of expressly rejecting it, and cooperated with the proceedings. Traditionally, ETA militants began their trials by declaring themselves to be members of ETA, rejecting the court's jurisdiction, and asking their lawyers to lay down their defense. The macro-trial defendants, in contrast, strongly refuted the allegation that they were members of ETA.

In order to argue that members of these left-nationalist organizations were members of ETA, prosecutors put the foundation and role of these organizations in the context of the history of ETA since the Franco regime, when ETA decided to enforce a process called "*desdoblamiento*," or "double track." This was the process (undisputed by the defendants) in which, with the emerging democratic structures, many of the Basque cultural and political organizations that had been prohibited under Franco's dictatorship began to work above-ground. Only the military wing of ETA stayed underground. According to the prosecutors, members of ETA would sit on the (above-ground) boards of various socio-political organizations, while simultaneously performing their illegal tasks within the underground armed organization, in order to maintain cohesion between the various left-nationalist organizations. During the trials, prosecutors also emphasized ETA's theory of national struggle on different "fronts." The armed struggle, in this theory, was just one of the organization's many battle fronts, while others included the political front and the "front of the masses," which encompassed popular grassroots organizations like prisoner support group Gestoras pro Amnistía.

The prosecutorial narrative in each of the macro-trials drew on the same themes and assumptions of the "ETA network." Each of the implicated organizations was claimed to fulfill a "function" within the ETA network. For example, in the proceedings against the newspaper *Egunkaria* – the only daily newspaper entirely in the Euskara language (which had been banned under Franco), founded in 1990 by a communal effort of left-nationalists – prosecutors raised a number of questions regarding the true purpose of the paper. Did it actually aim to inform people or did it primarily try to convince people of the legitimacy of ETA's struggle? As a profitable company, was the paper's real objective to function as a source of funding for ETA? The indictment by Instruction Judge del Olmo described *Egunkaria*'s "function" within the ETA network as "to facilitate the protection and diffusion (with the help of *Eusquera* [sic], or Basque language, as cultural cover for that) of the terrorist idea and the values and interests defended by that terrorist organization" (Case *Egunkaria*, auto del procedimiento, 2004:8).

The instruction judge in the trial argued that the newspaper explicitly sought to increase popular support among ETA's "population of reference" and achieve its mid- to long-term strategy objectives under the guise of legitimate activity, protected by constitutional provisions guaranteeing freedom of language, information, and expression (Case *Egunkaria*, auto del procedimiento, 2004:1). As evidence, he cited a letter written by someone who had refused a seat on the board of *Egunkaria* because the paper had described the death of an ETA member very differently than the death of an Ertzaina (a Basque policeman). He also cited an incident in which *Egunkaria* failed to mention that the victims of an ETA attack had been children (Case *Egunkaria*, auto del procedimiento, 2004:34). Victim organizations supported this narrative, explicitly recognizing that they endorsed freedom of expression, but rejected the notion that *Egunkaria* had been founded with a journalistic purpose (Asociación Dignidad y Justicia 2007).

The trial against the Basque-language newspaper *Egunkaria* was a special case, in that after the initial proceedings led by the instruction judge, the prosecutor decided to drop the charges against the newspaper for a lack of evidence. It marked the only macro-trial in which the state prosecution retreated from the case, while a victim organization, Dignidad y Justicia, decided to pursue the trial on its own in the form of a popular accusation (open for those representing a group of victims). This was quite extraordinary, causing left-nationalists to question the right of the organization to continue the popular accusation without the backing of a state prosecutor. While most of the macro-trials ended in convictions, all of the defendants in the *Egunkaria* trial were acquitted by the Audiencia Nacional on 15 April 2010.

In the trial against the Basque left-nationalist prisoner support collective Gestoras pro Amnistía, the prosecutor argued that the "function" of Gestoras within the ETA network was to control the collective of ETA prisoners; facilitate contact between ETA's inmates and leaders; collect information relevant to the security of ETA; indicate and legitimize targets in society for ETA to kill; publish pamphlets; and recruit additional militants to the struggle. For example, prosecutors argued that Gestoras members' criticism of the court rulings of Judge Lidón constituted "signaling" (*señalamiento*) to ETA to target him, as ETA militants subsequently killed him in 2001.

While the primary logic of these macro-trials was to show that the socio-political organizations – of which the defendants undisputedly were members – belonged to the ETA network, prosecutors still emphasized the "individualization" of their charges for each defendant (countering any allegation of "collective punishment," which is at odds with the liberal legalist framework). In a break during the hearing in Madrid, the Gestoras defendants cracked jokes about the unfalsifiable reasoning the prosecutor employed to demonstrate each individual's membership in the ETA network: "if you had many documents, you're in trouble. But if you had no documents at all, like the group's president, then you're in even more trouble! You then had such responsibility that you didn't need the documents, or had someone else to carry them for you." The same applied to phone calls, they joked: "If there were many phone calls registered to you, you are in trouble. However, if there were only a few phone calls linked to you, then it proves that you were taking security precautions" (field notes June 2008, Case Gestoras pro Amnistía).

In proceedings against a Basque youth organization known at various times as Jarrai, Haika or Segi,[2] prosecutors accused the organization of coordinating *kale borroka*, or left-nationalist street struggle by youth in the Basque Country, to further the aims of ETA (Case Jarrai/Haika/Segi,

---

2   After the suspension of Jarrai, it was re-founded as Haika and after that as Segi, the trial was against members of Jarrai-Haika-Segi.

concluding statement, 11 April 2005). The prosecutor drew upon a theory elaborated by ETA leader "Txelis" in the late 1980s, which differentiated between x, y and z struggle. Journalist Gurruchaga writes in her book on ETA's leaders that, according to Txelis, the first were engaged in political agitation, the second (y-groups) in sabotage and the third were the ETA commandos. As it would be a pity if ETA members were detained for low-level actions, Txelis intended for minors to engage in actions of *kale borroka*, especially also because they would be prosecuted only for misdemeanors (Gurruchaga 2006:300–1). The concept of y-groups was heavily criticized by left-nationalist activists, who claimed it was an invention in order to link the youth organization Jarrai to ETA (Interview S-23; Arzuaga 2010:137). The private accuser argued that the organization Jarrai/Haika/Segi was responsible for 6,263 acts of *kale borroka* between 6 January 1992 and 5 March 1999, and the prosecutor charged 42 separate members of the youth group with "membership of a terrorist organization" as part of the ETA network (Case Jarrai/Haika/Segi, Conclusiones, 6 January 2005: 84). In 2005, the Audiencia Nacional convicted 24 of the defendants and declared the youth organization to be *illegal*, but clarified that it was not a *terrorist* organization. On 19 January 2007, however, the Supreme Court reversed the verdict and declared Jarrai/Haika/Segi to be a terrorist organization, citing the distinction between an *armed* organization and a *terrorist* organization (Case Jarrai/Haika/Segi, verdict, 46th consideration, para. 8).

Thus, the image of the "ETA network" enabled a series of prosecutions expanding the kind of defendants that had previously been put on trial in relation to ETA's crimes. By developing the notion of the "ETA network," Spanish prosecutorial narrative changed its conceptualization of a terrorist *organization* as well as its understanding of *terrorism*. As described in chapter 1, the novel prosecutorial qualification of *kale borroka* as a terrorist offense had already broadened the meaning of terrorism toward including property destruction, thus shifting such prosecutions from local courts in the Basque Country to the Audiencia Nacional. In order to establish a link between the defendants in such cases and ETA, they were alleged to have acted in support of the same ideology as ETA or to have been instructed by ETA. In some of these cases, the prosecutorial narrative pulled together those allegedly part of a same "cell" to hold each responsible for all actions of *kale borroka* attributed to that cell. For example, in October 2007, Judge Baltasar Garzón employed this narrative when he decided about the preventive detention of eight defendants:

From the information we gather that the terrorist organization ETA in the development of its criminal action gives a special relevance to the so-called street struggle or "Kale Borroka" as an element more to its terrorist activity complementing the armed action of ETA. [...] The groups (Cells "Y") of the "Kale Borroka" are formed around one or various responsible persons or dynamizers who propose, proportion, and order the execution of the different violent actions per zone. Within these activities, the zone Uribe-Costa (Vizcaya) and its area of influence is one of the permanent scenes of terrorist action, and it is in this framework that the activity of the group of imputed persons took place, between the years 2004 and 2007. [...] According to police investigations, the organizers and dynamizers of the "Cell Y" operating in the zone of Uribe-Costa who followed the instructions of the terrorist organization ETA were: ... . (Case Kale Borroka, Diligencias Previas, 19 October 2007)

Single events of, for example, burning waste containers or ATMs were put in the context of *kale borroka* as part of the cell's activities and connected to ETA. The decision in this case listed eight "cell" members and leaders as well as the various actions for which they were deemed responsible, even though each time they acted in various different constellations of two, three or four persons. At times only the participation of one of them was alleged, in none of the actions did all eight defendants act together or at least, that was not alleged. Thus, individual responsibility and the categorization as terrorism were often established by linking the individual to a group and an alleged pattern of actions.

A further widening of the net was evident in prosecutions against those alleged to have voluntarily paid ETA (Colli 2006). This fitted a new prosecutorial narrative pushed by, for example, the director of Dignidad y Justicia, Daniel Portero, who stressed the need to "follow the money" in order to destroy ETA (Interview S-14). During the 1980s and 1990s, the payment of money ("revolutionary taxes" as ETA called it) was generally understood as "extortion," given the pressure ETA exerted on those who refused to pay and the risk of kidnapping or worse. With time, however, interest groups began to advocate for prosecuting such payments as "financing of terrorism." Portero (2007b:14) reported that, after 2000, ETA initiated a new form of collecting money in which it asked businessmen in left-nationalist circles to contribute voluntarily, without any threats. In June 2011, the Audiencia Nacional for the first time convicted two sisters (Maribel and Blanca Bruño) for – allegedly voluntarily – paying the "revolutionary tax," sentencing them to one year and three months imprisonment. Prosecutors identified their active participation in left-nationalist political parties that had been made illegal as an indication of their voluntary payment. In contrast, the convicted sisters self-identified as "victims of ETA" (EFE 2011). Thus, while prosecutors cast the net wider, these prosecutions were strongly supported by some and contested by others.

The macro-trials were closely followed by the defendants' supporters in the Basque left-nationalist movement and also by organizations of victims of ETA. In all of the "ETA network" cases, prosecutors argued that the evidence they presented in the courtroom demonstrated close cooperation between ETA's military wing and certain socio-political organizations. One point of controversy was the alleged contact between left-nationalist activists and ETA. While some defendants and their supporters denied the very existence of contact with ETA's armed members, others refuted the notion that talking to ETA members would always be criminal in nature. For instance, left-nationalist activists pointed out the absurdity of criminalizing simply talking to ETA members given that the Spanish government frequently spoke with ETA militants for the purpose of negotiations. In a courtroom discussion about the nature of a meeting between an ETA member and a journalist from the newspaper *Egin*, the prosecutor argued that the meeting was an "organic meeting" and a fundamental part of the relationship between the ETA member and the journalist, while the journalist argued that the meeting was purely for journalistic purposes; it was supposed to be an interview for the newspaper. Relating this exchange in an interview with me, the frustrated defense lawyer commented: "everyone who wants to talk with ETA talks with ETA! Everyone talks with ETA, even prime ministers Aznar and Zapatero!" (Interview S-3). In other cases, defendants and their supporters disputed whether contact with ETA militants by individual members in a socio-political organization could be attributed to the organization as a whole, to the extent of holding other members responsible for fulfilling a particular "function" in the ETA network. For example, Gestoras pro Amnistía activists contended that if one or two persons within the organization had indeed recruited ETA members, they had done so of their own personal accord (field notes, trial Gestoras pro Amnistía June 2008).

Supporters of the macro-trials hailed the shift in prosecutorial narrative as a response to what they saw as left-nationalist activists "abusing" the spaces the law provided for the pursuit of socio-political activities. In the words of a representative of the victim organization Fundación Fernando Buesa, "the left-nationalists and the sympathizers of ETA, they laugh about the legality of [Spain's] democracy. They cheat on the law, they make fun of it. In this, they are experts and it becomes their life's obsession, all their energies go into it" (Interview S-15). In a similar vein, the president of the association of victims of ETA violence Dignidad y Justicia noted that various left-nationalist organizations mocked the law by simply changing their name after they were made illegal, like the Basque left-nationalist youth organization *Segi* which continued its work under several different names after courts ordered it to disband (Asociación Dignidad y Justicia 2009:1).

The Supreme Court did not, however, always accept the decisions taken by the Audiencia Nacional. For example, it reversed charges of membership into collaboration for many of the defendants in the Sumario 18/98 and significantly reduced their sentences from in total 525 to 239 years while acquitting 10 of the 47 convicted defendants (*El País* 2009). Still, the prosecutorial narrative in the macro-trials effectively coined the notion of the "ETA network," which was quickly adopted in mainstream media. The trials also successfully challenged and changed the traditional understanding of a terrorist organization.

In the negotiations with prime minister Zapatero in 2006, ETA asked the government to stop the macro-trials as a gesture of goodwill toward the left-nationalist movement, which – as journalists noted – coincided with state prosecutors dropping the case against *Egunkaria* (Villanueva and Colli 2011). Whether this was a coincidence or not, after the negotiations broke down, the macro-trials against the alleged ETA network continued, even after ETA laid down its arms in 2010. In July 2014, for example, the Audiencia Nacional convicted 20 people for membership in or collaboration with a terrorist organization due to their involvement in the left-nationalist cafés (*herriko tabernas*) that allegedly financed ETA. In subsequent trials, a change was observed in the defense strategy of those accused to be part of the ETA network. In the 2016 proceeding against the parties that had been made illegal – Batasuna, Partido Comunista de las Tierras Vascas (PCTV) and Acción Nacionalista Vasca (ANV) – there was an agreement between the defendants, the prosecutors and the popular accusation. The defendants agreed to acknowledge that their parties were instrumentalized – in an illegal manner – for the goals of ETA. In return, their sentences were set below two years, which kept them out of prison

(Europa Press 2017). Four months later, defendants belonging to the left-nationalist political organization Ekin[3] accepted a similar agreement, after having been accused of leading the left-nationalist movement in 2009 and 2010.

The image of a terrorist organization influences who is prosecuted for what

The shift toward the concept of the "ETA network" in the Spanish prose-cutorial narrative regarding ETA from the late 1990s onwards exemplifies a debate about the nature and make-up of allegedly terrorist organizations that was also visible in courtroom conversations in Chile and the United States. Of course, organizations with a political goal, such as the estab-lishment of an independent Basque Country, never exist in a vacuum, but are often part of a vibrant movement. This raises the question of how membership in such organizations should be defined. In each of the episodes in Spain, Chile and the United States, prosecutors selected who to prosecute for such membership[4] and who not to; this meant they had to create a narrative justifying their choice of defendants and explaining why the defendants belonged to that organization. The construction of these prosecutorial narratives involved choosing what acts, events and details to include and how to contextualize them within the broader scope of the respective episodes. Similar to the *kale borroka* prosecutions in Spain, prosecutorial narratives in Chile and the United States proposed framing property damage as a terrorist offense.

By moving to a conceptualization of ETA as a network, Spanish juris-prudence came to distinguish between an armed organization and a terrorist organization, enabling the so-called macro-trials against a large number of members in socio-political organizations of the Basque left-nationalist movement. After years of focusing on members in ETA's armed commando units, Instruction Judge Garzón (2006:289) criticized the Audiencia Nacional for having "played the game" in accordance with the rules imposed by ETA. Instead of accepting the separation between ETA as a military organization and the left-nationalist movement as a col-lection of legitimate socio-political organizations, he spearheaded a shift

3   In the earlier judgment by the Audiencia Nacional (Sumario 18/98), Ekin was considered to be the political apparatus of ETA.
4   Even though in the United States it is not a crime to be a member of a terrorist organization, US prosecutors select those who are considered to be a part of a conspiracy to commit a crime.

in the prosecutorial narrative by contextualizing Basque socio-political activities in the context of a presumed network with different functions, on the basis of which Spanish prosecutors began a series of trials.

In the new narrative, the work of members in the newspaper *Egunkaria* and prisoner support organization Gestoras pro Amnistia as well as youth organization Segi was conceptualized as performing a function in the ETA network. Arguably, the turn toward prosecuting members of the broader left-nationalist movement was facilitated by increasingly wide-spread rejection of armed struggle in the Basque Country. A lawyer for the victim association Dignidad y Justicia told me that, back in 1997, it had been unthinkable to imagine prosecuting the board of the left-nationalist political party Batasuna on charges of collaboration with ETA. Everyone assumed it would be explosive ("*la bomba*"), as she put it, but when it finally occurred in 2002, "nothing happened" (Interview S-27).

Thus, throughout the years, prosecutors cast a wider net as they defined cases as "ETA cases." For example, during a protest against the planned high speed railway (TAV) in the Basque Country on 3 November 2006, two activists from the town of Beasain were arrested and charged for "public disorder" (Alonso et al. 2008). On 15 January 2008, their case was finally scheduled to take place at the court house in Tolosa. However, at the last moment, the Audiencia Nacional intervened, redefining the conduct as terrorism and transferring the case from the local courthouse in the Basque Country to Madrid. Just over a week earlier, on 5 January 2008, the newspaper *Gara* had published an interview with ETA in which the organization announced its opposition to the railway project. With this information, the Spanish authorities viewed the earlier protests in a new light. It is not clear whether or how that case proceeded, but in a different case in 2015, the Audiencia Nacional convicted four anti-TAV activists to up to two years in prison for having thrown pies in the face of the president of Navarra for building the railway (*Diagonal*, 16 July 2015).

By 2008, criminal prosecutions even targeted officials in the moderate Basque Nationalist Party, PNV, for allowing, in their role as mayors of Basque villages, homecoming celebrations for ETA prisoners. A left-nationalist lawyer interpreted these prosecutions as "another leap" in the expansion of the scope of activities and defendants that had come within the purview of the criminal justice arena (Interview S-3). These prosecutions, narrating the praise of ETA prisoners as the humiliation of victims, thus casting the net even wider to include expressions in support of ETA militants, are the topic of the next chapter.

7

Narrating Praise for ETA
Prisoners as Humiliation
of Victims

The liberal separation between ideas and conduct

When I visited the Basque Country in 2008, I observed many symbols of solidarity with "Basque political prisoners." Pictures of prisoners hung on the walls in many bars, while numerous balconies were decorated with flags saying "bring the prisoners back to the Basque Country," referencing the Spanish state's policy of dispersing ETA prisoners across Spain to punish and prevent in-prison organizing. Contentious ETA-related trials and allegations of torture in custody brought large numbers of people to the streets. Similarly, activists organized protests and coordinated hunger strikes to demand better prison conditions. Upon release, "Basque political prisoners" could expect an official honoring ceremony in their village to welcome them home. Associations of victims of ETA viewed such solidarity as highly problematic and equated it to support for ETA. This also became the narrative presented in legal proceedings. For example, during a trial in 2008, a police expert claimed that a Basque mayor had openly called for support for two ETA members who were detained and allegedly tortured. When the defense lawyer asked whether she actually used the word 'ETA' in her speech, the expert responded: "she said 'Basque political prisoners' which everyone understands as ETA prisoners" (Personal observation during the trial June 2008, on making the left-nationalist Basque political party ANV [Acción Nacionalista Vasca]/PCTV [Partido Comunista de las Tierras Vascas] illegal, Supreme Court). Over the period from 1990 to 2010, public expressions of support for ETA and its prisoners became increasingly controversial as victim associations mobilized to gradually push the issue into the criminal justice arena.

The shift in Spanish prosecutorial narrative toward criminalizing verbal and symbolic expressions of support for ETA, including its prisoners, highlights the tension in liberal legalism's dichotomy between ideas and conduct. The principle of harm is the foundation of criminalization in democratic societies (Wallerstein 2007).[1] Yet the meaning and impact of speech acts, and whether, when and to whom they cause harm, are subjective determinations open to considerable contention. While liberal democratic frameworks champion the notion that ideas should be free, they allow restricting the public expression of ideas when they pose a threat to public order. In such cases, liberal democratic states must determine when speech or symbolic expressions in support of particular acts or actors cross the threshold between simply expressing an opinion and facilitating or inciting unlawful conduct.

In 1979, Spain's Attorney General berated the media for providing exposure to terrorists: "Terrorism needs publicity for its ends. The terrorist sees his injustice crowned and completed as his name appears on the front page" (MA 1979:72). Therefore Spanish prosecutors mounted cases against individuals and institutions involved in the publication or distribution of ETA communiqués. Only a few of these attempts succeeded, however. On 9 January 1980, the Audiencia Nacional convicted Luis Felipe of a "crime against citizen security" for editing and publishing ETA communiqués and other information about the group's actions given to him by ETA members to spread. Almost a year later, however, in a case against the director of a newspaper, *Egin*, the Constitutional Court ruled that publishing ETA communiqués did not constitute endorsement of terrorism but rather comprised activity protected under the right to inform and be informed (Vercher 1991:425). In 2004, in a case against the Basque-language newspaper *Egunkaria*, the act of publishing ETA communiqués, as such, was not conceptualized as a crime, but was narrated as a key aspect of the newspaper's alleged "function" within the "ETA network" (Case *Egunkaria*, auto de procedimiento, 4 November 2004).

Belief in the harmful effects of public approval for crimes and the need to address such speech in the criminal justice arena is not limited to Spain. Actors in Chile and the United States have also sought to criminalize public expressions of support for criminal activities. For example, on 5

---

1   In defining the principle of harm, liberal philosopher John Stuart Mill noted that "the only purpose for which power can rightfully be exercised over any member of a civilized community against his will is to prevent harm to others" (in De Roos 1987:36).

December 2003, the Chilean newspaper *El Mercurio* reported that several senators sought the detention of Mapuche leader Aucán Huilcamán, arguing that he "justifies and promotes" indigenous land occupations "in the form of interviews, conferences and communiqués," by which he "publicly backs the means of pressure of the Mapuche communities." The senators declared that "[t]his support constitutes incitement to commit the crime of usurpation" (*El Mercurio* 2003). Despite their call for his prosecution, however, Huilcamán was never charged. In the United States, prosecutors began to explicitly highlight the harmful effects of press communiqués related to environmental and animal rights protest actions in the 1990s. For example, in the criminal case against animal rights activist Rod Coronado for arson at a university research lab, the prosecutor argued that "the threats Coronado circulated were at least as important as the arson attacks themselves since they furthered ALF's goal of threatening violence against other scientists, farmers and consumers if they did not bow to the ALF's demands" (Case Rod Coronado, Government's Sentencing Memorandum 1995:13, footnote 2).

This chapter traces changes in prosecutorial narrative in Spain that led to the criminalization of speech and symbolic expressions in support of ETA as "endorsement" and "glorification" of terrorism. Throughout the 1990s, prosecutors and a number of victim spokespersons sought to penalize a wide range of expressions that they perceived to endorse terrorism. For a long time, judges ruled against their efforts, arguing that the mere approval of ETA's actions was insufficient to constitute endorsement of terrorism. They maintained that endorsement required the direct incitement to commit a crime, meaning that there must be a real intention to commit a future crime (see also Belloch 2000; Biurrun 2000; Landáburu 2002). However, in 2000, mobilization by victims of ETA led to the passing of a new law on "glorification" (*enaltecimiento*) of terrorism, which enabled the prosecution of expressions without inductive intent, as well as expressions glorifying the author of a crime, not just the conduct itself (LO 7/2000, new Article 578 of the Spanish Penal Code), imposing a sentence of up to two years. The law introduced the humiliation of victims of terrorism as a relevant and separate legal interest, thus giving victims an important role in bringing cases to the attention of the authorities and in defining the meaning of "humiliation." Victim associations immediately grabbed the opportunity to generate prosecutions under the new law, actively filing petitions against displaying photos of ETA militants in public places, naming streets to commemorate them, and honoring them in homecoming ceremonies upon their release from prison.

Solidarity with detained ETA militants: the acquittal of five municipal councilors

In 1992, after several ETA leaders were detained in a major police operation in Bidart, France, five municipal councilors from San Sebastián issued a statement saying: "We extend our most firm solidarity to all militants of our sister organization ... at the same time we express our profound admiration for their patriotic consistency, their heroism and human fortitude." In response, a Basque prosecutor indicted them for "endorsing terrorism." While the municipal councilors clearly expressed solidarity with the detained ETA militants, the Tribunal Superior de Justicia de Bilbao acquitted them on 17 November 1993, reasoning that mere approbation of an act was not punishable unless it negatively influenced the social community and clearly stimulated the commission of crimes. Critics of the prosecution also argued that criminalization should be limited to the endorsement of a specific crime, not its author.

Following the prosecution's defeat in this case, the 1994 Annual Report by Spain's Attorney General contained a lengthy discussion regarding "endorsement of terrorism" (apología) as a crime. Over six pages, the Attorney General acknowledged the contested place of "endorsement" within criminal law and described the history of its use in various court decisions and related interpretations of words like "approval" and "solidarity." He made clear, though, that endorsement should not be taken lightly, especially in the case of terrorism and committed to continuing the appeal in the San Sebastián case, and possibly other cases, until he obtained a judgment favorable to his interpretation.

In his analysis, the Attorney General contended that it was not necessary to show a concrete harmful result in order to prove the crime of endorsement (MA 1994:154). Instead, he argued that verbal expressions like the statement of the San Sebastián municipal councilors did not endorse the detainees' political ideology, but instead, endorsed them *as militants of the terrorist organization ETA*, which was recognized as an illegal organization. He asked rhetorically: "Is it necessary to emphasize that the terrorist band ETA is known, not primarily for its political ideology, but for the ways its members use to realize, or better, impose it?" The Attorney General held that the reference in the municipal councilors' statement to the detainees' "brave struggle" against "foreign imperialism" clearly amounted to "praise" and "exaltation" of the *conduct* of the prisoners, as in his view, the foreign imperialism they cited was not foreign imperialism at all, but "nothing more than the integration of Euskadi in the Spanish State" (MA 1994:149).

On 4 July 2001, the Supreme Court rejected the cassation arguments of the prosecutor in the San Sebastián case, thus closing this avenue for criminalizing such verbal expressions. By this time, however, the new law had been passed that provided prosecutors with the tools needed to prosecute acts of solidarity and approval without having to argue that there was an inductive intention in the relevant verbal expression. While the prosecutors lost this particular case, it had played a role in preparing the grounds for the new law. The new legal interest shifted prosecutorial and societal attention to the plight of victims of terrorism and their family members.

The shift from normal to socially unacceptable to crime

During much of the 1980s, few people in the Basque Country openly criticized ETA's armed struggle. From the late 1980s onward, however, critics and victims of ETA increasingly formed alliances and mobilized in condemnation of the organization. In 1986, the organization Gesto por la Paz was formed as one of the first public platforms for opposing ETA violence. Later, the organizations Basta Ya and the Forum of Ermua were formed explicitly to oppose ETA's violence. Throughout the 1990s, public demonstrations against ETA's abductions and assassinations of civilians enabled people in Basque villages and cities to speak more openly about their ideas, even though the majority would still choose to avoid the subject rather than explicitly oppose ETA. Sociologist Van den Broek writes that according to many political comments in those days "the so-called 'Basque conflict' had gradually turned into a 'conflict among Basques'" (2004:719). When public anti-ETA demonstrations were held that called for the liberation of hostages held by ETA, some left-nationalist activists organized counter-demonstrations, yelling slogans like 'ETA kill them' and harassing the anti-ETA activists (Van den Broek 2004:719).

During a conversation in January 2010, a Durango resident recalled a funeral ceremony that he saw at some point in the late 1980s. The coffin was covered with the *ikurriña*, the Basque flag. An ETA member had died in prison and, during the funeral ceremony, someone with his face masked handed a memorial object with the symbol of ETA to the mother of the deceased. She lifted it above her head and shouted "*Gora ETA militarra!*" (Long live military ETA!). After relating this memory, he shook his head and said it would be unthinkable nowadays. It would also be unthinkable for youth to stand in the streets in a counter-demonstration like he had done ten years previously, yelling "ETA, kill them, ETA kill them" to the so-called "blue-ribbon" wearers who demonstrated for the liberty of a businessman abducted by ETA. I pushed him on his participation in these counter-demonstrations, pointing out the horrible meaning of such slogans. He shrugged and could only say, "it was normal." He and his friends celebrated when ETA killed someone and they idolized specific ETA members, who they thought seemed really "cool or sympathetic."

He was a young teenager at the time, but his attitude was typical and embedded in a broader social environment. He recalled that his parents, for example, who were voters for the moderately nationalist Partido Nacionalista Vasco (PNV), would comment indifferently or even with a smirk when they would see the windows of a bank had been smashed as a result of *kale borroka* actions in his village, which happened regularly. He recalled that the office for temporary jobs had to close because it got its windows smashed every three months. There was no general outrage. When we spoke in 2010, however, the same attitude and behavior would be considered far from normal. He had also changed his opinions over the years and was no longer in favor of ETA's armed struggle, although he had not changed his view that ETA had been very important to the Basque people. "But now things are different," he said, noting that he thought ETA should lay down its arms and politicians should resolve the situation through political dialogue. Shortly thereafter that is indeed what happened.

Throughout the 1980s and 1990s, prosecutors closely followed the developments and shifts in public support for ETA. In 1993, the Attorney General reported that he was "hopeful" that, day by day, Basque society was taking a firmer position against the "terrorist phenomenon" (MA 1993:147). In a survey conducted by the Basque government that year, 70 percent of Gipuzkoans (residents of a province in the Basque Country) rejected terrorism as a vehicle for the expression of any idea, repudiating it as unjustifiable, while "only" 7.3 percent of respondents thought ETA's violence was justified (MA 1993:148). In 1997, popular support for ETA dropped significantly after the assassination of Ermua town councilor Miguel Angel Blanco. Six million people took to the streets in protest. By the 2000s, social support for ETA and its arguments about the necessity of the armed struggle had become the subject of public campaigns in the Basque Country to de-legitimize violence. In 2006, for example, the grassroots anti-ETA organization Gesto por la Paz organized a colloquium around this theme and in 2010 the Basque regional government launched a "Plan for democratic coexistence and the de-legitimization of violence" (31 May 2010).

During my interviews in 2008, many left-nationalist activists still refused to see ETA as a *terrorist* organization, but also thought it should stop killing. Despite steadily declining public support, ETA did not waver in its commitment to armed struggle for a long time. Even in 2007, ETA still announced that "[t]oday, in the conditions our country is in, we consider that the reasons for carrying out armed struggle are still applicable and as long as that is the case we will continue" (Interview in *Gara* 8 April 2007). In June 2010, however, a significant turn was set in motion when the left-nationalist political party Batasuna asked ETA to relinquish its arms and pursue dialogue. In this plea, Batasuna had the support of the majority of ETA prisoners. On 11 January 2011, ETA announced a permanent ceasefire (Aizpeolea 2011).

The increasing public rejection of violence in the Basque Country also led to louder calls for the criminal prosecution of public support for ETA and its actions. After the 2000 enactment of legislation banning "glorification" of terrorism, victim organizations filed complaints leading to numerous criminal cases in which the prosecutorial narrative came to address practices that were previously beyond the purview of the criminal justice system. References to and symbols of ETA that could be found in many places throughout the Basque Country for decades – in graffiti in the streets, in public speech or in songs – came to be framed as acts of glorification of terrorism. As a consequence, several expressions of support for ETA and "Basque political prisoners" that, for a long time, were habitual practice in the Basque Country, slowly disappeared or changed now that they were subject to criminal prosecution. By 2010, what used to be perceived as normal during the 1980s had not only become socially unacceptable, but had also been effectively translated into criminal conduct. Drawing on selected cases which were made possible by the new law, the next sections illustrate changes in prosecutorial narrative and highlight the discursive battle of interpretation over the usage of ETA symbols, honoring ceremonies and the public display of "political prisoner" pictures.

Eliminating ETA symbols from the public sphere

In 2006, two young Basques (25 and 27 years old, respectively) were taken to the Audiencia Nacional in Madrid and accused of glorifying terrorism because they waved a flag with the ETA emblem during a soccer match. In the verdict, the alleged facts were related as follows:

> On the afternoon of the fifth day of February, 2006, the defendants Ander [...] and Jagoba [...] are together in the soccer stadium of Anoeta to watch the soccer match between the teams of Real Sociedad of San Sebastián and Real Mallorca, occupying spaces in the amphitheater's southern section, carrying a flag on which is painted the word ETA, and its corresponding emblem, consisting of an axe with a snake coiled around it, in addition to the words "Bietan Jarrai" along with a star with five points that coincides with the emblem of the youth terrorist group ETA Jarrai, inside of which is painted an emblem of the soccer team of the Real Sociedad, from which they have eliminated the crown that it officially carries. (Case flag wavers, Audiencia Nacional 15 November 2007)

These facts were confirmed by the defendants. The Audiencia Nacional found that the intention of the defendants could have been nothing other than to glorify terrorism, as "knowledge of what the letters ETA mean and the symbol of the coiled snake and the axe are public and notorious" (15 November 2007, second consideration). As evidence of the criminal conduct, a video of the soccer match was shown. In its verdict, the court noted that the video footage did not show any gestures of rejection by the defendants with regard to the flag. The two young men were sentenced to one year in jail each.

In a dissenting opinion in the case, however, Judge Ramón Sáez Valcárcel disputed that the perpetrators had the required intention ("*dolo*") needed for the crime of glorification and argued for their acquittal. The defendants, he suggested, could well have been fervent and aggressive supporters of their club Real Sociedad who randomly picked up a flag that was lying on the floor of the stadium – as testified by the defendants – while not noticing or caring that it had the ETA symbols among several other symbols, such as a piracy skull. They cheered for the game, never uttering any political phrases, possibly not caring about politics at all, and left the flag after the game was over. Judge Sáez concluded that the flag waving did not constitute glorification of any concrete criminal offense or its authors and, "in addition, it is doubtful that it represents, without further evidence, an exaltation of the group and its methods [...] even though it expresses in a confused manner a pseudo-ideological position that may seem aberrant" (dissenting opinion 4/2007).

By increasingly bringing such cases, prosecutors sent a clear message about the public use of ETA symbols. Often, such prosecutions were initiated after complaints were filed by victim associations. For example, in March 2008, after ETA murdered a municipal council member, the board of the soccer club Athletic Bilbao decided to introduce a one-minute silence in his memory before a Sunday match. During the minute of silence, someone in the stadium shouted *"Gora ETA."* After a criminal complaint by the victim organization Dignidad y Justicia, the Audiencia Nacional opened an investigation to search for the alleged suspect.[2]

Public support for "Basque political prisoners": glorification of armed struggle or criticism of state repression?

Viewed as soldiers (*"gudaris"* in a war of liberation, ETA members who were killed by Guardia Civil or right-wing paramilitaries were celebrated annually as heroes on days of commemoration (Casquete 2017). Similarly, throughout ETA's existence, it has been common practice among nationalist Basques to organize honoring ceremonies for ETA prisoners when they are released and return to their villages. During the 2000s, such honoring ceremonies slowly came to play a role in criminal prosecutions. In 2006, Batasuna leader Arnaldo Otegi was convicted and sentenced to 15 months' imprisonment for glorifying terrorism due to a speech he gave during a ceremony commemorating the 25th anniversary of the death of ETA militant "Argala" (Reuters 2006). In the indictment of leaders of the prisoner support group Gestoras pro Amnistía for membership in a terrorist organization, the prosecutor argued that one of the "functions" of the group within the "ETA network" was to organize honoring ceremonies in memory of ETA members who passed away, in which "they endorse a crime, mocking the victims and the juridical order" (Indictment Gestoras, March 2008, para. 12).

Victim organizations, as well as anti-ETA groups, used the new law on glorification of terrorism passed in 2000 to petition for the criminal-

---

2   No information could be found on whether the case proceeded.

ization of such honoring ceremonies. For example, on 29 January 2008, the right-wing platform España y Libertad wrote a petition to the prosecutor's office of the Tribunal Superior de Justicia (the highest regional court) in the Basque Country. The platform referred to Article 264 of the criminal procedure to explain that it approached the authorities because of the general obligation of citizens to report crimes and called attention to an upcoming honoring ceremony in the town of Santurce for Endika Iztueta, an alleged ETA militant, who had passed away in Cabo Verde. By 2008, honoring ceremonies had become subject to prosecution as stand-alone crimes. In that year, the mayor of the Basque village Amurrio was prosecuted because he allowed an honoring ceremony to take place in the village.

Left-nationalist activists and family members of prisoners disagree with the criminalization of honoring ceremonies. As the nephew of a well-known ETA militant who spent 17 years in prison put it, "We are honoring my uncle. He has suffered so much ..." (Interview S-28). When I asked him whether he would agree with victims who argue that honoring ceremonies are humiliating and insulting to them, he seemed surprised by the suggestion. "Humiliation ... ? We wouldn't do it, if it were humiliating," he stuttered. According to him, honoring ceremonies are about honoring the person, not what that person did or did not do. The whole family suffers when someone is imprisoned, particularly when that person is imprisoned far from their home due to Spain's dispersion policy for ETA prisoners. The ceremonies, he insisted, are meant to honor those who have suffered, who have served their time and finished their punishment. He argued that such ceremonies should not be outlawed or criminalized, as they represent the exercise of freedom of expression, and because every individual who attends such ceremonies does so with his or her own motivations:

We are not protecting or justifying, but it is our family. I can't put myself into their skin, but I don't think it is humiliating. [...] I don't want to offend anyone, but it is my uncle. I have to support him. Not only because he is in prison, but also because it is a continuing extortion with blackmailing and threats. For example, he puts pictures of his family and an "*Arrano Beltza*" (Black Eagle, symbolizing Euskal Herria) on the wall of his cell and they tell him to take it away, otherwise he won't get dinner. That is why he has done several hunger strikes and has been put in isolation. (Interview S-28)

Another contested practice in which "Basque political prisoners" are memorialized is by regularly displaying their pictures in bars throughout the Basque Country and during towns' annual *"fiestas del pueblo."* For example, on 17 September 2009, Dignidad y Justicia presented a complaint about a photo displayed during the *fiesta del pueblo* in the city of Durango. The instruction judge took the case up and considered the photo to be a "clear homage" to ETA members Harriet Iragui and Igor Solana. This interpretation was not only disputed by left-nationalist activists, but also by moderates. In this case, one of the municipal councilors of the festivities in question, Natxo Martínez from the moderately nationalist PNV, defended the practice, arguing that "the photo of a prisoner who fulfills a sentence is only a record that the inmate cannot be present during the fiestas of his home village" (Europa Press 2009). Meanwhile, victims of ETA's violence pointed out that not every inhabitant or prisoner who was unable to attend the *fiestas* was similarly memorialized with a photo. In 2010, the related practice of memorializing ETA militants by naming streets after them also came under scrutiny by victim organizations. Several criminal prosecutions were launched that posed the question of whether such pictures or street names signified support for armed struggle and glorified ETA and its militants, and whether they humiliated victims.

In 2008, the mayor of the Basque village Hernani was prosecuted for glorifying terrorism after making a public statement following the arrest of two suspected ETA militants. In the offending statement, she thanked the crowd for showing support for the two village members: "First of all, thank you for this spirit, hug and shower of applause that you have shown, as warm as possible, for Igor Portu, Mattin Sarasola and all the Basque political prisoners who are scattered in the jails of France and Spain. We love you!" (EFE 2009). The judge dropped the case, however, reasoning that her words should be taken in the context of reports that Portu and Sarasola had been tortured during their detention. He also noted that it had yet to be proven whether Portu and Sarasola were members of ETA (Case Portu and Sarasola, Audiencia Nacional, 25 January 2008). Relying on an earlier verdict from the Supreme Court (21/1997), the judge emphasized that the defense of ideas – even if they question the constitutional framework – should be allowed, otherwise the crime of glorification could convert into an instrument to control political dissidence (Case Portu and Sarasola, Audiencia Nacional, 25 January 2008). The prosecutor appealed the decision to drop the case, emphasizing that the mayor had given support to Portu and Sarasola as members of ETA and to the activities of the "armed organization" (Audiencia Nacional, 3 April 2008). The case was reopened on 5 June 2009 and the Audiencia Nacional sentenced the mayor to one year in prison (Yoldi 2009). On appeal, on 19 March 2010, she was finally acquitted by the Supreme Court (Sáiz-Pardo 2010).

Throughout the 2000s, these "glorification" prosecutions served as a site for ongoing debate about the identity of "Basque political prisoners" and ETA militants. Typically, supporters of honoring practices for prisoners emphasized state repression as the relevant context of their symbolic expressions. They held that the photos, speeches, and ceremonies referenced the suffering of prisoners and their families. Victims of ETA and prosecutors, however, emphasized ETA's violent activity and terror campaign as the relevant context and interpreted the photos and ceremonies as glorification of that violence.

Public speech and expressions in the Spanish prosecutorial narrative

The 2000 law on "glorification" opened new possibilities for prosecuting speech acts, not only for their potential incitement to commit crimes but also because of the glorifying or humiliating nature of the speech itself when put in the context of ETA's armed struggle. After years of neglect, victims of ETA's violence, their family members and their associations finally attained influence in the criminal justice arena. Some grabbed the opportunity with both hands, turning the courtroom into a new site of contestation over the meaning of symbols and expressions related to ETA and its prisoners. In response to this mobilization, the prosecutorial narrative expanded its reach to translate public support for ETA and its militants into the condemnatory language of criminal law.

In the glorification cases that followed the passing of the law, judges often defended the strict separation between ideas and actions, thus acquitting defendants. In one case, the Supreme Court even reversed an earlier conviction holding that the judge of the Audiencia Nacional had not been impartial to the defendant.[3] Even though many cases ended in acquittals, the prosecutions still had a real impact on defendants and the willingness of society to accept such contested speech. For example, Martxelo Otamendi, the director of the Basque-language newspaper *Egunkaria*,

---

3   Former Batasuna leader Otegi was prosecuted for having glorified ETA leader Sagarduy in an honoring ceremony in 2005. After the reversal, he was ultimately acquitted in July 2011.

which was closed due to allegations that it was part of the "ETA network" (see chapter 6), often spoke in public about the terrorism charges against him. In one instance, the dean of the University of Gran Canaria refused his presence in a forum, fearing that it could constitute "endorsement of terrorism" (Martín 2003). In making this decision, the dean took heed of the developing prosecutorial narrative and drew his own conclusion.

In interviews in 2008, left-nationalist activists also frequently expressed insecurity about whether their words and actions could potentially be prosecuted as endorsement or glorification of terrorism. At times, they adjusted their actions accordingly. For example, in June 2008, I spoke with the municipal assistant of a mayor in a Basque village. He was preparing the annual *fiesta* and was not sure how to describe some of the activities in the official program. He decided to rename the annual "amnesty day" as the "day in favor of the rights of the repressed." He added that on the public billboards people would still use the widely known term "amnesty day," but those were not made by the municipality and his concern was to prevent criminal prosecutions against his mayor (Interview S-3).

By 2010, the prosecution of activities glorifying terrorism, specifically prohibiting the exhibition of symbolic images in public spaces, had become an important and explicit prosecutorial focus in the struggle against ETA (MA 2010:262). This explicit emphasis was remarkable in that it signified a radical change from the silence that characterized much of the prosecutorial narrative during the 1980s. The change can only be understood in light of the active mobilization by and on behalf of the victims of ETA, who tirelessly pushed these issues onto the agenda. It took years before their voices were recognized and the harm-definitions that they proposed were adopted into the prosecutorial narrative. Speech and symbols supporting ETA changed from being normal occurrences to being socially rejected and, finally, to being criminalized and subject to punishment. After ETA laid down its arms, prosecutions for glorification of terrorism continued. Between 2014 and 2016, the Guardia Civil launched "Operation Spider" to counter glorification of terrorism (of ETA but also of organizations like GRAPO) in social media, which led to the detention of 73 persons (Amnesty International 2017:183). In 2016 alone, the Audiencia Nacional convicted 25 people for glorification. In that same year the tribunal opened a case against two puppeteers who had used a banner with Gora ETA in a play in the streets of Madrid. After an outcry over freedom of expression, in 2017 their case was abandoned. Finally,

Spain's recent Ley de Seguridad Ciudadana (Law on Public Safety 2015) was widely criticized for not respecting freedom of expression and for criminalizing social protest, thus opening up a new site for contestation about public expressions.

"MAPUCHE CONFLICT" CASES IN CHILE

8

Vacillating between Criminalization and Negotiation

After Chile's return to democracy in 1989, the Chilean public widely recognized the legitimacy of indigenous Mapuche communities' demands for land restitution (CEP 2006:48). The dialogues between the new Chilean government and Mapuche representatives triggered high expectations for land reforms. As early as 1992, however, a few Mapuche activists expressed frustration with the political limitations of the Indigenous Act, the law designed to facilitate land redistribution. After the Act came into force the following year, the National Corporation for Indigenous Development (CONADI) administered the land redistribution program. This state agency could not seize land for redistribution, but only buy it if the owner was willing to sell voluntarily, which was often not the case. This process of land transfer was also at odds with the perspective of some Mapuche activists. As a member of a Mapuche community exclaimed: "Buying lands?! That is ridiculous. The lands were ours to begin with!" (Interview C-61). In addition, the CONADI mechanism only focused on Mapuche communities that were already in possession of a land title. By default, this excluded Mapuche communities' demands for lands beyond the reservations, which they had owned *before* the war that ended in 1882, the so-called "Pacification of the Araucanía." Moreover, actual progress in resolving pending Mapuche land claims has remained slow and underfunded.[1]

In turn, Mapuche organizations and communities have attempted to mobilize pressure on the state and current landowners to fulfill their

---

1 According to Correa and Mella (2010: 207–8), between 1994 and 2006, only 73.045 hectares were acquired by CONADI and transferred to Mapuche communities. In comparison, in 2010 forestry companies owned about 1.5 million hectares.

obligations. They have written letters to the president, issued public declarations opposing major infrastructure projects on contested lands, protested in street demonstrations, and engaged in civil disobedience by staging ceremonial temporary recuperations of disputed property, erecting road blockades, and occupying the office of CONADI in Temuco. From 1997 onwards, having become increasingly frustrated with the lack of actual land transfers, a small number of activists began to destroy property as a means of increasing pressure on the state and landowners. Further, the Mapuche organization CAM introduced non-ceremonial land occupations in which the communities would harvest the existing plantations and agricultural produce. This shift in tactics on the part of some Mapuche activists led private landowners to stoke public fears that property destruction signaled an escalation in violence that was likely to lead to injuries and even death. Indicative of the perception of escalation, in 2001, the Chilean newspaper *El Mercurio* ran the headline: "The Mapuche intifada: The indigenous uprising worsens" (Barria 2001). The article quoted commercial Chilean farmers willing to defend their property "by all means" and described Mapuche actions as increasingly "pseudo-guerrilla" in nature.

Meanwhile, Mapuche activists disputed the notion that their protests sought or would necessarily lead to such violent escalation. From the late 1990s onwards, confrontations between police, landowners, or private security guards and activists during the dispersal of land occupations or road blockades did, however, occasionally lead to injuries on both sides. While landowners and media painted Mapuche protesters as purveyors of violence, activists noted the long history of unnecessary and disproportionate police violence used against Mapuche communities following the violent colonization of their lands in the first place. Although there have been incidents leading to personal injuries, the majority of actions by Mapuche activists have always constituted symbolic actions or property damage.

In response to Mapuche protests, Chilean prosecutors have pulled alleged perpetrators into the arena of criminal justice. At the same time, the legitimacy of Mapuche land claims has frequently led to negotiation – in the political arena – with the very communities whose members were put on trial. This chapter traces the vacillating prosecutorial narrative as it justifies assigning the Mapuche protests to the criminal justice arena on some occasions, while leniency in sentencing or even silence at other times seem to recognize the political character of and legitimate grievances behind the criminalized actions. Ever since the Mapuche land recuperations re-emerged in the early 1990s, commercial landowners have mobilized around a claim to victimhood, criticizing what they perceive to be impunity for illegal incursions onto their property (see chapter 4). They have sought to have Mapuche land occupations dealt with in the criminal justice arena and, later on, incidents of arson to be redefined as acts of terrorism. Against the victimhood claims of landowners, Mapuche activists have asserted the legitimacy of occupations ("recuperations" in their words) as a political tactic to highlight their demand and right to land restitution, while largely denying involvement in arson.

In 2002, the Attorney General requested that the number of public prosecutors be increased after the Chilean Public Ministry reported that the "Mapuche problem" had significantly enlarged prosecutors' daily work load (Ministerio Público 2002:158). Notably, the increased burden on prosecutors related primarily, if not solely, to investigating Mapuche protest actions, as reflected in Chilean government statistics on crimes in the context of the "indigenous conflict" (Comisión de Constitución 2003:78 and 2006:12).[2] Meanwhile, investigations into allegations of police violence against Mapuches, such as teargas used against women and children during community raids, have been rare (Correa and Mella 2010:275).

Mapuche activists criticized the criminal prosecutions against them and continued to push their protests back into the political arena (see chapter 5). Mapuche activists viewed "usurpation" charges against them as pure cynicism, as their history reflects the constant usurpation of their lands. As a community member from the Lumaco area said about their occupation of a disputed estate: "We don't steal from anybody: the Mapuches reclaim their rights" (Interview C-60). The counter-narrative mobilized by Mapuche activists obtained quite some leverage due to support from within the Chilean society as well as from outside actors, such as the Inter-American Court of Human Rights. Secret cables published by Wikileaks also showed that American officials thought Chilean media coverage of Mapuche protest actions exaggerated their gravity, indicating instead that they were hardly violent and mostly targeted property (Gallego-Díaz 2010; US Embassy in Santiago 2010).

This chapter shows how Chilean prosecutors had a hard time legitimizing their criminal cases on the basis of the narrative pushed by present-day

---

2   For example, in 2001, the governor of the Malleco province counted 22 arsons, 22 land occupations, 6 road blockades, and 8 incidents of property destruction (Comision de Constitución 2006:12).

landowners and its particular interpretation of the Mapuche conflict and their land claims. In the prosecutorial narrative, only rarely was the "Mapuche conflict" a reference to the larger context of historic colonial dispossession and Chilean–Mapuche relations throughout the entire 20th century. At the same time, the ethnic label "Mapuche conflict" conveniently worked to downplay non-Mapuche landowners' *economic* interests. Given the lack of social consensus on whether the Mapuche protests constituted crimes (and if so, what crimes), prosecutorial narrative vacillated between pulling the issue into the criminal justice arena, symbolically trumping up charges on some occasions, while reducing the actual punitive effect or refraining from prosecution at other times, even as the underlying land claims were being negotiated in the political arena.

The symbolic crackdown on land occupations

In 1990, the Mapuche organization Consejo de Todas las Tierras (the "Council of All Lands" or Aukiñ Wallmapu Ngulam in the Mapuzugun language) was founded. Activists from the Consejo did not feel bound by the 1989 "Agreement of Nueva Imperial," in which other Mapuche organizations had negotiated with President Aylwin and promised to stick with institutional paths. Instead, activists decided to carry out direct action modelled on "the much-feared and remembered land occupations" of the 1960s and early 1970s (Bengoa 2002 [1999]:196). Elderly people, traditional authorities and children participated in these symbolic events, in which they entered a contested estate, performed a ceremony, and left again. The Consejo also started a newspaper called *Aukiñ*, or the "Mapuche Voice." In March 1992, the organization inaugurated a Mapuche tribunal to strengthen Mapuche "institutionality" (*Aukiñ* 1993a). In light of later events carried out by other Mapuche activists, especially incidents of arson, these earlier activities seem pretty innocent. Yet, both the land occupations and the Mapuche tribunal challenged Chilean laws and jurisdiction, and as such, were perceived as a threat by the governor (*Intendente*) of the 9th Region, leading him to file a petition for a criminal investigation into the group's activities.

On 23 June 1992, investigative Judge Antonio Castro Gutiérrez initiated an investigation against the Consejo leader Aucán Huilcamán and 143 others, as members of the allegedly criminal organization Consejo de Todas las Tierras, for the usurpation of lands and theft. Different incidents of land occupations, for which complaints were sitting at local police offices across the 9th Region without successful prosecution, were pulled together to construct a pattern which, relying on an alleged common objective, served as the basis for the charge of a criminal organization. The investigative judge shifted prosecutorial attention away from the occupation of specific estates on precise dates and particular damage done to fences or crops, to a broader scope, both in terms of the time-frame and geographical reach.

In 2009, I interviewed an activist with the Consejo who was one of the defendants in the case about the group's activities and the subsequent prosecution. He recalled the hopes and expectations of the organization's members when they began mobilizing in the early 1990s:

> Those who participated were elderly, traditional authorities, and children. [...] There was a lot of hope. The idea at the return of democracy was that we were going to be listened to, that there would be an opening in the attitude toward the Mapuche. At that moment, Patricio Aylwin was president and had adopted a dialogue with the Mapuches. They said that we were against the state. We were not at all against the state. We were just demanding compensation for the historical debt. It was an opportunity. Our position was entirely legitimate. We thought it would be received positively. (Interview C-53)

The indictment against the Consejo de Todas las Tierras sparked strong resistance. "We demand acquittals" was the front page headline in the organization's newspaper *Aukiñ*, in November 1992, accompanied by pictures of a grand demonstration portraying an assembly of older men and women wearing traditional clothing and holding typical musical instruments affirming their Mapuche identity. The *Aukiñ* (1992a) editorial framed the land occupations as "the crime of reclaiming historical rights". As *Lonko* (community chief) Juan Coliqueo publicly declared: "We Mapuches have not committed any crime; we have only demanded our rights to the lands. [...] The *winka* [Chileans] are the usurpers, not the Mapuches" (*Aukiñ* 1992c). Leader Aucán Huilcamán defended the Consejo as a legitimate organization: "We haven't organized to commit a crime, but to promote our rights" (*Aukiñ* 1992c). The *Aukiñ* newspaper emphasized the context of dispossession as the proper framework within which to judge the Consejo's actions, noting that "[a]ccusing Mapuche communities of usurpation of lands is the most aberrant accusation that exists in the Chilean and

Mapuche history. With this, they refuse to recognize that the Mapuche are the real owners of the land. It pretends to reverse history" (*Aukiñ* 1992b).

The prosecutor had selected the 144 defendants because they had signed a letter that explained the Consejo's demands for land and their actions of recuperation. According to one of the activists, not everyone who signed the letter had actually participated in the land recuperations, but they were all members of the organization. Thus, they were charged for their membership in the Consejo, with the letter used as evidence of their membership. The investigative judge justified this move by stating in the indictment that, for the Chilean state, far more was at stake than the harm inflicted by single acts of land occupation: "The illegal character of this association is sufficiently accredited in ignoring the authority, the creation and functioning of a Mapuche tribunal, the creation of a flag and an emblem, the clandestine newspaper called *Aukiñ*, and pressuring the authorities" (official indictment, republished in *Aukiñ* 1993b).

The trial became a battle about the identity and legitimacy of the Consejo de Todas las Tierras as well as the legitimacy of the Mapuches' land claims. After the conviction of 141 defendants on 11 March 1993, the Consejo appealed, but lost again and was later rejected at the Supreme Court. The Consejo defendants then decided to bring a petition to the Inter-American Commission for Human Rights (IACHR). In its pre-trial assessment of the case in 2001, the commission proposed a "friendly settlement agreement" that included dealing with land demands, thus clearly pushing the situation back into the political arena.[3] Meanwhile, the defendants lost their political rights (they were blocked, for example, from running for president), but none of them spent time in prison. Thus, while the state obtained a symbolic legal declaration that the Consejo constituted a criminal organization, the group continued to exist and did not cease mobilizing Mapuche communities and organizing land occupations. A 2006 survey confirmed that a significant number of Mapuches still felt the Consejo represented them (CEP 2006). For many activists in

---

3   According to the website of the Organization of American States, "The friendly settlement mechanism provides an opportunity for dialogue between petitioners and states, in which they can reach agreements that introduce reparation measures that benefit both the direct alleged victims of the violation and society at large" (www.oas.org/en/iachr/friendly_settlements/).

The Consejo petitioners rejected the settlement proposal subsequently offered by the Chilean state for being insufficient and, in 2002, the IACHR declared the case admissible to the Court (www.cidh.oas.org/annualrep/2002sp/Chile11856.htm). However, the case was not pursued and was closed in 2017; (http://formu.info/informe-anual-2017-captulo-ii-sistema-de-casos-peticiones-y-me.html?page=20).

the Mapuche movement, the respected social status of Consejo members within their communities and the widespread participation of the elderly as well as women and children in the symbolic land recuperations made the group's criminalization a symbol of repression against "the Mapuche people" as a whole. That message caught on and became a shared belief among a considerable segment of the Mapuche communities, despite explicit efforts by prosecutors to counter this image (see chapter 9).

After the prosecution of the Consejo de Todas las Tierras, symbolic land occupations by Mapuche activists in Chile were rarely prosecuted.[4] A survey conducted at the end of the 1990s showed that land occupations, used by Mapuches as a protest action, enjoyed widespread legitimacy among Chileans, indicating that 80 percent of Chileans thought that "the Mapuches are right in the conflict between forestry companies and Mapuche communities" (CERC 1999:1). Indeed, between 2001 and 2005, it even became government policy not to prosecute such occupations. As Jorge Correa Sutil, the former Undersecretary of the Department of Internal Affairs described it: "The government of that period abstained from action in cases known as 'virtual land occupations,' in which coordinated groups pacifically entered the lands, convoked the press and then left without the necessity of massive police intervention and without leaving behind significant damages to the property" (Comisión de Constitución 2006:32). This gave Mapuche activists and communities the *de facto* space to claim that such occupations, as political actions, belonged to the political arena, to be responded to within the logic of persuasion and negotiation, even though landowners continued to claim that the occupations were criminal and should be prosecuted.

Arson and the narrative of state security

In 1977, a legal decree (*Decreto Ley* 701) issued by Pinochet gave forestry companies financial incentives to invest and plant commercial plantations to avoid further erosion of agricultural lands. Many of those plantations were in the south of Chile surrounding Mapuche communities, partially on disputed lands. As the tree plantations took about twenty years to reach maturation, 1997 marked the year when forestry companies started to exploit the plantations that had been planted immediately following the decree's enactment. In October 1997, 50 members of a Mapuche

---

4 Nevertheless, whenever activists opposed evictions, confrontations with the police did lead to detentions. But only a few of these arrests led to prosecutions.

community in Lumaco occupied a forestry plantation on Estate Pidenco, owned by the company Bosques Arauco, and blockaded the main road leading to the plantation. They protested for a fair share of the profits from the pine and eucalyptus trees, rather than watch the wealth of the contested lands go abroad. The Mapuche community claimed to be the legitimate owner of the land that was, at the time, legally in the hands of the company. The community members who participated in the land occupation and road blockade perceived themselves to be pioneers in the struggle for land reform after a long period of silence. Some of them recounted how, during the Agrarian Reform in 1970, their fathers had actually possessed the disputed land, but were removed from it during Pinochet's Contra Reform. One summarized their point of view: "If I had 1,800 hectares then and now I have only 800, and I have never sold anything, then there is usurpation" (Interview C-60).

On 1 December 1997, after ensuring that the truck drivers were brought to safety, a group of activists set three company trucks of Bosques Arauco on fire (Interview C-23). As a member of the Mapuche movement later explained:

> The arson in Lumaco was a response to the limits of the Indigenous Act. A lot of people had confidence in that Act; they thought it would create a better place for their community, but it wasn't what they expected. The discrimination, racism, misery and arrogance experienced by the community members of Lumaco – that led to the burning of those trucks. (Interview C-57)

This incident led newspapers, forestry companies and the state to speculate about the existence of an underground organization and a "Chilean Chiapas" in the country's Araucanía region.[5] Contrary to these suspicions, an activist who participated in the event emphasized that the arson had not been planned, but occurred spontaneously in the heat of the moment due to their anger (Interview 2003, C-23).

Similar to the criminal case against the Consejo activists, the regional governor intervened to push for a criminal investigation. Regional Governor Oscar Eltit even requested that the Law on State Security be used, which radically changed the legal interest at stake from mere

---

5   The newspaper El Mercurio reported with the heading "*Nuestro Pequeño Chiapas*" [Our Little Chiapas] on 28 February 1999 (cited in: Barrera 1999:74).

property damage to state security. To sustain this claim, the governor argued that "[t]his action put in grave risk the life and physical integrity of the drivers of the trucks, and provoked serious economic damage both to the company Forestal Bosques Arauco and to the different truck owners, thus gravely disrupting the normal development of economic activities involved in the transport of goods" (Request for Investigation, 2 December 1997). In the search for the perpetrators of the arson, Governor Eltit gave orders to look for those who had been involved in an earlier occupation of the CONADI offices by Mapuche organizations, thus making a connection between the arson in Lumaco and broader Mapuche land struggles. He specifically called for punishment of the "intellectual authors" of the crime, noting – in line with the widespread perception of escalation – that crimes related to Mapuche land claims "have become progressively more violent, and they are instigated by leaders who maybe do not participate in the material action, but they are the intellectual authors, whose responsibilities should be determined in the investigation" (Request for Investigation, 2 December 1997). Shortly after, 11 community members from Lumaco and an additional student activist were charged for their alleged involvement in the burning of the three trucks.

The proceedings drew international attention. Explicitly disputing the legitimacy of the criminal prosecution, the Spanish non-governmental organization WATU Acción Indígena sent a letter to Antonio Castro Gutiérrez, the investigative judge on the case. The organization viewed the arson in the context of legitimate land demands and asked him to withdraw the charges and start a process of negotiation and dialogue instead (29 December 1997). The charges were not withdrawn, however, and the defendants were convicted. Despite the strong vocabulary of "state security," though, the community members were allowed to serve their sentences on probation, while regularly reporting to the nearest police station. Moreover, after the conviction, the Chilean government did indeed negotiate with the Lumaco community. Their land claims were recognized and the community was awarded a land title to a larger estate elsewhere in the 9th Region. In contrast with the probationary sentences of the community members, the student activist had to serve three years in prison.

The emergence of productive land occupations as a loss of control

In 1998, the Mapuche community of Temulemu carried out what came to be called a "productive" land occupation. Contrary to earlier symbolic occupations, they not only entered contested land, but also started felling trees in the plantations on the Santa Rosa de Colpi and Chorrillos estates. As justification for their action, the community claimed ownership of the land based on a 1930 judicial decision by the then existing Tribunal de Indios (with jurisdiction on land ownership) (Barrera 1999:69). As one participating urban activist narrated the story:

> We entered [the forestry plantations] and started a little company. People from the community simply came to work. Instead of occupying the field as a symbolic action, we did a "productive" recuperation. That meant that instead of asking attention for our demand and hoping that it would get solved, we just put the land to our use. We started cutting the trees and transporting them. People from the community, who came to work, would get their pay at the end of the day. [...] With a hundred people, we occupied it for three months. We made a camp and installed a wooden campground. We had an industrial saw machine and a modern production. (Interview C-59)

The productive land occupation was based on the concept of "territorial control" advanced by José Huenchunao, a leader of the Mapuche organization CAM. In 1998, during a meeting in an old school building in Arauco in Chile's 8th Region, CAM was founded as a new type of Mapuche organization. In response to dissatisfaction with other Mapuche organizations, CAM was established with the explicit intent to further radicalize the movement (Interview C-46). For many CAM members, the new organization was an inspiring force, leading rural communities to stand up for their rights.

While symbolic land occupations were rarely criminalized after the Consejo conviction, this new "productive" occupation at the estates of Santa Rosa de Colpi and Chorrillos led to a criminal prosecution (Case Temulemu). The indictment accused different participants of "usurpation" and "theft" between 20 September and 16 October 1998, and on 16 November 1998. Only *Lonko* Pascual Pichún, the chief of the Temulemu community, was accused of participating in both instances. In the end, 15 participants in the incidents were convicted of usurpation and theft of wood, but – as was typical – none of them actually spent time in prison. Instead, they were released on probation that required them to report regularly to the police station. Thus, the state responded symbolically through prosecution and conviction, yet refrained from harsh punishment. Similarly typical, in 1999, CONADI acquired and returned 58.4 hectares of land from the Santa Rosa de Colpi estate to the community of Temulemu on the basis of their land title (Richards 2013:85).

Following this example, many more communities started to do productive land takeovers. They would simply start working the land during the day and patrolling at night. As a Mapuche community member from the coastal area said, "we are guarding the territory in order to prevent the company entering. We get up early and work in shifts" (field notes April 2009). These occupied estates would be transformed into no-go areas for the landowners and Chilean authorities. Moreover, instead of being clandestine operations they were often publicly announced. For example, on 13 January 2003, a Mapuche community sent out a public declaration stating that they had occupied estate Nupangue:

> This occupation develops with productive activities inside the estate and will be done for an undefined time. [...] This action expresses our rejection of the usurpation of the ancestral Mapuche lands that both individuals and transnational companies, especially forestry investors, have previously carried out. (Mapuche community "José Millacheo Levío" 2003)

Many productive occupations did not lead to criminal prosecutions. According to the lawyer for the Governor of Malleco (a province in the 9th Region), the government was generally more concerned with removing the participants in an estate takeover than mounting an effective prosecution (Interview 2009, C-56). Instead of criminal prosecution, in May 1999, the government proposed a dialogue upon which the Consejo de Todas las Tierras and 60 Mapuche communities agreed to stop their occupations of contested estates, while CAM refused to stop its occupations and rejected the dialogue.[6] In the few cases of productive occupations that were prosecuted, the prosecutorial narrative followed the narrative of the commercial landowners as it tended to emphasize the damage done to the trees and produce, affirming the economic value in financial vocabulary. In the Temulemu case, for example, there was considerable debate about the value of trees and whether 1 cubic meter was worth 10,000 pesos. Further, Chilean prosecutors reproduced the narrative that forestry activities benefit the common good, in line with statements by the director of the forestry council CORMA (2002), who claimed that "the private sector

6   www.archivochile.com/tesis/03_tpo/03p00004.pdf

continues to be the principal motor of development of the country." This contrasts with the view of those Mapuches who see a plantation as a desert and regard arson as an opportunity for the land to regenerate and become nature again.

To summarize, in the prosecution of Mapuche community members and activists for their role in land occupations throughout the 1990s as well as the Lumaco arson, the prosecutorial narrative reflected and reproduced the narrative of the commercial landowners, and found Mapuches guilty of crimes, but hardly enacted harsh punishment. Criminal law was symbolically relied upon to establish order. The prosecutorial narrative reproduced a particular conception of land ownership (on the basis of valid land titles) and what benefits the common good (production for profitable sale). Sentences, or their execution, were relatively lenient and were often followed by recognition of the legitimacy of Mapuche claims, demonstrated by increased state efforts to restore some of their land rights, the dispute over which landed them in court in the first place. However, this process of the restoration of land rights has been slow. Only in 2011, after years of further mobilization by the communities of Temulemu and neighboring Didaiko, did the Chilean government return the entire 3,000 hectares of the estates Santa Rosa de Colpi and Chorillos to the Mapuche communities.

The controversial terrorism label

Landowners continued to reject the legitimacy of land occupations and kept pushing for criminalization. As described in chapter 4, forestry companies and private plantation owners in Chile mobilized to collectively argue that not only was private property at stake, but also the national economy and security. In 1999, the forestry association CORMA wrote: "It is not, as we see it, a conflict between private parties" (1999a:2). In that same year, CORMA wrote a letter to Investigative Judge Archibaldo Loyola to request the use of the anti-terrorism legislation in prosecuting the actions of Mapuche activists in Temulemu and Lumaco (Barrera 1999:100). In a public speech in 2002, the director of CORMA criticized the state's permissiveness toward Mapuche land occupations. He argued that the social order would weaken when the application of the law was made dependent on "the popularity of a cause, the socioeconomic situation of the criminals or their capacity to voice their demands in the media." He called for the law to be applied "with rigorous equality" to all members of society (CORMA 2002):

Without a doubt, Sir Parliamentarians of the Region, we are very tired, worse, discouraged. We have knocked on many doors and we haven't been listened to [...] Can one occupy with force the property of a neighbor when one has been waiting several years for a solution to housing? Can a group of Mapuches attack a patrol of *carabineros* (police) with an axe in Lumaco, or a farmer in Victoria and others in Collipulli with bullets? Can someone systematically steal wood from his neighbors because he believes that the lands belonged to him at some point? Can one burn woods and houses, attack and intimidate workers, assault trucks and build clandestine sawmills when one is dissatisfied with the actual situation, established in the Chilean laws? (CORMA 2002)

In response to a growing number of incidents of arson (Comisión Especial 2000), non-Mapuche commercial landowners pushed for the use of anti-terrorism legislation because it allows an investigation to remain secret for six months (instead of the normal 60 days) and permits a longer period of pre-trial detention, the protection of witnesses through anonymity, and the interception of telephones (Univisión 2009; Vargas 2010). They hoped that ensuring anonymity for witnesses would help Mapuches critical of arson overcome the fear of testifying against fellow community members and lead to more convictions. A lawyer representing one of the biggest forestry companies in Chile asserted, however, that seeking the qualification of terrorism was not just about its practical advantages for prosecution, but also about giving the actions their appropriate name (Interview 2009, C-44).

In the early 2000s, prosecutors initiated four cases involving terrorism charges. In the criminal case against the *Lonkos* of Traiguén, for example, leaders from the Mapuche communities of Temulemu and Didaiko were charged, along with one non-Mapuche activist, with committing two "terrorist" arson attacks in December 2001, one against the house of a landowner on the contested Nancahue estate and another on a pine plantation in the estate of San Gregorio. During the trial in April 2003, the prosecutor commented that after pieces of land were "unilaterally" declared to be in conflict, "those terrains left the sphere of Chilean legality. They became a no man's land. [...] From Temulemu onwards, it is another world, that's another Chile" (field notes, Case *Lonkos* of Traiguén, April 2003). Instead of sticking to the specific conduct attributed to the defendants in the case, the prosecutor put the alleged facts in the context of what he viewed as the "Mapuche conflict": "If 400 arsons in this region, if burning houses within an estate, if burning 80 hectares of a plantation … if that is not terrorism, I don't know what is." He described farmers as threatened with the choice: "you give me half of your house, or we burn it." This pressure had an effect, according to the prosecutor, and that was the problem: "What the defendants seek is that those lands can be bought. They demand from the authorities that they buy. And sadly, we have seen that the strategy has worked" (field notes, Case *Lonkos* of Traiguén, April 2003).

Although the prosecutorial narrative increasingly aligned with the landowners' efforts to criminalize Mapuche protests under Chile's Anti-terrorism Law, these efforts were also widely criticized, both within Chile as well as internationally. In 2003, then UN Special Rapporteur on the rights of indigenous peoples Rodolfo Stavenhagen asserted that "[c]harges for offences in other contexts (such as terrorist threat and criminal association) should not be applied to acts related to the social struggle for land and legitimate indigenous complaints" (Stavenhagen 2003: paras 69–70), suggesting that to do so criminalized a legitimate demand (Stavenhagen 2003: para. 40).

In each of the four terrorism cases, Chilean prosecutors had a hard time getting the terrorism charges to "stick," as they initially faced judges who refused to accept the terrorism qualification. It took numerous retrials and, finally, a determination by the Supreme Court, before the terrorism qualification was accepted, at least in some of the proceedings. The first judge to hear such a terrorism case, Judge Nancy Germany, rejected the prosecutors' qualification of arson as terrorism. Even though the Court of Appeals in Temuco confirmed her judgment, the prosecutors filed a complaint against Judge Germany at the Supreme Court. In January 2004, the Supreme Court rejected the complaint, but found that the judge had exceeded her competencies in dismissing the terrorism qualification and she was removed from her position. Other cases led to partial acquittals. For example, *Lonko* Pichún was acquitted of the more serious "terrorist arson," but convicted of "terrorist threat," still leading to five years of incarceration. In the case against 18 members of CAM for membership in a terrorist organization, prosecutors had to give up and drop charges after two trials. In the second judgment, the court explicitly pointed out that CAM's goals are legitimate, as Chile's Indigenous Law No. 19.253 recognizes land as "the main fundament for the existence and culture of indigenous people" (Case CAM, Verdict Tribunal de Temuco, consideration 11, 27 July 2005). Furthermore, the court stated that any concept of "terrorism" should include "contempt for human life," but asserted that no indication of such contempt could be drawn from the available evidence.

In those terrorism cases that led to convictions, the sentences handed down ranged between five and ten years in prison. The defendants brought their cases to the IACHR. Already in its *prima facie* assessment in 2007 in the case against one of the Mapuche leaders, the IACHR considered that the application of a "special penal regime [terrorism charges] more severe than the common regime, because of his ethnic origin" could constitute a violation of Article 24 of the American Convention (Case Ancalaf, IACHR, 2 May 2007). Finally, in 2014, the IACHR ordered Chile to annul the terrorism convictions of the eight Mapuche activists who were convicted in the early 2000s (Acevedo 2014). In addition, Chile was ordered to pay compensation to the former prisoners.

Former President Bachelet was also critical of applying anti-terrorism legislation to Mapuche land activism. During her presidential campaign in 2006, she vowed not to use the Anti-terrorism Law due to the controversies in the Mapuche cases (*Cooperativa* 2006b). For a while, between 2004 and October 2008, no new criminal prosecutions were initiated under the Anti-terrorism Law. During this period, incidents such as the burning of trucks on the highway by Mapuche activists, which had previously been qualified as "terrorism," were prosecuted as "common arsons." Yet in the end, Bachelet did not keep her promise. In October 2008, the application of anti-terrorism legislation returned when a number of non-Mapuche students gathered on the highway of Temuco, intending to block the road to highlight the injustices toward the Mapuche people. They were indicted on terrorism charges for allegedly throwing a Molotov cocktail at a police car, which the defendants denied. Since then, more Mapuche activists have again been charged with terrorist offenses for the arson of trucks, buses, plantations and houses in relation to demands for land restitution. These terrorism charges led to a long hunger strike, initiated in 2010 by detained Mapuche activists, demanding that the terrorism charges be replaced with common criminal charges. In September 2010, there was an open confrontation between Chile's executive government and the Attorney General after President Piñera promised Mapuche hunger strikers that their charges would be changed from terrorism to ordinary crimes. The Attorney General refused to do so, arguing that it would be illegal and unconstitutional (*Cooperativa* 2010).

In 2013, the death of one of the non-Mapuche landowners together with his spouse led to an outcry. Five years earlier, on the very same estate, CAM activist Matías Catrileo had been killed by the police after an occupation of the land. In a protest to remember his killing, the landowners' house was set on fire, resulting in their deaths. Prosecutions were initiated on the basis of the Anti-terrorism Law and, following multiple trials, four members of a Mapuche community were convicted. Overall, however, the same dispute about the appropriateness of the application of anti-terrorism legislation described above continued in this case, as well as other terrorism proceedings between 2010 and 2018. In some instances, the judges convicted the defendants on the basis of common crimes, but refused to accept the terrorism charges. In other cases, judges outright acquitted the defendants. Some of these acquittals were later overturned by a superior court, leading to a re-trial in which some defendants were eventually convicted while others were acquitted yet again. Some of the convicted activists chose to flee and remain fugitive (see Amnesty International 2018).

In sum, the prosecutorial narrative's shift in the legal interest from ordinary crimes to state security and terrorism matched the escalation narrative propagated by present-day non-Mapuche landowners, such as when the prosecutor in the CAM proceedings argued that a conflict that starts with damages, threats and robberies may end with violence against people (Case CAM, oral proceedings, June 2005). In these terrorism cases, there was no leniency in the punishment, even though the proceedings were characterized by intra-state disputes about the appropriate categorization of Mapuche protest actions. Even in the cases of full acquittals, many defendants spent time in pre-trial detention and suffered stigmatization. At the same time, the Mapuche movement was able to mobilize a strong counter-narrative, which received backing from the IACHR and other international spokespersons, including UN Special Rapporteurs, who pushed the issue back into the political arena.

Dealing with unresolved legitimate grievances

In many of the criminal prosecutions against Mapuche activists for their involvement in land occupations or arson, the Chilean prosecutors were not able to authoritatively draw a boundary between the criminal justice arena and the political arena. The prosecutorial narrative of land occupations as crimes did not sit well with the context of legitimate demands for land restitution. The narrative of a "terrorist" organization was countered by judicial criticism that no contempt for human lives could be proven. In 2006, a parliamentary commission in Chile made a comprehensive proposal that included provisions for land transfers and pardons for those Mapuches who had been convicted for crimes connected to land demands and who rejected violence (Comisión de Constitución 2006:75; Comisión de Derechos Humanos 2006). The significance of this proposed law lay in the fact that the legislature attempted to modify judicial verdicts that were understood to be final. Another legislative effort tried to add a provision to the Indigenous Act stipulating that indigenous people should be punished under ordinary laws (instead of terrorism charges) if they were to commit crimes in the process of demanding the rights protected by the Act. While both proposals were rejected, they clearly connected criminalized protest actions to the underlying land demands. Thus, wherever prosecutors attempted to exclude "politics," other actors brought it back in, be it supporters of Mapuche prisoners in the Mapuche movement and abroad, the Chilean government itself in negotiations by CONADI, Chilean parliamentarians, or the IACHR. The prosecutorial narrative is bound to remain highly contentious as long as there is no social consensus on whether Mapuche protests belong in the criminal justice arena or the political arena.

The vacillation in the prosecutorial narrative about where Mapuche protests should be placed, with different state actors taking different positions at different times, led to both present-day commercial land-owners, as well as Mapuche activists, accusing the criminal justice system of bias and politically influenced decisions. As described in chapter 5, Mapuche activists routinely accuse the state of criminalizing the Mapuche protests. Landowners often argue the opposite: their concern is that Mapuches can actually get away with certain crimes only *because* they are Mapuche. Both propositions can point to existing legal practices to back up their claims.

The Chilean state and landowners have often been permissive of Mapuche protests and mobilization related to land claims. While land occupations and road blockades were generally (violently) dispersed by the police, many have not been followed by criminal prosecutions. Many Mapuche activists have been briefly arrested, but often were never subsequently indicted. It was not until 2000 that the first Mapuche activist actually had to spend time in prison for a conviction, as previous convictions led to a sentence on probation. In 2003, a parliamentary commission recognized that many criminal cases remained unresolved. The reported "statistics on the indigenous conflict" between 2000 and 2003 in the regions of the Araucanía and Arauco lists 90 pending and closed investigations of crimes categorized as arson, property destruction, usurpation and terrorism offenses. Only six cases led to convictions (Comisión de Constitución 2003:76). According to a lawyer of the farmer's association SOFO, some business farmers even preferred that Mapuche activists received a so-called "alternative solution" instead of a conviction, as the farmers sought to avoid accusations of "unjust repression" and "political prisoners" (Interview 2009, C-42). Leniency was also recognized in the recollection of Mapuche activists. Reflecting upon an occupation in the Arauco province at the end of the 1990s, a former student leader agreed with the idea that they were able to get away with it because they were Mapuches. He recalled that, after being convicted for usurpation and theft, he told his co-defendants: "We got off with minor sentences! If we were Chileans, we would still be in prison" (Interview C-59).

At the same time, there have been many instances in which the Chilean state did indeed react with a heavy hand. For example, it has applied anti-terrorism legislation, arrested and convicted many activists over time,[7] used trumped up charges, and employed disproportionate police violence in Mapuche communities (Observatorio Ciudadano 2008; Instituto Nacional de Derechos Humanos 2017). There have been numerous raids in the zone leading to the destruction of doors and windows as well as fear and personal injuries (Correa and Mella 2010:275–94). Further, the zone is characterized by a permanent police presence due to the police protection of forestry activities (Informe Especial 2016). Several activists have suffered long periods of pre-trial detention, despite subsequent acquittal, and newspaper headlines have branded Mapuches as terrorists.

Prosecutors were slapped on the wrist by judges though, as the latter sometimes refused to accept the qualification of terrorism for mere property destruction. Mapuche activists were therefore frequently acquitted of the more serious charges – such as arson and belonging to a terrorist organization – that led to stigmatizing headlines after their arrests, but were nevertheless convicted on minor charges, such as arms possession or issuing threats (Le Bonniec 2008:2). While such acquittals

---

7   For example, one source estimated that in 1998 there were 285 people arrested and in 1999 at least 400 (Comunicaciones Mapuche Xeg-Xeg 1999). Another count lists 145 prisoners between January 2000 and May 2009 (Correa and Mella 2010:305).

may be interpreted as an indication of a well-functioning and independent judiciary that adequately scrutinizes cases, their frequency has led to criticism as well as doubt about the legitimacy of initiating such criminal investigations in the first place, hence raising questions about their validity (HRW 2004; Guerra 2010; Sepúlveda 2011). According to a defense lawyer, the prosecutors "want to convict someone, guilty or innocent" (Interview 2003, C-25).

The simultaneous harshness and leniency in dealing with Mapuche protest actions in the criminal justice arena reflects the dilemma facing Chilean prosecutors in processing cases in which the underlying demand for land restitution – widely viewed as valid – remains unaddressed. Usually, the legitimacy of grievances is not a problem for liberal legalist systems, as prosecutors can point to the difference between means and ends. Rhetorically, both public prosecutors, as well as present-day commercial landowners acting as private accusers in Chile, have recognized the "legitimate aspirations" of the Mapuche people in court, while also emphasizing the "legal avenues" available for their pursuit (for example, field notes, Case *Lonkos* of Traiguén, March 2003). During my visit to the Public Ministry in January 2003, one of the prosecutor's attorneys commented: "I can't commit crimes the whole day, while I have the idea that I fight for something, whatever that may be!" (Interview 2003, C-12).

Over the course of the episode of contention since the early 1990s, the Chilean state has intervened in the "Mapuche conflict" in many ways: with poverty programs, a land redistribution scheme, and through criminal prosecutions. The state recognized the legitimacy and validity of a part of the Mapuche land claims, while at the same time condemning any extra-legal actions undertaken in the name of those demands. This strict separation between ends and means is typical for liberal democracies and was also invoked regularly by prosecutors in Spain and the United States to distinguish between "legitimate" protesters and those put on trial.

The emphasis on existing procedures for solving the land claims sits uncomfortably, however, with the Chilean state's failure to effectively address long-standing structural inequalities, poverty, and the lack of indigenous access to decision-making, while promoting the expansion of the logging industry and other infrastructure projects in the areas where Mapuche communities live – even forcing their continued expropriation. The fact that the legitimate demand for land restitution remains unaddressed creates a dilemma: what should Mapuche communities do in the meantime? Are productive land occupations legitimate (though illegal) due to the fact that the state has not adequately facilitated land restitution for so long, or should they be prosecuted as long as society thinks that the Mapuches have not waited long enough before taking such drastic measures? And if they are prosecuted, should leniency in the sentencing compensate for the legitimate demands underlying the crime? Instead of prosecutors dealing with underlying political claims, the focus for criminal justice agents is on the appropriateness and legality of the means used by the challengers to the status quo in order to back up or enforce their claims. As this chapter has shown, though, this clear separation between the two arenas is difficult to uphold. In October 2010, in a rare admission of the limits of the criminal justice system in such cases, the Attorney General said: "We don't pretend that the Public Ministry can solve a 200-year-old problem" (*Cooperativa* 2010).

9

Responding to Allegations of Racism and Repression against the Mapuche People

"They are not the Mapuche people"

In 2001, two *Lonkos* (community chiefs) of the Mapuche communities of Temulemu and Didaiko near the village of Traiguén in the 9th Region of Chile were arrested and indicted for the allegedly "terrorist" arson of the house of a private landowner, Agustín Figueroa, as well as "terroristic" threats against him. Later, the non-Mapuche activist Patricia Troncoso was also arrested and charged for the same incident. While indeed demanding the estate currently in the hands of the Figueroa family, the defendants denied the charges against them. Their first trial took place in 2003 and began with the prosecutor proclaiming "This is not a trial against the Mapuche people." During the trial, the *Lonkos* presented themselves as Mapuches, as they appeared in their traditional clothing and addressed the audience in Mapuzugun, the language of Mapuches. The prosecutor, however, sought to set the defendants apart from the larger Mapuche population. He argued that the majority of people within their communities did not share "their violent ideas" and declared that they "use the name of the Mapuche people," but do not represent them (field notes, March 2003). Countering this claim, the Mapuche communities of Temulemu and Didaiko expended enormous effort to arrange travel and lodging for at least 40 people – including the elderly, children, men and women – to be present during the week-long trial to support their *Lonkos*. Outside of the courtroom, supporters played Mapuche musical instruments and performed Mapuche ceremonies (field notes, April 2003). Meanwhile, the prosecutor argued that such identity performances should be ignored and, in line with the liberal notion that everyone is equal before the law, claimed that the defendants should only be seen as "Chileans."

The territorial demands of Mapuche communities rest on the basis of their belonging to the Mapuche people, who were forcibly removed from their lands during the so-called Pacification of the Araucanía in the late 19th century. Accordingly, when Mapuche activists are prosecuted for protest actions, they actively bring their identities into the courtroom to claim the legitimacy of their mobilization. Mapuche identity thus has become a political identity (Tilly 2007b:9), as it refers to a collective that makes claims in relation to the Chilean government. Yet, Chilean prosecutors often explicitly ignore or even deny these identity claims. For example, during the criminal proceedings against the *Lonkos* of Traiguén, the prosecutor argued that, since 1992, various intellectuals, such as Chilean anthropologist José Bengoa, had spread "theories" about the history of Chile and the Mapuches, spurring Mapuches to make ancestral land claims. The prosecutor thus reduced Mapuche land claims to mere "theories" of recent origin, ignoring the extensive history of Mapuche claims made in Chilean courts and mobilization efforts, including staged occupations, long predating 1992 (Mella and Le Bonniec 2004).

The first trial against the *Lonkos* ended in an acquittal, but Supreme Court nullification led to a re-trial in September 2003. This time, the prosecutor referred to an anthropological account from the 1950s by American academic Louis Faron to argue that the defendants did not represent real "traditional" authorities of the Mapuche communities they claimed to represent (Le Bonniec 2004:6, footnote 13). This and several other prosecutorial attempts to reverse acquittals and convict Mapuche activists under terrorism charges (see chapter 8) were interpreted within Mapuche communities and the broader movement as persecution for claiming Mapuche identity and demanding restitution of Mapuche lands. In response to the terrorism charges against the *Lonkos*, a Mapuche leader publicly accused the prosecutor of Traiguén of racism and called the trial discriminatory (ORBE 2002). He criticized how Mapuches were portrayed as criminals and suggested that the defendants had been targeted due to their position as community chiefs. He therefore demanded that the prosecutor step down. Commenting on different terrorism proceedings between 2001 and 2005, defense lawyer Fuenzalida criticized how, in the courtroom, it seemed to be sufficient that the defendant was Mapuche to assume that he or she was part of an organization or movement that aimed to create fear (Fuenzalida no date:§E-15).

In response to such allegations of racism and repression by the Chilean state against the Mapuche people, prosecutorial narrative came to draw upon identity images that isolated "radical" Mapuche activists and reified the "true" Mapuche as peaceful and opposed to activists' "violent" actions. As anthropologist Le Bonniec (2004:2) points out, the construct of the "bad" Mapuche on trial is the counterpart of the "good" Mapuche who opposes violence and is the beneficiary of state assistance and social programs directed at eradicating poverty and supporting education. Similarly, in her analysis of the position of Mapuches in Chile, sociologist Richards argues – based on concepts developed by Charles Hale – that a dichotomy between the "authorized Indian" ("*indio permitido*") and "insurrectionary Indian" has long governed the Chilean state's response to Mapuche land claims (Richards 2010:72).

In the trial against the *Lonkos* of Traiguén, the prosecutor accused the defendants of abusing their identity, thus raising questions of what it means to be "Mapuche," what rights Mapuche people have and who represents them. This chapter describes the development of the distinction in Chilean prosecutorial narrative throughout the 1990s and 2000s between the "bad Mapuche" on trial and the "good Mapuche" who cooperate with the state. It shows how the prosecutorial narrative responded to discursive mobilization by Mapuche activists, on the one hand, as well as present-day landowners, on the other. Within these narratives, prosecutors inevitably engage in and influence broader societal debates on ethnicity and identity, which sits uncomfortably with the liberal call to treat everyone equally before the law.

Prosecution of defendants as Chilean citizens

Activists in the Mapuche movement base their demands for land restitution on a collective Mapuche identity grounded in the historical relationship between the Chilean state and the Mapuche people. For radical Mapuche activists, their ethnicity is not just the justification for reclaiming lost lands, as the descendants of those who were pushed out of them and into reservations. Their ethnic identity also forms the basis of a national claim and, thus, the right to self-determination for the Mapuche people as a nation. In 2002, 4 percent of the Chilean population self-identified as Mapuche. In Chile's 9th Region, however, the Mapuche population in 2002 was 30.6 percent of the inhabitants (Instituto Nacional de Estadística 2002:14). In contrast to other Latin American countries, Chilean identity is not generally perceived to be "*mestizo*," or a mixture of racial and ethnic origins, usually meaning a combination of Spanish and indigenous identities. As a commentator in a newspaper wrote, Chileans have always viewed themselves to be the Englishmen of the continent (Jaramillo 2005). For radical Mapuche activists, their ethnicity is not just the justification for reclaiming lost lands, as the descendants of those who were pushed out of them and into reservations. Their ethnic identity also forms the basis of a national claim and, thus, the right to self-determination for the Mapuche people as a nation.

Some Mapuche activists refer to their Mapuche identity when they claim that, contrary to forestry companies and commercial farmers, they seek to live in harmony with nature rather than exploit it. They advocate an alternative vision for the use and purpose of the lands they seek to reclaim, rooted in their Mapuche identity. Present-day commercial land-owners generally downplay or denigrate such identity-based claims. For example, according to a forestry engineer of a major company, the theft of wood by Mapuche activists is primarily a profit-driven business; "ideology" is just a handy excuse, but not their primary motivation (Interview C-34). Forestry company Mininco's chief of public relations said that "living in harmony with nature" is not what "the" Mapuches really want. In his view, "They only want that their kids will study and have another life" (Interview C-17). A commercial farmer expressed another view, declaring the Mapuche way of life and desire for "harmony" to be mere laziness:

It is not possible to transfer lands to the Mapuches ... that will be an absolute misery, because they do not work. That won't resolve the problem. That won't end their miserable state. Have you seen how their lands are that the state has purchased for them? Nothing remains, not one tree, they don't produce anything! ... Indians never work. The Mapuche is predatory, doesn't have intellectual capacity, no will, no economic means, no equipment, nothing ... The Mapuche is sly, twisted, disloyal and abusive. (Private landowner, cited in Cayuqueo 2005b)

Discarding the identity-based claims, commercial landowners and the Chilean government also frequently reduce the "Mapuche problem" to a poverty issue. Poverty is indeed widespread among Mapuches[1] and, accord-

---

1   A 1998 report from the private Chilean think tank Libertad y Desarrollo stated that the percentage of the population living in poverty in the regions where the Mapuches had their original territory, and where the majority of the Mapuches (apart from those in Santiago) lived at the time (8th, 9th and 10th regions), was

ing to the Gini index, Chile is one of the most unequal societies in South America.[2] Yet, while Mapuche activists denounce structural inequality in Chile in general, they also insist that they "are not poor Chileans" (Barrera 1999:72, footnote 14). Instead, they emphasize their right to the contested lands on the basis of history and their identity as a *pueblo*.

When I visited the Public Ministry in Temuco, the capital of the 9th Region, in January 2003, the prosecutors were keen to emphasize that they had participated in the movement that disposed of the infamous Chilean dictator Pinochet. They clearly saw themselves as being on the right side of history and bristled when I mentioned Mapuche activists' allegations of racism and repression by prosecutors in ongoing criminal proceedings against the *Lonkos* of Traiguén and other cases (Interview C-12/13). When I asked the head prosecutor of the 9th Region about how she dealt with prosecuting Mapuche activists given that they are Mapuches and make claims on the basis of their identity about historic land rights, she claimed to "investigate crimes independent from the motivation that lies behind it." She continued:

It is about objectivity. When we let that go, it becomes dangerous. It is about juridical security. That gives citizens confidence in the justice system. It would create uncertainty if we would distinguish between races, colors, political parties or religion. We believe in transparency of the justice system. (Interview C-10)

In the framework of liberal legalism, everyone is equal before the law. As such, ethnic identity should not play a role in prosecutorial decision-making. This basic liberal principle was echoed by the prosecutors, who insisted that Mapuche defendants "are ordinary Chilean citizens. We don't make a distinction between Mapuches and Chileans" (Interview C-11).

33.9 percent, 36.5 percent and 32.2 percent, respectively, whereas countrywide 23.2 percent of Chileans live in poverty (de la Luz and de los Angeles 1998:5). The same report cited illiteracy among the national rural indigenous population at 19 percent. The national mean for illiteracy was reported at 4.4 percent, whereas the national rural mean was reported at 12.2 percent (1998:6). A 2003 paper from the same institute reported similar findings related to inequality (Camhi and de la Luz 2003).

2   In 2010, Chile rated 54.9 on the Gini index, while in all of South America, only Brazil, Colombia and Bolivia had a higher Gini coefficient. The Netherlands, in comparison, had a rating of 30.9 (CIA 2010).

Commenting on the recent arrests of members of the radical Mapuche organization CAM in December 2002 and the accusation that they were members of a terrorist organization, the head regional prosecutor explicitly denied that CAM was an *indigenous* organization. At the same time, she emphasized her respect for *"la etnia"* [the ethnic group] and recounted: "I grew up in the countryside and know the people; I have a lot of respect for them" (Interview C-10). Similarly, denying the relevance of the Mapuche identity of detained CAM activists, in 2002 the Chilean Minister of Internal Affairs commented:

This is not a detention of Mapuches. This is a detention of persons about whom criminal information has been collected. Among these persons are Mapuches. There are [also] persons who, judged by their last names, are mestizos and there are Nordic persons, who can hardly link themselves to the Mapuche people. If one looks at persons with double Mapuche last names,[3] there are only three. (Del Valle 2005:91)

In the subsequent trial of the CAM members, the lawyer representing the Department of Internal Affairs argued that "the defendants will try to demonstrate their representativeness of the Mapuche people, but without democratic elements of national or popular representation, they only represent themselves" (Case CAM, opening statement, oral proceedings, June 2005). Some non-Mapuche landowners also expressed an interest in portraying activist defendants as Chileans. For example, in August 2008, landowner Jorge Luchsinger's lawyer urged the Minister of Internal Affairs not to view a recent arson attack at Luchsinger's house as a matter concerning the Mapuche people. In his opinion, there was "a specific group that commits these terrorist acts, absolutely oblivious to the origin, ethnicity, race or condition" (cited in *El Mercurio* 2008).

The rhetoric of non-representation and insistence that defendants be prosecuted "as Chileans" can be contrasted with trial transcripts, which show that defendants were often identified as "Mapuches" or belonging to the "Mapuche ethnic group." Both the trials I attended, and those for which I could gather the transcripts, often turned into a debate about whether the defendants were Mapuches or not, and to what degree they represented the Mapuche people. Prosecutors, Mapuche activists and landowners all participated in this debate, discussing whether "the" Mapuches really

---

3   In Chile, people carry the last name of both father and mother.

supported protest mobilizations for land redistribution, or whether they were being manipulated by urban Mapuches, other Chileans, or foreigners. These debates about the identity of defendants in criminal trials were embedded in broader societal debates about Mapuche–Chilean relations, the characteristics of Mapuche ethnicity, rules about who qualifies as Mapuche or not, as well as the obligations of the Chilean state toward the Mapuches and their rights as a people.

While prosecutors typically insisted that they do not distinguish between defendants on the basis of ethnic identity, agents throughout the Chilean criminal justice system used the "Mapuche conflict" as a relevant category to classify criminal cases. For example, the police have photo-collections with the label "Mapuche conflict," in which they keep pictures of protest participants and those previously detained in relation to Mapuche mobilization. During one trial, the lawyer representing the Ministry of Internal Affairs as private accuser explained that the ministry had decided to participate in the trial because the alleged crimes had been executed "in relation to the so-called Mapuche conflict" (Case CAM, oral proceedings, June 2005). Judges also used the "Mapuche conflict" as a relevant category in their verdicts (variously labeled as "territorial conflict" or "Mapuche Problem") to contextualize the alleged facts.

Since January 2008, the 8th and 9th Regions have even had specific prosecutors exclusively dedicated to the prosecution of offenses arising in the context of the "Mapuche conflict" (Leiva 2008). The Public Ministry justified the appointment of specialized "Mapuche conflict" prosecutors by citing the need for specific expertise. Yet, at the same time, such a denomination can unduly cement certain assumptions about the relevant context of certain crimes. In my interviews with non-Mapuche landowners in 2009, it turned out that widespread incidents of wood theft – often associated with Mapuche communities and their land claims – may have been unrelated to Mapuche claims. In their view, wood theft constituted a problem far beyond the "Mapuche conflict." The director of the association of commercial farmers SOFO even used the word "mafia" to describe the organized practices of professional thieves unrelated to Mapuche demands (Interview 2009, C-55). In such cases, the involvement of a specialized "Mapuche conflict" prosecutor can lead to basic assumptions about motive and possible defendants that may not be true. Not surprisingly, many Mapuche activists call them the "anti-Mapuche prosecutors," making it even more important for the prosecutors to counter allegations of racism and repression against the Mapuche people. In many trials, the prosecutors therefore emphasized the context of the Mapuche conflict as relevant for the criminal proceedings to justify certain charges (such as terrorism), while downplaying or denying the relevance of defendants' Mapuche identity to avoid allegations of discrimination.

The prosecutorial narrative aims to legitimize its choices of defendants and victims

In 1999, only 18 percent of Mapuches surveyed supported the Chilean government, while 25 percent of those surveyed reported confidence in the government. Mapuche support for and confidence in Chile's national parliament was even lower, both hardly reaching 10 percent, and confidence in the Chilean state's judicial institutions only amounted to 13 percent (survey by CERC [Centro de Estudios de la Realidad Contemporánea], in Lavanchy 2003:13). On the basis of these survey results, Lavanchy (2003:13) concluded that the Chilean state had lost legitimacy in the eyes of the Mapuches in general, not just among activists. This lack of confidence made it difficult for the prosecutors and judges to perform a legitimizing function regarding their decisions in judicial proceedings. Activists referred to an unfavorable court decision against a land claim as proof of the way in which "the system" works against Mapuches when they demand restitution through judicial proceedings, providing justification for civil disobedience such as land occupations. Meanwhile, favorable decisions served as evidence that Mapuches were historically dispossessed. Similarly, in criminal proceedings, whereas Mapuche activists viewed an acquittal as proof of "unjustified persecution" by prosecutors, they interpreted convictions as merely an affirmation that the trial was rigged and that Mapuches are not granted equal rights in courts.

Aware of the resentment against him, one of the Chilean prosecutors routinely started his trials by declaring his objectivity and adherence to the rule of law. For example, in 2009, he opened a case against 11 members of the Mapuche community Chequenco, who were accused of crimes during a land occupation, by saying that "we will hear talk of 'set-ups,' 'state terrorism' and a 'racist and militarized state,' but here are crimes [...] which the Public Ministry tries to prove" (Case Chequenco, audio proceedings 19 February 2009). As described in chapter 5, the Mapuche movement has been quite successful in establishing its narrative that the Chilean state unjustly criminalizes legitimate Mapuche protest for land restitution. Prosecutors, in turn, have attempted to counter this narrative and legitimize the specific prosecutions initiated. Thus, in response to the allegations by the Mapuche movement that prosecutions of activists and community members were part of a long-standing repression of the Mapuche people, turning Mapuches into political prisoners, Chilean prosecutors explicitly denied that defendants represented the Mapuches and emphasized their equality before the law as Chilean citizens.

Key elements in this prosecutorial narrative on Mapuche protest have included a focus on "outsiders" selected as defendants, the construction of a dichotomy between "true" and supposedly peaceful Mapuches and the "violent minority" on trial, and a portrayal of present-day landowners as innocent victims caught up in a dispute in which they played no part.

The focus on outside influence in Mapuche communities

It was a recurring theme in media and interviews with present-day landowners that Mapuche protest mobilization, particularly land occupations and arson attacks, resulted from outside influence. In their denial of "authentic" Mapuche involvement in protest actions, private landowners often blamed mobilization for Mapuche land claims on outside "manipulation," "infiltration," and "indoctrination" (for example, Barrera 1999:72). According to the lawyer for the farmer's association SOFO, such outsiders included foreigners (in particular American and European students), radical leftists, communists, ecologists, international terrorist groups (such as FARC and ETA), and "academics from the seventies" (Interview C-42). The former owner of a disputed estate asserted, "They [Mapuches] are used. They don't invent it themselves" (Interview C-37). Indeed, in 1999 a French student writing his Master's thesis about the Mapuches was invited to spend a few nights in the Mapuche community of Temulemu, while the community was engaged in a land occupation (see chapter 8). He was subsequently accused of involvement in the occupation and deported from Chile (Case Arnaud Fuentes, verdict 1999). Landowners frequently referred to his case as evidence of foreign involvement. Throughout the 1990s and 2000s, this view also appeared in prosecutorial narrative, as prosecutors repeatedly asked the police to specifically search for and investigate external activists.

In 2001, an independent Mapuche media collective made fun of the constant allegations against them of having links with foreign terrorist groups by writing the words "Bin Laden Corporation" on their website with a fake address in Saudi Arabia. The issue was immediately reported in newspapers and the Undersecretary of Internal Affairs ordered an investigation into the group (Ansa 2001; Fredes and Gómez 2002). The website editor commented: "We just wanted to laugh about all the paranoia, such as that people thought that there could be suicide attacks here. [...] We had black humor; this was typical of our media collective. But others did not identify this as humor" (Interview C-28). The Mapuche media collective's website was subsequently analyzed in a report on "cybernetic terrorism" published in the Chilean newspaper *El Mercurio*, which also referenced various academic, advocacy and human rights websites allegedly involved in promoting Mapuche "violence" (Richards 2010:75). The media collective's website was also cited in the trial of the *Lonkos* of Traiguén as evidence that the arson incident had been a "terrorist" act of arson (field notes, Case *Lonkos* of Traiguén , April 2003).

Present-day landowners and prosecutors not only viewed foreigners as "infiltrators," but also activists from Mapuche organizations like CAM and the Consejo de Todas las Tierras. For example, in 2003, a Mapuche community announced a land occupation and claimed that it was done "with the help of the neighboring communities in conflict and the Coordinadora Mapuche Arauco Malleco" (Mapuche community "José Millacheo Levío" 2003). Instead of "help," a prosecutor framed CAM's involvement as "infiltrating the communities, creating fractures in the communities" (Case CAM, opening statement, oral proceedings, June 2005).

In several cases, prosecutors specifically sought out external "radicals" to indict in relation to land occupations and other (alleged) Mapuche protest actions. In a case of alleged violent usurpation of land, theft and arson in Nueva Imperial, a prosecutor specified to the police that: "It is equally solicited to investigate if members of some organization *unconnected* to the sector [of the Mapuche community] has brought about, planned or participated in these events, and if there are persons who participate *as activists* in illegal takeovers" (19 February 2002, emphasis added by author). Similarly, in the case of a productive land takeover in Temulemu, Investigative Judge Archibaldo Loyola explored the existence of an "underground organization composed of Mapuches and non-Mapuches who take advantage of the situation for their own benefit in order to transport and commercialize stolen wood" (Barrera 1999:77).

The search for "instigators" is also visible in the transcripts of interrogations of Mapuche community members by the police and prosecutors, in which frequent questions were: Who gave orders? Who directed the rest? Who was the spokesperson? This purposive selection of defendants from a larger group of participants actually reproduces the image of a radical minority of "activists." An urban activist from the Consejo told me, he was convicted for usurpation when he was supporting a community in reclaiming land through a land occupation, while the community members who participated were acquitted: "They accused us of being activists. The others were acquitted. [...] The community had more legitimacy" (Interview C-53).[4]

The prosecutorial emphasis on outside infiltration sought to de-legitimize protest actions and legitimize their criminalization and choice of defendants by suggesting they were not initiated by the Mapuche communities themselves. Activists from Mapuche organizations like the Consejo and CAM – especially those external to the rural communities – were more likely to be prosecuted and convicted, often with the argument that these groups do not represent "the" Mapuche people. In turn, Mapuche activists have criticized the prosecutorial notion that the supposedly authentic Mapuches are "manipulated" by external elements and foreigners, framing such portrayal as a continuation of the subordinate position that Mapuches have long occupied within Chilean society, in which they are assumed to lack agency and the capacity for autonomous decision-making.

The construction of the "true" Mapuche

Complementing the image of external radicals and infiltrators as criminals, Chilean prosecutorial narrative has also construed an image of the "authentic" or "true" Mapuche. The construction of the "good" Mapuche fits well within the multiculturalist discourse that has dominated Chilean society since the early 1990s, used to generate consensus for neoliberal policies (Richards 2013:101). This multiculturalist discourse does not question power structures that benefit some ethnic groups more than others. While it recognizes the indigenous populations of Chile at a cultural level, it has been hesitant to recognize that they hold any rights. This was evident in the long delay in ratifying the International Labour Organization (ILO) Convention 169 on the rights of indigenous and tribal peoples, which was only achieved in 2008, and the degree of right-wing opposition to constitutional recognition of Chile's indigenous peoples. Chile is one of the few Latin American countries that is still without constitutional recognition of its indigenous peoples.

---

4   This shows the negative connotation that "activist" has in the Chilean context. Lacking a better word, I continue to use the term "Mapuche activist" to refer to those who are involved in the Mapuche movement.

In their construction of the "true" Mapuche, the Chilean government and present-day landowners have regularly emphasized that ordinary Mapuches reject the "violence" promoted by a "radical minority." The governor of the 9th Region, for example, stated in 2001 that "the rest of the communities live in peace and don't want this. They don't want it!" (in Barria 2001). Similarly, a forestry manager said: "it is only a small group that makes trouble. With the rest of the indigenous people we have a good relationship, we give them work" (Interview C-7). The police have also drawn upon and reproduced this dichotomy. For example, a police report on a contested tract of land described how "minorities" were "agitating" and "dividing" the community, as they "introduce violent formulas" in the struggle for land (Police report on Estate Rucañanco 2001). According to the Chilean sociologist Saavedra, the frequent use of "*los encapuchados* [the hooded persons]" as a reference to activists in newspapers dehumanizes this minority (Saavedra 2002:5). The image of "radicals" as dangerous has been further reinforced by newspapers publishing allegations of "paramilitary training" and possession of "weapons" (for example, Notimex 2009).

In line with this narrative, prosecutors repeated during trials that even Mapuche community members ask for police protection and are afraid to testify in court. The prosecutorial narrative in the proceedings against the *Lonkos* of Traiguén exemplifies the construction of the image of the "true" Mapuche in contrast to the defendants. The prosecutor argued that the "true" Mapuches have calluses on their hands because of their hard work on the land (field notes, Case *Lonkos* of Traiguén, April 2003). In the courtroom at the time, Mapuche supporters inspected their hands and cracked jokes about their authenticity as Mapuches. These jokes were later repeated among themselves: "Show me your hands, let me see if you are a Mapuche according to Mr. Bustos [the prosecutor]!" (field notes April 2003).

The prosecutor further argued that those within the communities who disagreed with violent tactics (such as the alleged arson incidents in that case) were ostracized by the rest of the community and had their own pieces of land burnt. He asserted that the fear was "inter-ethnic *and* intra-ethnic" (field notes, Case *Lonkos* of Traiguén, March 2003). There has indeed been tension within the Mapuche movement about the legitimacy of tactics. For example, the organization Alianza Territorial Mapuche publicly condemned an attack on a small farmer in the district of Ercilla in the 9th Region: "When actions by CAM do not harm persons, clearly we will not say anything. But we are against injuring persons or attacking life, including that of police officers ..." (in Cayuqueo 2009). Such sentiments are relevant for law enforcement agencies, as they depend on citizen cooperation to solve crimes. The prosecutorial narrative also refers to such tensions to legitimize criminal proceedings.

After the *Lonkos'* unsuccessful appeal against their five-year sentences for a "terroristic threat" (they were acquitted of the arson charges; see chapter 8), they took the case to the Inter-American Commission for Human Rights (IACHR). In its statement before the commission in 2006, the Chilean state reiterated its narrative based on the notion of a "violent minority" and downplayed the relevance of the *Lonkos'* Mapuche identity, arguing that of the more than 3,500 Mapuche communities comprising 203,950 individuals in the 9th Region, only 60 people had ever been involved in criminal activity such as that alleged in the case. The Chilean state further emphasized that some of those 60 people did *not* belong to the Mapuche people and, therefore, those who carried out illegal acts "represent a percentage that is considerably small in relation to the universe of members of that [Mapuche] people" (Case *Lonkos* of Traiguén case, CIDH/ IACHR, report on admissibility, 21 October 2006, consideration 35).

The same prosecutorial narrative dominated the proceedings against the Mapuche organization CAM. In December 2002, the police arrested many CAM members, charging them with "membership of a terrorist organization." Shortly after their detention, the head prosecutor of the 9th Region asserted that, "also the Mapuches are afraid of the radicals" (Interview C-10). In total, 18 alleged CAM members were indicted. In the opening statement of the lawyer for the Ministry of Internal Affairs during the second trial in June 2005, the notion was frequently repeated that "there are a total of 2,500 Mapuche communities, of which not more than 300 demand lands and not more than 60 have been involved in illicit acts" (Case CAM, verdict, 27 July 2005). The prosecutor juxtaposed violent activists with "the peaceful families, which are the majority, the people that want the institutional ways, with CONADI [National Corporation for Indigenous Development], with the government" (Case CAM, oral proceedings, 2005). He further drew a distinction between good and bad Mapuches to argue that the trial was specifically meant to protect the interests of the "real" Mapuche people:

> In this case, we don't persecute an ethnic group or a specific community. In fact, several of our witnesses are Mapuche community members. To

them, they have only ended up impoverished because of the destruction of sources of labor and their own goods. They have been threatened, including physically, for not adhering to the violent methods of this association, or because they improved their economic situation through institutional avenues, with CONADI, or through the state. They are the primary interested parties that this rural terror stops. (Case CAM, Prosecutor statement, cited in verdict, 27 July 2005)

In this statement, the prosecutor referred to situations in which Mapuche activists who had negotiated a land deal with the state were accused of selling out. Aware of the dominant prosecutorial narrative, some Mapuche activists argued that there was a specific state policy intent on dividing communities. "We are [considered] the violent ones," said a young leader from the Mapuche community Temucuicui in the 9th Region. According to him, "they [the state agents] are trying to divide us. They love it when we fight between each other, that de-legitimizes us" (Interview C-68). In his analysis, there is a conscious strategy by the state to stigmatize "bad" communities. "They only say that [some communities are violent] in order to keep the Mapuche in their place."

Thus, in addition to pointing out that activists are a numerical minority, the prosecutorial narrative leverages intra-movement disagreements about the legitimacy of violence, on the one hand, and negotiating with the government, on the other, to produce a discursive dichotomy between "real" Mapuches and "radicals." Prosecutors then use this distinction to legitimize the criminalization of the "radical minority."

The portrayal of the present-day landowners of contested lands as "victims"

In these trials against Mapuche activists, the prosecutorial narrative not only construed a particular image of the defendants, but also portrayed present-day landowners as victims of land occupations and arson attacks, adopting the perspective of commercial farmers and forestry companies. In January 2003, the head prosecutor of Chile's 9th Region insisted, "We feel responsible to protect the victims. We care about the victims," pointing out that "victims were asking how long they had to wait for the state to act" (Interview C-10). Yet, while prosecutors often refer to "the" victims to legitimate their prosecutions, who the victims are is highly contested. Activists in the Mapuche movement insist that the Mapuches are the victims of land usurpation, water shortages and soil degradation due to erosion in forestry plantations. However, their narrative has not been adopted in criminal proceedings.

The prosecutorial narrative in the trial of the *Lonkos* of Traiguén exemplifies the way in which the present-day owners of contested lands are described as victims. The prosecutor's closing argument emphasized that "In this trial, those people were given voice, who normally don't have a voice: the victims." He claimed that "the victims," the owners of the estates where the arson incidents occurred, "don't have a voice, don't appear on television and don't give press conferences" (field notes, April 2003). Thus, not only did the prosecutor refer to the ways in which supporters of the *Lonkos* of Traiguén had indeed strategically used the media to call attention to the trial against them, he also inverted the slogan that Mapuche activists use to describe and legitimate their own aim, to "give voice to those without a voice" in marginalized Mapuche communities.

The prosecutor even warned the court that the defendants would present themselves as the weaker party. "According to them, we are the racists, the violators of human rights," he cautioned. Meanwhile, he emphasized that Chilean smallholder Juan Sagredo Marin, owner of the San Gregorio estate, lost "the only patrimony that he had" in the alleged arson attack. He stressed that the victims "are not millionaires, magistrate, they are not tall blonds with green eyes. They are Chileans, and as Chileans they need their rights to be respected." The owner of the other contested estate in the case, Agustín Figueroa, was at the time a lawyer at the Constitutional Court and former Minister of Agriculture. The prosecutor even consciously countered Mapuche portrayals of him as a rich and powerful man by insisting, "We are not talking about forestry companies. We are talking about middle and small-scale landowners" (field notes, Case *Lonkos* of Traiguén, April 2003).

The prosecutor further exclaimed in his opening statement that the landowners "have done everything possible, everything humanly possible, to live in peace. What can one say, as the landowner of a property, when your neighbor after decades and decades suddenly says: 'this is declared to be in conflict'"? (field notes, Case *Lonkos* of Traiguén, March 2003). As Mella and Le Bonniec (2004) point out, this reference to Mapuche communities as mere or random "neighbors" leaves out the history of the creation of private property and how those landowners and Mapuche communities *came to be* neighbors. While Mapuche activists view landowners and forestry companies as complicit in the ongoing dispossession of Mapuche lands and resources, the prosecutor in the trial of the *Lonkos* of Traiguén described the status quo as a situation of "peace," thus marginalizing the perspective of Mapuche activists.

In criminal proceedings, landowners often feed the narrative that they are already doing "everything possible" to live in peace. For example, a private accuser stated during a trial that "days earlier he had taken [the defendant] a part of the way in the truck and offered him clothes for his children" (Del Valle 2001). Another landowner reported to the police that "until the conflicts between Chilean landowners and Mapuche community members started, the relations with the adjacent communities were very good. One gave work to the Mapuche community members and attempted to incorporate an important number of them into agro-forestry jobs on the land" (Case *Lonkos* of Traiguén, Declaration to the police, 3 August 2002, Traiguén).

Richards observed similar references to paternalistic "generosity" in her interviews with the Araucanía elite and concluded that "the Mapuche provide convenient evidence for the European farmers' benevolence and superiority" (2010:82). This narrative is also presented by landowners in the courtroom, in their testimonies as witnesses for the prosecutor or in their statements as private accusers. One landowner, for example, claimed that his grandfather built a public school and a health clinic for the communities after acquiring the disputed property around 1942 (Case CAM, witness testimony, verdict, July 2005). Richards (2010) points out that landowners often selectively remember a good relationship with the Mapuche communities and place recent Mapuche mobilization efforts in a very short timeframe. Indeed, in their courtroom utterances landowners often ignored the history of previous land occupations during the period of Agrarian Reform in Chile in the early 1970s. In the CAM proceedings, the prosecutor echoed the landowners' view when he argued that they had followed strategies of implementing Good Neighborhood Programs, offering work and firewood to Mapuche community members, specifically to avoid any trouble (Case CAM, opening statement, oral proceedings, June 2005). The selective focus of prosecutors and landowners on good relationships contrasts with the discourse of Mapuche activists, which tends to go back to Mapuche relations with the Spanish Crown. Thus, by representing present-day landowners as victims in these trials, the prosecutorial narrative accepts, argues and reproduces certain victim identities while marginalizing others.

Identity politics and representation in the courtroom

In the trials discussed in this chapter, Chilean prosecutors explicitly attacked the notion that defendants legitimately "represented" their communities or the broader Mapuche people, despite it being irrelevant for the determination of guilt regarding the alleged criminal conduct. The identity boundary erected in the prosecutorial narrative between "manipulative activists" and "the Mapuche people" reinforced the boundary between the political and the criminal justice arenas, legitimizing the criminal prosecutions of the "radical minority" and the definition of their protest activity as "crime," while reassuring "peaceful" Mapuche communities that they were welcome as patient petitioners of CONADI or passive recipients of poverty reduction programs. In attempting to discredit the *Lonkos* of Traiguén for not representing authentic Mapuche chiefs, the prosecutorial narrative sought not only to provide redress for the alleged arson attacks but also strove to cut off community support and deter other activists. In addition to countering Mapuche allegations against the state of racism and repression, this narrative sought to legitimize the criminal prosecution by invisibilizing potentially legitimate land demands and portraying the defendant's motivations as driven by profit or terror.

Prosecutorial narratives thus strategically or inadvertently reject certain identities, while reproducing others. This phenomenon is not limited to cases connected to the "Mapuche conflict" in Chile, but can also be seen in prosecutions in Spain and the United States. The prosecutorial narrative in Spain did not dwell on a dichotomy between Basque and Spanish identities. Instead, in identifying defendants in the so-called "macro-trials" (see chapter 6), prosecutors equated general ties to the left-nationalist movement with membership in ETA's network. Although people always have multiple identities, in a prosecutorial narrative one identity can be chosen as the "relevant" or "dominant" identity. Tilly (2003:32) argues that the government sorts political identities into legitimate/illegitimate and recognized/unrecognized. In the US, prosecutors strategically emphasized the anarchist credentials of activist defendants and downplayed their environmentalist motives (see chapter 10). These labels – invariably contested – communicate something about the role of defendants, their motives, dangerousness, or disposition toward violence.

The reality of contestation over identity politics in the courtroom challenges the liberal ideological underpinnings of criminal law in two ways. First, identity can be understood to imply certain political motives, which can become criminally relevant in terrorism legislation and cases. Second, social identities reference a collective, thereby moving away from the abstract individual that is the subject of criminal law in liberal legal systems. Social identities assume the existence of a category or group of people as well as a continuance of that identity through time. Such assumptions render the default mode of prosecutorial narrative, which strives to decontextualize acts from identity in determining criminal conduct, particularly difficult. The Chilean prosecutorial narrative negated the reference to the collective of the Mapuche people, while also reinscribing it. This chapter thus demonstrates how prosecutors – inadvertently or intentionally – engage in societal debates on identity politics as they (de)contextualize the alleged facts of a case, thus co-constructing and reproducing images and identities of defendants and victims that are deeply contested.

"ECO-TERRORISM" CASES IN THE UNITED STATES

10

Shifting from Reactive to Proactive Prosecutions

In September 2007, I attended the trial of Eric McDavid in Sacramento, California. He was ultimately convicted of conspiracy to commit arson in the name of the Earth Liberation Front (ELF) and, because of a terrorism enhancement, sentenced to almost twenty years in prison. "Anna" testified during the trial against McDavid. As an informant for the United States' FBI, she played a pivotal role in McDavid's arrest and prosecution. Activists claimed that she also played a crucial role in manufacturing and funding his alleged crime. "Anna" had met McDavid during an annual gathering of anarchists. McDavid's supporters accused the government of playing dirty and violating its own rules by luring McDavid into conversations and attempts to fabricate an "explosive device." The FBI, though, presented his arrest as a timely intervention, preventing potentially serious harm:

> In early 2006, eco-terrorist Eric McDavid and two associates met in a secluded cabin in Dutch Flat, California to discuss making improvised explosive devices and to choose targets to bomb. Soon after, they began casing the targeted facilities and buying supplies to make bombs. But before they started mixing the ingredients, we swooped in and arrested them. (FBI 2008)

In an unexpected turn of events, in 2015, federal prosecutors admitted they had potentially violated evidentiary rules by withholding approximately 2,500 pages of documents from McDavid, which would have revealed his manipulation by the FBI informant Anna. In an unusual settlement with the government, McDavid pleaded guilty of a lesser charge and was immediately released from prison (Aaronson and Galloway 2015).

The prosecutors presented the case against Eric McDavid as an "eco-terrorism" case. By the 2000s, this term had become a routine frame in governmental assessments of the threat posed by environmental and animal rights activists. The concept was coined in 1983 by a representative of the Center for the Defense of Free Enterprise, who defined it as a "crime committed to save nature" (Potter 2011b:55). In 2002, the Subcommittee on Forests and Forest Health of the House Committee on Resources held a hearing in Washington DC on "The Threat of Eco-Terrorism" in which the FBI Domestic Terrorism Section Chief cited acts of "eco-terror" as dating back to 1977, when the Sea Shepherd Conservation Society was formed as a breakaway group from Greenpeace. He described a rise in eco-terrorism incidents from the late 1990s onwards and outlined the FBI definition of eco-terrorism as "the use or threatened use of violence of a criminal nature against innocent victims or property by an environmentally-oriented, subnational group for environmental-political reasons, or aimed at an audience beyond the target, often of a symbolic nature" (Jarboe 2002).

This chapter examines prosecutorial narrative in the US related to the perceived threat of "eco-terrorism" connected with contentious environmental and animal rights protest. Tracing its development from 1979 onwards, the chapter shows how US prosecutors' conceptualization of "eco-terrorism" came to center on the claimed dilemma of needing to prevent acts of "terrorism," while liberal criminal procedure puts restrictions on the incarceration of suspects before a crime has occurred. It describes the discursive shift in prosecutorial narrative from a focus on punishing past harm to avoiding future danger, which led to an increase in proactive as opposed to reactive investigations, as well as harsher sentences meant to deter similar acts. These investigations came to include the use of undercover FBI informants and the systematic infiltration of activist groups. Because proactive investigations focus on potential criminal conduct, they heavily depend on contextual analysis of movements, organizations and gatherings. Powerful interest groups, including industry-sponsored organizations, successfully engaged in "victim mobilization" in the criminal justice arena to push for effective "results" in terms of preventing intimidation and attacks on "animal enterprises" and other targets of environmental activism. The chapter shows how their discursive mobilization was instrumental in shifting prosecutorial narrative over time, leading to an increase in conspiracy charges and terrorism enhancements.

The emergence of eco-terrorism prosecutions

Environmental protest tactics such as tree-spiking by activists began to be referred to as terrorism in public discourse as early as the 1980s

(Scarce 2006:77). Over the next two decades, discursive mobilization by targets and opponents of such protest influenced the threat assessment of law enforcement agents and gradually shifted the conversation about such activism as terrorism into the criminal justice arena, leading to the emergence of "eco-terrorism" prosecutions. For example, even though ALF activist Rod Coronado pleaded guilty to common arson, during the 1995 sentencing hearing his actions were framed as part of a "terrorist" campaign, meaning that "[a] terrorist combines violence and threats so that those that disagree with him are silenced, either because they have been victimized by violence or because they fear being victimized" (Case Rod Coronado, Government Sentencing Memorandum, 1995:19). In the end, he was sentenced to four years and nine months in prison, much less than the nearly twenty-year sentence defendants received for (conspiracy to commit) arson attacks just ten years later, in which a terrorism enhancement was applied.

In 2006, the FBI publicly released a chronological list of "terrorist incidents in the United States" between 1980 and 2005, providing insight into the government's classification of environmental and animal rights protest activity as terrorism. For each incident, the list describes the allegedly "terrorist" action, perpetrators, and any killings or injuries involved (FBI 2006). In this document, the FBI qualifies acts committed by a wide variety of groups fighting for an even wider variety of goals as "terrorism", ranging from the Jewish Defense League to the Armenian Secret Army for the Liberation of Armenia, the Justice Knights of the Ku Klux Klan, and the Red Guerrilla Resistance. Especially in the 1980s, these different militant organizations seem to have flourished, engaging primarily in bombings or shootings. The first environmental action on the list was an act of "sabotage" on 14 May 1986 in Phoenix, Arizona, attributed to the organization Earth First! The FBI noted that nobody was killed or injured in the incident (FBI 2006). The second environmental incident listed occurred at the veterinary building that was under construction at the University of California (UC), Davis in 1987, and was the first FBI-recorded arson attributed to ALF. A total of $11,500 was offered in rewards for the capture and conviction of anyone involved in the action. At the time, nobody was arrested (Scarce 2006:223).

Hardly any environmental actions were recorded on the FBI terrorism list for the 1980s and 1990s.[1] A hike, however, was clearly visible after

---

1   For the 1980s, a total of seven environmental actions are listed on the FBI chronology: four incidents of sabotage, two of arson, and one of malicious destruc-

1999. Indeed, by then, almost all of the terrorist incidents on the FBI list were attributed to ELF, ALF, or other animal rights groups.[2] The environmental and animal rights actions listed for 1999–2005 included four bombings, seven incidents of malicious destruction of property (some including theft), 24 arsons (some multiple, some attempted), one burglary, one tree-spiking incident, and two incendiary attacks. Comparison of the limited information provided in the FBI list with activist accounts allows one to conclude that some of the charges of "vandalism/ destruction of property" refer to mink releases, such as in Harborcreek in 2002, and others to the destruction of SUVs and Hummers at multiple car dealerships, such as in West Covina in 2003.

A further comparison with other available information about environmental and animal rights actions *not* recorded by the FBI demonstrates a considerable shift in their categorization of incidents. For example, whereas the FBI considered mink releases to be "terrorist incidents" from the 2000s onward, earlier well-known mink releases were not included on the list. Other animal rights actions from the 1980s that resulted in considerable property damage were also missing from the list. For example, on 9 December 1984 at the City of Hope Research Institute in California, $500,000 of damage was registered when ALF organized a break-in, stealing dogs, cats, rabbits, mice and rats. On 2 June 1987, a fur store in St. Louis, Missouri was firebombed, with allegedly $1 million in damages (Guither 1998:221–4). However, neither of these incidents appear in the FBI chronology.

Contrary to a dataset compiled by academic Loadenthal (2013) that shows a decline in ALF/ELF incidents after 1997, the FBI Deputy Assistant Director for Counterterrorism John Lewis testified before the Senate Committee in 2004 that "eco-terrorism" attacks were growing in frequency and size, "targeting of sports utility vehicles and arsons of new construction homes or commercial properties," while the list of potential targets and willingness to use arson were also expanding at the same time. He pointed to an activist communiqué as an example of an "escalation in violent rhetoric," highlighting threats of "potential assassinations of researchers"

---

tion of property. From 1990 until 1999, the list only mentions one incident of malicious destruction of property, one fire bombing, and one arson incident.

2   The only non-environmental actions listed by the FBI after 2000 include two attacks by anti-abortion activists, the 9/11 Al Qaeda attack, the anthrax mailings, a shooting involving an Egyptian immigrant, and one arson attack carried out on behalf of the "Aryan Nations." The other 47 "terrorist" actions are all attributed to ELF, ALF, or other animal rights groups.

and the possibility that there may be a "new willingness on the part of some in the [environmental] movement to abandon the traditional and publicly stated code of nonviolence in favor of more confrontational and aggressive tactics designed to threaten and intimidate legitimate companies into abandoning entire projects or contracts" (Lewis 2004).

By 2005, Lewis had declared "eco-terrorism" and the animal rights movement the number one domestic terrorism threat in the US (see chapter 4 on the role of victim mobilization by animal enterprises in influencing this assessment). In 2006, a bulletin addressed to law enforcement by the Department of Homeland Security warned that "[a]ttacks against corporations by animal rights extremists and eco-terrorists are costly to the targeted company and, over time, can undermine confidence in the economy" (Department of Homeland Security 2006). Similarly, in 2008, an online brief on eco-terrorism by the FBI highlighted the sheer volume of eco-terrorism crimes and their huge economic impact, citing more than 2,000 incidents and losses of more than $110 million since 1979 (FBI 2008). For perspective, compared to the more than 2,000 incidents classified as eco-terrorism over a nearly thirty-year period, in 2009 alone, the US saw 15,241 murders, 89,000 incidents of forcible rape, and 408,217 incidents of robbery (FBI 2009). Thus, the number of incidents was clearly not the only factor in the rise of "eco-terrorism" to the level of a serious domestic terrorism threat. Indeed, already since the early 2000s, there was a decrease in actions of arson claimed in name of ELF or ALF. By 2015, a journalist concluded that – possibly due to major prosecutions – "crimes of 'eco-terrorism' are practically non-existent now" (Kirchner 2015).

From the late 1990s onward, in line with the shift in FBI categorization, prosecutors in the United States increasingly framed criminal proceedings against environmental and animal rights activists as "cases of" eco-terrorism. Trials in such cases often started with expert witnesses (frequently from the police) explaining the "relevant context," such as the background of ELF and its ideology. The first witness in the 2007 trial against activist Eric McDavid, for instance, was a lieutenant from the Criminal Intelligence Unit of the UC Davis Police Department who took the stand to speak about ELF, ALF, and anarchism. One of the prosecutors explained the pragmatic reason for such a witness, arguing that "the jury should have some background or frame of reference" regarding the defendant's motive (Interview US-1). A motive was not required for a conviction, but according to the prosecutor, a motive could help the jury to better understand why a defendant did something, which could increase their belief in the defendant's guilt. Through this broad contextualization, McDavid was connected to arson attacks carried out in name of the ELF and ALF that had occurred ten or even twenty years prior, in which he was not alleged to have participated. Similarly, during a hearing against William Viehl, who pleaded guilty to releasing mink in Utah in September 2008, the prosecutor showed a slideshow that displayed images from incidents of arson attributed to or claimed by ALF, as well as communiqués for actions of which Viehl was not accused (Young 2010).

US prosecutors also emphasized anarchist credentials of defendants while downplaying environmental motives in a number of cases related to environmental and animal rights protest actions. The "anarchist" lifestyle of McDavid was discussed at length: the fact that he traveled by hitchhiking, engaged in shoplifting, and attended protests and anarchist conventions. His co-defendant explained how they would panhandle or steal in order to feed themselves, and how they would go train hopping and dumpster diving. The prosecutor also pointed out that McDavid had read the book *Evasion*, in which an anarchist describes her lifestyle. One of McDavid's supporters commented that if such books were suspicious, then her book shelves would certainly get her in trouble as well (Interview US-4). An affidavit by special FBI agent Walker also described co-defendant Zachary Jenson and the fact that one of his favorite books was *Days of War, Nights of Love* by CrimethInc. "This book contains a chapter-by-chapter description of anarchist values and objectives" commented the affidavit. The message from these discussions of anarchism was clear: whereas many groups may be environmental groups, only the dangerous ALF and ELF combine environmental activism with anarchist ideology. In the prosecutorial narrative, anarchist ideology and its call for "direct action" were considered relevant for criminal proceedings because activists used them to justify illegal or violent protest methods, while environmental motives were considered political and thus taboo for prosecutors to dwell upon.

The eco-terrorism narrative has real consequences for sentencing. Defendants facing a jury trial for a common crime can receive an enhanced sentence if the judge decides the crime involved or was intended to promote a "federal crime of terrorism," or was "calculated to influence or affect the conduct of government by intimidation or coercion, or to retaliate against government conduct" (US Sentencing Guidelines § 3A1.4).[3] From 2001 onwards, defendants in "eco-terrorism" cases were

---

3   While the provision introducing these enhancements was drawn up in 1994 in order to increase penalties in relation to international terrorism, lawyer

sentenced with these terrorism enhancements, often after some of the defendants accepted a plea agreement and cooperated with the prosecution by implicating other defendants. US activists have since criticized the severe impact the terrorism label has had on their sentencing and prison conditions. For example, in another case, in March 2008, Marius Mason, Frank Ambrose, Aren Burthwick, and Stephanie Lynne Fultz were arrested and charged with conspiracy to commit arson. It came out that Ambrose, Mason's ex-husband, had been extensively assisting the FBI in investigating environmental organizing since 2007. Despite his cooperation, his plea bargain resulted in a nine-year sentence, two years more than the prosecutor had requested. Mason pleaded guilty and admitted involvement in 12 other acts that totaled more than $2.5 million in property damage. While activists emphasized that "[n]o one was physically harmed in these actions" (supportmariusmason.org), he was sentenced to almost 22 years due to the terrorist enhancement applied during his sentencing.

The "eco-terrorism" narrative promulgated by the FBI and interest groups like animal enterprise alliances emphasizes that eco-terrorism is not just a local problem, but a national or even international threat. It highlights the enormous losses in terms of "the economy" and the "reasonable fear" of victims, and broadens the legal interest at stake in its shift to categorizing actions such as burglary or property destruction as terrorism. In line with this narrative, during criminal proceedings the FBI and prosecutors connect actions of environmental and animal rights activists into a pattern based on a shared ideology, thus justifying the application of terrorism enhancements leading to very long sentences meant to deter other activists. There has been a pushback, though, by activists and even some sections of the Department of Justice, against the eco-terrorism qualification and the FBI's prioritization of these investigations.

Pushback against the eco-terrorism label

While the FBI concluded that eco-terrorists are "one of the most serious domestic terrorism threats in the U.S. today" (FBI 2008), the same threat assessment was not shared by everyone. Activists denounced the FBI and prosecutors' disproportional use of the terrorism label in relation to envi-

---

McLoughlin (2010:51) argues that domestic incidents such as the 1995 Oklahoma bombing stretched the "draconian" provision's application beyond the terrain of international terrorism, "giving it far-reaching power and leading to devastating consequences" (2010:54).

ronmental and animal rights protest actions. Journalist Will Potter, for instance, argued that the eco-terrorism "threat" in the United States had been manufactured since the 1980s:

> They [industry groups] are doing everything they can to *create* this fear through scare-mongering: that's the point. In light of this political climate, it's impossible to discuss "reasonable fear," because industry groups are throwing all their weight into making the unreasonable seem reasonable – into making the public afraid of non-violent activists, so they can push a political agenda. (Potter 2007)

Apart from activists, other actors in the US Justice Department also disagreed with the FBI's threat assessment. In December 2003, the Audit Division of the Justice Department criticized the FBI for its disproportionate attention to eco-terrorism and recommended that it focus its intelligence reports on "the high risk of international terrorism and any domestic terrorist activities aimed at creating mass casualties or destroying critical infrastructure, rather than information on social protests and domestic radicals' criminal activities" (Office of the Inspector General 2003:xi). The audit advised the FBI to stop investigating animal rights and environmental activists through its Counterterrorism Division and recommended that it shift these cases to the FBI's Criminal Investigative Division, "except where a domestic group or individual uses or seeks to use explosives or weapons of mass destruction to cause mass casualties" (2003: x). In its May 2008 "Ecoterrorism Threat Assessment," the Department of Homeland Security wrote that "[c]urrently, ecoterrorist movement activities do not represent a serious threat to U.S. national security" (Department of Homeland Security 2008:34).

Whether the actions of environmental and animal rights activists pose a threat to human lives is deeply contested. Countering accusations of terrorism by prosecutors, US environmental and animal rights activists often claimed that they were careful to ensure that their actions did not hurt "human or non-human" animals. Activist Rod Coronado, for example, declared that actions were often postponed or cancelled when life safety could not be ensured. Even James Jarboe, the chief of the FBI's domestic terrorism section, recognized that animal rights groups like ALF "have generally adhered to this mandate" (Jarboe 2002). At the same time, FBI officials emphasized the *potential* danger that extremist environmental actions pose for human lives (FBI 2004). A prosecutor pointed out that with tactics like arson and bombing, it is never possible to guarantee total safety, adding that it was only by the "grace of god that people have not been killed" (Interview US-1). Similarly, the US Attorney from Oregon in the Operation Backfire case said, "It was pure luck that no one was killed or injured by their actions" (Case Operation Backfire, Terrorism Enhancement Hearing, 2007:12).

Underlying criticism of the terrorism label is the implicit or explicit comparison with other crimes deemed to be graver or more dangerous. For example, the imprisoned environmental activist Jeff Luers provided a long list of other crimes committed in the state of Oregon to demonstrate the discrepancy between his sentence (22 years and 8 months for burning three SUVs to draw attention to climate change) and lower sentences in other cases involving crimes like attempted murder, assault and rape (Luers 2011).[4] Such comparisons have been a major tool in the dispute on eco-terrorism in the criminal justice arena in which the boundaries between what constitutes terrorism or not are drawn. Activists have frequently invoked the fact that, historically, anti-abortionists have not been similarly labeled as "terrorists" in the US, even though they have engaged in killing doctors (Potter 2007).

To counter such criticism, US prosecutors have employed different analogies. During the sentencing hearing of an environmental group dubbed "The Family," the prosecutor drew a comparison with the white supremacist organization the Ku Klux Klan (KKK):

The defendants' argument is there was no injury to human beings, no danger to humans, and therefore, there was no terrorism. If that's the standard, the Ku Klux Klan did not commit terrorism when they traveled in the dark of night, three, four o'clock in the morning, burning black churches in Mississippi. No one was inside the churches, no one was there to be injured. They may not have wanted to injure anybody. They just burned buildings. So according to the defense theory, that's not a terroristic act. (Case Operation Backfire, Terrorism Enhancement Hearing, 2007:12)

This comparison upset the lawyer of defendant Daniel McGowan, who argued that the Ku Klux Klan did actively engage in murder and

---

4 After six years in a maximum security prison, he won his appeal and his sentence was reduced to ten years.

that, therefore, the comparison did not hold (Case Operation Backfire, Terrorism Enhancement Hearing, 2007:58).

In justifying their actions, animal rights activists frequently compared themselves to the Underground Railroad, supporting escaping slaves from the US South in the 19th century. However, the prosecutor argued that they "compare themselves to the wrong people, frankly. They should be comparing themselves to Jack Dowell." Dowell was sentenced to 30 years in prison for serving as a lookout while the US Internal Revenue Service building in Colorado Springs, Colorado, was burnt down, an arson in which "[n]o one was injured. Just property damage" (Case Operation Backfire, Terrorism Enhancement Hearing, 2007:13–14). The prosecutor's comparison with Jack Dowell portrays his indictments and sentencing requests against "eco-terrorists" as even-handed and appropriate. Thus, in competing narratives about the nature and dangerousness of environmental and animal rights protest actions, prosecutors and prisoner supporters advocate radically different events as suitably analogous.

Past harm and future danger: proactive investigations

For a long time, the US government was unsuccessful in obtaining convictions after contentious environmental and animal rights protest actions like raids on labs or fur farms. In response, the FBI gradually adopted a more "proactive" approach to criminalizing these actions. Rather than specific criminal conduct, their investigations often took certain individuals and organizations as a starting point, with a focus on future danger instead of past harm. In a public hearing before the Senate Judiciary Committee on the issue of "Animal Rights: Activism vs. Criminality" in 2004, the Deputy Assistant Director of the FBI's Counterterrorism Division addressed the "threat posed by animal rights extremists and eco-terrorists in this country," explicitly noting that, "The FBI's commitment to address the threat can be seen in the proactive approach that we have taken regarding the dissemination of information" (Lewis 2004). He described how, in March 2003, the FBI established a Domestic Collection, Evaluation and Dissemination Unit, which in its first year issued 20 Intelligence Information Reports related to "animal rights and eco-terrorism" activity. He described these reports as part of the FBI's proactive "information campaign" and "nationwide, strategic investigative approach to addressing the animal rights/eco-terrorism threat in the United States." This investigative approach involved a collaborative effort, he noted: "This campaign has included ongoing liaison with federal, state, and local law enforcement and prosecutors, relevant trade associations and targeted companies and industries" (Lewis 2004).

According to the FBI, extremist activists who commit their actions in the name of ALF and ELF present unique challenges for law enforcement. Because such entities have little, if any, known hierarchical structures, unlike traditional criminal enterprises, conducting criminal investigations into them can be problematic. A prosecutor similarly recounted that "in theory the mafia isn't that hard to wipe out" due to its hierarchical structure, while tackling networks like ALF and ELF is far more difficult, as traditional methods to pressure local people into testifying against those higher up the chain do not work with the horizontal networks (Interview 2007, US-1). Already in 1995, in a prominent case against animal rights activist Rod Coronado, the prosecutor acknowledged the difficulty of securing convictions against ALF members:

> The FBI has designated the ALF as a domestic terrorist organization. In terms of organization, this designation is particularly apt because the ALF has adopted the "cell" structure of such terrorist organizations as the Irish Republican Army, making investigation of the organization and identification of its members very difficult. As a result, until today, no known member of the ALF has ever been convicted of a felony. (Case Rod Coronado, Sentencing Memorandum, 1995:1)

In a number of trials throughout the 2000s, the FBI's proactive approach as described by Lewis materialized in conspiracy charges designed to punish preparatory activities before a planned crime takes place. It also included the use of undercover FBI agents, who monitored activists and meetings, and an increasing preoccupation with controlling the perceived process of activists' radicalization. For example, animal rights activist Peter Young said that he was offered a plea bargain in exchange for returning to the activist community as a mole following his sentence. Another offer required him to name other animal rights activists (Interview 2008, US-15). This illustrates a development from conduct-driven (reactive) to suspect-driven or organization-driven (proactive) investigations in relation to environmental and animal rights activism in the US.

In interviews prosecutors expressed a paternalistic attitude toward the use of proactive investigations and harsh sentences, often painting an image of defendants as young idealists who had gotten carried away in search for a way to give meaning to their lives. They perceived younger eco-activists as middle-class kids who had taken a "wrong" turn somewhere and just needed to be set back on the "right" path. One prosecutor spoke about "preventing these kids from doing stuff they later regret" (Interview US-1). He viewed young activists as "victims" of the anarchist ideology and older "cell" members to whom they were attracted. He lamented the fact that "the people that I *have* to prosecute are all babies" and hoped that one of the public "eco-terror" trials would deter other "kids" who might get swept up by romantic ideals and incisive writing of figures like Derrick Jenson. He said "I don't want to see these people sent to prison for stupid stuff" and told me that he hoped that his trial would make them think twice before they walked down this dangerous path (Interview US-1).

Another prosecutor also expressed hope that criminal proceedings against activists would deter others who may be eager to "save the world" and would otherwise be "lulled into" such activity (Interview US-13). Interestingly, mink liberator Viehl was quoted as having told the judge during his sentencing hearing: "I think it's noble to add a deterrence so other young people don't end up in my shoes [...] I truly wish I hadn't put myself through this, and I will respect any decision you make" (Morgan 2010). A young activist indeed affirmed that he, like many other activists, thought the "Green Scare crackdown" was intended to undermine his feeling of invincibility, his assumption that he and his fellow activists – white and upper-middle class – would not be prosecuted, and to instill fear in him and others like him (Interview US-5).

In contrast to those activists whom prosecutors identified as "babies" or "kids" were the so-called "big fish" or "masterminds." One prosecutor told me that he thought the people behind the ALF and ELF websites and the "ideologues in the movement" (for example, writers and filmmakers like Derrick Jensen and Craig Rosebraugh) were the real danger and, accordingly, bore responsibility for the crimes committed. He found it problematic that those who were enticing young and naïve kids into crimes were not serving any time themselves. He pictured them "behind the screens" and argued that "those people know what they are doing: they are sending the sheep to the slaughter" (Interview US-1). In line with this image, some prosecutors made a specific effort to prosecute those in leading roles for their influence on younger people. In one case, the prosecutor accused two organizers of a home demonstration against the animal-testing laboratory Huntingdon Life Sciences of "corruption of minors" because two of the demonstrators were younger than 18 (Nawrocki 2004).⁵ Thus, the particular images and threat assessment underlying the "eco-terrorism" narrative have shaped the FBI's proactive investigations as well as prosecutorial decisions. In particular, early intervention was combined with harsh sentences to deter young activists from the "wrong" path.

Conspiracy charges against environmental and animal rights activists

Within the framework of US criminal law, a conspiracy is an illegal agreement that, in and of itself, constitutes a crime. At the core of a conspiracy, there are two crimes. The conspiracy is a crime in itself, as is the crime that is the subject of the conspiracy. Prosecutors emphasize that conspiracy cases do not criminalize thoughts, as proving conspiracy generally requires an "overt act" toward the execution of a crime. However, nearly anything that can be construed as a step toward the execution of the crime can be considered an overt act for the purpose of proving conspiracy. As described in the jury instructions in the case against the Stop Huntingdon Animal Cruelty (SHAC) activists (detailed in chapter 11), the overt act need not be criminal in nature if considered separately and apart from the conspiracy. However, it must be an act that furthers, or tends toward, the accomplishment of the plan or scheme.

During the trial against environmental activist Eric McDavid, the prosecutor portrayed him, his two co-defendants, and the FBI informant "Anna" as a group of friends who, frustrated with the futility of demonstrations, were planning to do something "big" that involved making a bomb. Armed with the books *The Poor Man's James Bond*, *The Survival Chemist*, and some recipes provided by the informant "Anna," who had presented herself as a chemistry student, they began experimenting with mixing chemicals. They had not decided yet on what they were going to bomb, but did reconnaissance on several potential targets, such as the governmental Institute of Forest Genetics, which was engaged in genetic modification. While they were in this process, they were arrested.

In his closing arguments, the prosecutor emphasized that the defendant was about to start a "bombing campaign" in California and sketched the dilemma this posed for the FBI:

> But does the FBI make the risk assessment at that point that, well, these people, they are talking about the White House, and they are talking

---

5   The judge later threw the charge out, arguing that the state had failed to prove intent.

about the Pentagon, and they are talking about the World Trade Center, but they haven't decided on which one they are going to go after, so I guess we don't have a conspiracy. That's not what the conspiracy law requires. [...] We don't have to wait until the conspirators are crawling under the fence with bomb in hand or taking any closer steps, lighting the match. We just have to make sure we have a fully-formed conspiracy. (Case SHAC 7, Closing arguments, 25 September 2007)

In response to finding out about "Anna" and a number of other FBI informants during the 2000s, prisoner support groups for animal rights and environmental activists strongly criticized the government's use of undercover agents and informants in their circles. According to them, in those cases, the state was not uncovering existing crimes but actively manufacturing crimes by entrapping activists. Many environmental and animal rights activists in the US thus diametrically oppose the state's criminal definition of conspiracy, as they consider activists convicted on conspiracy charges as having "done nothing." Journalist Will Potter said about McDavid that "[t]he guy didn't *do* anything, [...] At the worst, he hung around with a group of people who talked tough. In court, Anna actually complained that the group spent too much time hanging around and smoking pot" (Bloom 2011). The support group of Eric McDavid called him a political prisoner and explained: "Eric was imprisoned for what amounts to thought-crime – no actions were ever carried out, and Eric was charged with a single count of 'conspiracy' – a powerful legal tool often used by the state to crush dissent" (Support Eric 2011). An activist leaflet pointed to the need to reach out to "people outside our social and political circles [...] to utilize this opportunity to discredit the state and delegitimize conspiracy-based cases. The broader the range of people who disapprove of this tactic, the more the hands of the authorities will be tied" (Conspiracy 2011:7).

The defense in the trial of Eric McDavid relied entirely on this line of argumentation. McDavid's impeccable courtroom behavior, his entrance into the courtroom wearing a formal white dress shirt, and the attendance of many of his family members all combined to communicate his obedience to the state, his belonging to the American community, and respect for its rule of law. His defense denied, or at least did not defend, the alleged plans to bomb a dam. The few fellow activists who attended the trial did not leaflet or protest, nor did they attempt to spread a message of environmentalism. Nobody during the trial attempted to justify the alleged plans of the conspiracy by pointing to grievances related to the environment. Instead, McDavid's defense focused solely on the government's abuse of its powers through "entrapment."

While entrapment is indeed a legally allowed defense, the judge made it clear that the trial was not going to be an indictment of the FBI, the Justice Department or the informant "Anna." Still, the defense argued that if McDavid was undergoing radicalization, it was only under the influence of "Anna," with whom he had been deeply in love. The defense lawyer argued that without her, there would have been no conspiracy, no get-together in California to start preparing a bomb, and no action in order to make it happen. Therefore, a major question during the trial was whether or not the defendants would have gone along with their plans if "Anna" had not been involved (field notes, Case Eric McDavid, September 2007).[6]

While activists referred to this trial as a prosecution of "thought crime" and "Orwellian," (Interview US-16; Support Eric 2011), the prosecutor argued during the closing arguments that the entrapment defense is meant to protect the unwary *innocent*, not the unwary *criminal* (Case Eric McDavid, trial transcripts, 25 September 2007). Merely providing an opportunity, she contended, did not constitute entrapment. The prosecutor emphasized that the role of "Anna" was to provide this opportunity and see whether the conspiracy would move forward:

And, yes, it's true that Anna did some things at the FBI direction to facilitate that meeting. [...] All the FBI did was bring these four co-conspirators together in one location to find out if they were serious about what Eric McDavid had talked about. [...] if they had gotten together that weekend, and if they had gone hiking, and there had been no discussion of any conspiracy or any bombing campaign, game over. [...] But that's not what happened. And fortunately, you have that on tape. (Case Eric McDavid, trial transcripts, 25 September 2007)

The approach to proactive investigation in the case of McDavid shifted the object of investigation from past crimes to the processes of radicalization. It was the observed radicalization of McDavid (after "Anna" had initially described him as "harmless") that led the FBI to provide opportunities

---

6   Once this defense was raised, the prosecution had to prove that (1) there had been no inducement by the government, or if that could not be proven, then (2) the defendant had a predisposition to commit the crime that was the subject of the conspiracy.

to see how "serious" he was. The prosecutor emphasized, however, that McDavid was not proactively targeted. "Anna" met him during protests and at an anarchist convention in Des Moines. When it turned out that he was talking about "something big" the FBI decided to provide further opportunity to find out if it was serious or just talk. The informant "Anna" was thus deployed initially with a focus on (anarchist) gatherings, spaces and events where it was suspected that crimes might occur or be prepared.

Dangerousness versus guilt

Traditionally, liberal criminal justice is a backward-looking affair, focused on punishing crimes that have already taken place in the past on the basis of guilt for wrongdoing. Punishment prescribed by the criminal justice system serves as an "answer" to an event and affirms that the norm violated by the conduct in question remains the norm in force. Criminal justice decisions based on the dangerousness of an individual (instead of past guilt) amount to what Jakobs and Cancio Meliá (2006) call "security measures," not punishment. For example, bail conditions and the possibility of spending time outside of jail while awaiting trial are frequently made dependent on the assessment of danger posed by a particular suspect. Pre-trial detention to ensure incapacitation cannot, in a liberal framework, take the place of punishment, which necessitates the proven guilt of the defendant.

A typical dilemma for prosecutors in the contentious episodes under examination in this book is that they expect challengers of the status quo to be willing and able to break the law in the future. In addition to punishing past harm, law enforcement agents also have the task of assessing such danger and possibly intervening beforehand to prevent crimes. However, if prosecutors intervene too early, they may forfeit the possibility of charging defendants with criminal conduct. Different criminal justice systems have developed various options for prosecuting crime before it occurs. The US system heavily relies on conspiracy charges in these types of prosecutions, whereas continental systems tend to criminalize preparatory activities and membership in criminal or terrorist organizations.

If people are in jail, the logic goes, they cannot commit crimes. Law enforcement agents can come to see such proactive prosecution as a short-cut to protecting the population against perceived danger. High sentences (such as McDavid's 20-year sentence) are another route through which prosecutors have hoped to deter those who might otherwise be inclined to replicate particular conduct. Even when a defendant was charged with a single incident, prosecutors contextualized the event in a pattern of ALF or ELF actions to justify application of the Animal Enterprise Terrorism Act (AETA) or terrorism enhancements. The sustained criticism leveled by prisoner supporters sometimes led to a reduction in sentencing, such as in the case of Jeff Luers or the early release of Eric McDavid. Still, a number of convictions were obtained on the basis of conspiracy charges, with the help of FBI informants and cooperating defendants who testified against fellow activists, while high sentences – meant to deter younger activists – were secured with terrorism enhancements.

Even in criminal cases against animal rights and environmental activists that were not qualified as eco-terrorism, prosecutors asked for deterrent sentences, explicitly aiming to communicate to those considering committing similar offenses. For example, in the case against climate change activist Tim DeChristopher, who participated in an auction of land in Utah national parks to raise the bids, the prosecutor construed speech acts in which he defended his acts as legitimate civil disobedience as "unapologetic" and therefore as one of the grounds for demanding a "significant term of imprisonment." The prosecutor argued that "[a]mong the many listening to the Court's sentence" there are those who consider "the defendant's invitation and encouragement to join him outside the bounds of law, and inside jail. Accordingly, the defendant's sentence should effectively communicate that similar acts will have definite consequences" (Case Tim DeChristopher, Prosecution sentencing recommendations, 19 July 2011). On 26 July 2011, DeChristopher was sentenced to two years in prison, an additional three-year probation, and a $10,000 fine. This sentence was subsequently confirmed on appeal. Online commentaries publicly hailed him as a "hero."

In sum, the discursive mobilization by alliances of animal enterprises and other lobby groups during the 1990s for the term "eco-terrorism" succeeded in creating a shift toward proactive investigations by the early 2000s. By contextualizing animal rights and environmental protest actions within anarchist ideology and labeling such actions as "eco-terrorism," the US prosecutorial narrative changed the legal interest at stake and shifted to an emphasis on future danger and preventing attacks. The FBI and prosecutors therefore turned criminal investigations toward settings and movements in which such ideology was present. They sought to intervene in the process of radicalization to set an example and steer "kids" participating in environmental and animal rights activism away from "doing things they would later regret." Thus, the discursive shift toward eco-terrorism involved a change in the assessment of danger as well as proactive investigations while prosecutorial narrative in the 2000s moved toward a contextualized mode to construct conspiracy charges and secure higher sentences. After the enactment of the AETA, there were a few more convictions of activists for animal releases and damage done to mink farms and labs with sentences up to three years (for example, Scott DeMuth in 2010, Lang and Oliff in 2015, and Buddenberg and Kissane in 2016/17). In line with the steep decline in arson attacks claimed in name of ELF or ALF, though, since the Operation Backfire proceedings in 2007, there were no large prosecutions against supposed cells of environmental or animal rights activists.

11

Drawing a Boundary between Raising Awareness and Intimidation

Criminalizing the publication of addresses of potential targets for animal rights protests

Huntingdon Life Sciences (HLS, currently known as Envigo) is a non-clinical contract research organization founded in 1951 in the United Kingdom that tests pharmaceuticals, industrial chemicals, food additives and other substances for safety and side effects before companies take them to market. Such research is often legally required to bring medicaments and chemicals to market, and controversially for many animal rights and animal welfare activists, often involves testing substances on animals. After the application or injection of the substance being tested and lab observation, the animals are typically killed and dissected for further research. Sometimes, however, animals are anesthetized and dissected while still alive in a practice called vivisection. In addition to Huntingdon's two laboratories in the UK, it has also operated an experimental facility in New Jersey in the United States since 1995 (Cook 2006).

Toward the end of the 1990s, anti-vivisection activists, frustrated with ineffective public demonstrations and lobbying for legislative reform, decided to experiment with a new kind of campaigning. In 1999, the Stop Huntingdon Animal Cruelty (SHAC) campaign was formed in the UK with the aim of forcing HLS to close down. The SHAC campaign quickly became an international effort. In 2000, SHAC USA was founded to extend the focus of the campaign to HLS activities in the US, where the campaign claimed "Every day an average of 500 animals – including dogs, cats, mice, primates and rabbits – die inside HLS." Undercover investigations by animal rights activists hired as employees revealed workers "punching 4-month-old beagle puppies in the face, dissecting a live monkey, falsifying scientific data, and violating Good Laboratory Practice laws over 600 times" (SHAC 7 2008).

In their campaign, SHAC USA activists tried to use protest as a means to tarnish HLS's reputation, scare away investors, and upset other business relationships in order to pressure HLS to stop animal testing. As part of the campaign, activists used tactics ranging from public street rallies and campaigning letters to the alleged firebombing of houses. The SHAC campaign website posted addresses of CEOs and other employees working at client companies and investors of HLS, calling on fellow activists to target them through various means of protest. Using this information, animal rights activists began to conduct so-called "home visits" to the private residences of HLS employees and the CEOs of HLS suppliers or otherwise affiliated companies.

These "home visits" often consisted of chanting and leafleting to raise awareness among neighbors about animal rights and the controversial animal-testing practices of HLS. During these protests, activists sometimes showed vivisection pictures and shouted messages through megaphones, such as "puppy killer" and "your neighbor is a murderer," as a way to name and shame people for their involvement in such practices.[1] In several instances – according to the subsequent indictment of SHAC USA campaigners – activists conducted "home visits" at night and damaged property by spray-painting houses, throwing rocks through windows, or damaging cars. When the police and FBI failed to catch those engaged in such acts of vandalism, an alliance of animal enterprises mobilized to put pressure on law enforcement officials to secure convictions.

This alliance pushed the "eco-terrorist" narrative and lobbied for the Animal Enterprise Terrorism Act (AETA) to be passed to overcome the limitations of the existing Animal Enterprise Protection Act (AEPA) and more successfully prosecute those behind these protests (see chapter 4). During a hearing of the Judiciary Subcommittee on Crime, Terrorism and Homeland Security at the US House of Representatives on the proposed AETA, Brent McIntosh, Deputy Assistant Attorney General of the US Justice Department, acknowledged that "considered individually" the various actions in the SHAC campaign were "state crimes" (that is, not federal) against "law-abiding employees." However, he argued that local

---

1   For an example of such a home visit, see the video of "Huntingdon Life Sciences Andrew Baker Home Demo 8-30-09," uploaded by nyc4animals on 31 August 2009, available at: www.youtube.com/watch?v=9zE48-xVc30.

police lacked investigative resources and the "nationwide perspective" needed to "put these local offenses into context as a multi-jurisdictional campaign of violence." Claiming the need for a new law, McIntosh further noted that while federal prosecutors were "well equipped" to prosecute activists using arson or explosives, "not all animal rights extremists use arson and explosives" (23 May 2006, Washington). This contextualization into a "nationwide perspective" came to characterize the prosecutorial narrative in the 2006 federal criminal case against six activists behind the SHAC website plus the organization SHAC USA Inc. (Case SHAC 7).

In their defense, the SHAC defendants claimed that attempting to close down a company was not a crime, just as "[c]ampaigning against the tobacco and liquor companies and agreeing or arguing for their demise is not a crime" (27 February 2006:149). Legitimizing his choice to prosecute the activists, a prosecutor differentiated such campaigns by criticizing the "tyranny of the minority" of the SHAC activists, asserting that "Bullying the NYSE [New York Stock Exchange] is not what this country is about, this country is about protesting legally. It is well within their right to write letters" (Interview US-13). This chapter explores the prosecutorial narrative around the publication of addresses of targets for animal rights campaigning and so-called home visits. It looks at a common prosecutorial device across the contentious episodes studied here: creating a narrative that holds a known defendant responsible for criminal acts committed by unknown others. It traces the narrative construction of a pattern and the framing of the protests as stalking and intimidation. Finally, it describes how this narrative enabled the criminalization of the activists behind the SHAC website without having to prove any direct involvement of the defendants in the controversial home visits.

The SHAC campaign: home visits, nuisance campaigning and secondary targeting

Campaigners for SHAC USA launched a website listing the home addresses of CEOs of companies making use of HLS test results or with shares in HLS, identifying them as "secondary" targets for campaigning. They included banks, cage suppliers, lawyers that brokered contracts with HLS, investment banks, auditing companies, and HLS shareholders. Among HLS's direct clients and customers, targets included pharmaceutical companies, biotech companies, and companies selling household products such as Colgate toothpaste. The logic behind secondary targeting was simple: HLS needed its shareholders, but shareholders did not need HLS. This logic was explained, for example, in a call by an animal rights activist group supporting the SHAC campaign for a demonstration at the house of the CEO of the office supplies company Staples:

> Staples might not seem to be an important part of the equation, but try running a business or a laboratory without paper, pens, paperclips and printer ink. Will Huntingdon Life Sciences simply switch to another vendor for their supplies? Probably so, but first they have to find a company that is not only willing to partner with animal abusers, but equally important, they will need to find a supplier that is willing to deal with the aggressive attention of a relentless global campaign by animal activists. (On file with author)

The activists accused "secondary targets" like Staples of "condoning" the animal cruelty practiced by HLS, calling them "collaborators in torture." In another example of the SHAC campaign's logic, a sample campaigning letter directed at the Swiss multinational pharmaceutical company Novartis, a client of HLS testing services, stated: "Novartis are condoning and encouraging this lawbreaking and cruelty by their continued financial support of HLS" (Novartis Global Week of Action 2008).

One of the defendants in the SHAC 7 case, Josh Harper, referred to SHAC's tactics as "nuisance campaigning." In his words from a 2002 speech at the University of Washington, the SHAC campaign "was people like all of us making that phone call every day. It was people like us setting [sic] at home on our computer, and maybe we've got a graphic design program, so we make up a poster that says anything, bike for sale, something like that, and it has Stevens' phone number on it" (Case SHAC 7, tape of speech in exhibit 8018:27). Stephens was the CEO of an investment bank that cancelled a $33 million loan to HLS following rioting at his offices in Little Rock and vandalism of his property (CrimethInc 2011). He was quoted as saying, "We were aware of the activists, but I don't think we understood exactly to what lengths they would go." Many companies incurred enormous costs due to SHAC tactics of "Electronic Civil Disobedience" or "virtual sit-ins" like phone or email "blockades" in which many activists would call or email at the same time to tie up companies' employees, make it hard for customers to reach them, and crash their websites. Another tactic was the "black fax," which makes a company essentially unreachable by fax by tying up the fax line with black pages that exhaust the ink cartridge. In another instance of "nuisance campaigning," an activist threw a stink bomb into an office, prompting people to leave the building for the day, costing the company $750,000 (Case SHAC 7, tape of speech in exhibit 8018:28).

Home visits challenge some of the assumptions regarding freedom of speech in the political arena, such as the accepted division between "public" and "private" spheres. Home visits turn the politics of animal testing from a public issue subject to collective social debate and a simple business decision based on legislative requirements into a matter of personal choice and, thus, subject to notions of private accountability. For SHAC activists, working at HLS or being affiliated with HLS did not count as a "business" decision, but was rather seen as a personal, moral decision. According to Harper, workers "hide behind their corporate logo," (Case SHAC 7, tape of speech in exhibit 8018). In challenging the boundary between "private" and "public" that is so central to liberalism, SHAC activists targeted "people who are just flesh and blood, like you and me ... in a manner that we know is going to [...] cause them discomfort and force them to make that decision [to withdraw from HLS]" (Case SHAC 7, tape of speech in exhibit 8018:74). As the activists made it personal, they disregarded business hours, business locations or pure business arguments. Instead, they might conduct a "home visit" on Christmas Day and make jokes about the alleged mistress of a CEO (Case SHAC 7, tape of speech in exhibit 8018:78).

The campaign challenged liberal politics

The SHAC campaign was incredibly effective in driving investors, shareholders and customers away from doing business with HLS. In the UK, Huntingdon was unable to obtain any loans from banks after the harassment of employees of the Royal Bank of Scotland by animal rights activists. The British government had to step in and provide loans to HLS (Murray-West 2001). In 2001, HLS moved its headquarters from the UK to the United States, thinking that US privacy laws would make it harder for SHAC to identify and target the company's shareholders (Case SHAC 7, transcripts of hearing, 7 February 2006:44). However, the company's stock dropped from $15 per share in 1999 to $1 in 2004 (Cook 2006). During the 2006 trial against SHAC activists, the prosecutor acknowledged that SHAC's tactics had been "absolutely" effective. In reference to SHAC campaigning against the insurance brokerage company Marsh, the prosecutor noted that other companies "didn't want any part of that. That's why [they] got out" (Case SHAC 7, summation, 2006:12). Companies pulled out of doing any kind business with HLS because of the disruption that SHAC campaigning caused to their business operations and the fact that the lives of their employees were turned upside down.[2]

Whereas animal rights activists were excited to have found a model that actually worked, this was exactly the fear of companies, as pointed out by the Foundation for Biomedical Research:

> Beyond the issue of research and the debate surrounding animal rights, there is a larger and more troubling message surrounding this regrettable pattern of capitulating to activist attacks. This is because those who seek to attack any corporation for any reason have, thanks to SHAC, now been provided with an effective model to gain publicity for their cause, seriously harm the company with which it has any complaint, as well as its employees, customers and vendors. (Foundation for Biomedical Research 2006)

Similarly, Brian Cass, the Managing Director of HLS, reportedly claimed that "[t]he number of activists isn't huge, but their impact has been incredible.... There needs to be an understanding that this is a threat to all industries. The tactics could be extended to any other sectors of the economy" (CrimethInc 2011).

Unfortunately, company representatives of HLS in the United States were unwilling to be interviewed (due to "security reasons"). Instead, I had the chance to speak with representatives of a European pharmaceutical company, who – similar to the animal enterprises alliance in the United States – expressed frustration with the global SHAC campaign and the lack of governmental response. They wanted police to be aware that graffiti saying "Stop HLS" is not just harmless graffiti, but should be reported. They demanded police be more aware in order to understand that such graffiti is "not just a stupid boys' joke" but "more organized" (personal communication). Emphasizing the importance of noting the pattern, they thought that the legality of "polite" campaigning letters sent to a company "asking" it to stop animal testing should be reassessed in light of the context of "vandalism" and "terrorizing" of employees of secondary targets.

---

2   In 2007, Brian Cass, the Managing Director of HLS called upon the financial community to stop treating HLS as "radio-active" (Jack 2007).

The tactics used by some SHAC activists also led to internal debate in the animal rights activist community. Some activists viewed secondary targeting as a legitimate campaigning tactic that was also used by anti-apartheid activists (Potter 2007:2). In relation to the nuisance campaigning, a journalist once asked a SHAC activist what gives them the mandate to employ a campaign of harassment and intimidation, to which the activist responded: "our knowledge of the suffering animals endure at HLS is all the mandate we need to rescue them using any means at our disposal."[3] However, not all fellow activists were so easily convinced. During a speaking engagement in 2002 in which Harper called upon other animal rights activists to participate in the campaign, one activist criticized SHAC's methods, saying "I wouldn't want these things to happen to me." Harper was brief in his answer: "well, you are not a puppy killer." For him, a few annoying phone calls were not comparable to the horrific HLS practices that SHAC's targets were supporting through their association with the company (Case SHAC 7, tape of speech in exhibit 8018:49). When another activist in the audience asked whether SHAC's tactics would be considered appropriate if they were applied by anti-abortion activists, Harper openly rejected the liberal separation of means and ends by arguing that the justifiability of means can only be assessed with an eye to the ends: that is, the righteousness of the cause.

In sum, the SHAC campaign and its tactics of nuisance campaigning and home visits to secondary targets became controversial as it challenged basic principles of liberal politics by breaching the division between public and private, being a nuisance instead of persuasive and targeting people only secondarily connected to the practices of animal cruelty being protested. These aspects of the campaigning blurred the boundaries between protected speech/protest and potential criminal activity in the form of intimidation/harassment, which formed the basis for contention around the subsequent criminal prosecution against the SHAC campaigners.

Prosecution of SHAC campaigners running the US website

Police were frequently unable to find the perpetrators of illegal actions that occurred during or after SHAC campaign visits, such as the flipping

---

3   Video "The Mandate," uploaded by Netverkett on 13 November 2007, available at www.youtube.com/watch?v=KeJgeKCmlgU (accessed 10 May 2011).

over of a car or the spray-painting of a house. When they did manage to find the perpetrators and prosecute such actions, sentences for the acts of vandalism were low. Mobilization by an alliance of "animal enterprises" (as described in chapter 4), however, led to a shift in prosecutorial narrative from a focus on isolated cases of vandalism to the people that ran SHAC's campaign website.

The nationwide coordination and federal investigation in the SHAC prosecution, in which more than one hundred agents from the FBI and the Bureau of Alcohol, Tobacco and Firearms participated, indicates that the issue was allotted the priority and status of a national problem. FBI Director Lewis indicated in his testimony before a Senate Judiciary Committee that the SHAC members "appear to engage in conduct that, while criminal (such as trespassing, vandalism or other property damage), would not result in a significant, particularly federal, prosecution." However, he continued, "given SHAC's pattern of harassing and oftentimes criminal conduct, and its stated goal of shutting down a company" the FBI searched for other options of investigation and prosecution (Lewis 2004).

In 2004, six SHAC activists as well as the organization itself, SHAC USA Inc., were indicted for conspiracy to violate the AEPA, in addition to several counts of violating the Interstate Stalking Statute and conspiracy to use a telecommunications device to abuse, threaten and harass persons. Three of the charges identified three specific victims. However, in the prosecutorial narrative, these individual victims were meant to be illustrative of the broader problem and, in that sense, represented many more families. Thus, in line with the narrative proposed by the alliance of animal enterprises and lab scientists in their mobilization as victims of "small-scale terrorism," the prosecutor explicitly contextualized single events into a larger pattern. This was apparent, for example, when the prosecutor began his opening statement with the story of Sally D. and her little son who feared the "animal people," explicitly stating: "And that fear, ladies and gentlemen, is why we are here today, because what was happening to [S.D.] and her family was happening to families all across of [sic] America" (Case SHAC 7, stenographic account, hearing, 7 February 2006:39).

The AEPA could not be used in relation to incidents in which SHAC's campaign targets were not animal enterprises. Therefore, the Senate Judiciary Committee described environmental activists as "[a]rmed with a knowledge of existing law" that led them to "avoid direct involvement with the animal enterprise" that was the primary target of their activism (Senate

Report 2006). This perceived gap also led to the passage of the AETA. At the time of the SHAC case, though, AETA was not yet in force. Therefore, in incidents involving secondary targets, the prosecutorial narrative framed the actions of the SHAC defendants as charges under the Interstate Stalking Statute instead (McIntosh 2006). While stalking is usually associated with a different type of situation, a prosecutor argued "we interviewed a lot of people, and these people were truly stalking-victims. They were so scared, so victimized" (Interview US-13). Regardless of Huntingdon's worth on the stock market, a prosecutor emphasized that, for him, prosecuting the SHAC activists was about the individual victims and their right to a secure life (Interview US-13). In March 2006, the activists were found guilty by a jury and convicted to sentences ranging from one to six years. The convictions were affirmed on appeal.

"The generals are guiltier than the foot soldiers"

The SHAC indictment construed a causal story of actions in which the SHAC USA activists coordinated and directed the campaign:

> 19. On or about February 15, 2001, the SHAC Website posted an announcement which stated in part: "we'll be at their offices, at their doorsteps, on their phones or in their computers. There will be no rest for the wicked."
>
> 20. On or about March 6, 2001, the SHAC Website listed the "top 20 terror tactics" that could be used against organizations and individuals in order to harm HLS and ultimately cause it to shut down.
>
> 21. On or about March 31, 2001, after the SHAC Website postings described above, protesters appeared at the New Jersey residence of HJ, an HLS employee, and banged on the windows and doors at his home.
>
> 22. On or about April 2, 2001, after the SHAC Website postings described above, rocks were thrown through windows of HJ's home; one of the cars in HJ's driveway was overturned and vandalized; and a second car in HJ's driveway was also vandalized. (Case SHAC 7, indictment, 2004)

At no point during the trial did the prosecutors prove that the defendants were themselves present on 31 March or 2 April 2001 at HJ's house. On the contrary, one of the prosecutors argued that their presence at the events described was not necessary. In an interview he reflected: "The charge is not that they did this, only the conspiracy to do it. Sometimes they were there: that was not necessary, but made it easier" (Interview US-13).

The case against the SHAC activists in the US was not a case in which the facts (that is, the website and its content) were disputed, or even in which responsibility for those facts was disputed. The issue disputed was the qualification of those facts as a "crime." Indeed, SHAC activists, including the defendants, repeatedly explained their tactics in detail in public speeches. The defendants did not hide their role in running the campaign's website. The activists were not fugitives on the run or hiding underground. Instead, they had well-known offices (even included in pictures in the prosecutor's exhibited evidence).

Yet, the prosecutor painted the defendants as "generals in a war," a war in which other activists served as "foot soldiers." Within this narrative, the prosecutor argued that the defendants could not exempt themselves from the illegal actions that happened as part of the broader campaign, asserting that "The law is not naïve" (Case SHAC 7, stenographic account, Summation, 2006:14). The prosecutor pointed out that it is legally possible to conspire without knowing all of your co-conspirators (2006:69). What is required is that everyone be aware of the agreement and acting in furtherance of it. According to one of the defense lawyers, this meant that "The government is making the entire universe of animal rights activism and activists unindicted co-conspirators" (2006:158). Indeed, the prosecutor argued that the SHAC defendants entered into a conspiracy not only with each other, but also with unknown others who would read and act upon the calls and information posted on the SHAC website. To prove that argument, during the trial, a young student testified as a witness for the government that he had engaged in the tactics described on the SHAC website. For example, he sent black faxes to the investment banker Stephens because it was announced as a SHAC tactic.

In his closing statement in front of the jury, the prosecutor described how the SHAC website listed actions like smashing the windows of a home, vandalizing a car, making threatening calls at all hours of the night, sending email "bombs" to crash computers, and ordering goods and services in other people's names. He pointed out that above this list, the SHAC website included the words: "don't read this as an extensive list of accomplishments to be proud of, which [it is], but a list that can be outdone and surpassed" (Case SHAC 7, Summation, 2006:26). The prosecutor emphasized that the website called upon activists to "make your home visits count" accompanied by three pictures: one of a home demo, one of an HLS worker's car flipped, and one of an HLS worker's house with red paint on it. He asked rhetorically: "where does it say, write a letter to these people? It certainly doesn't say that, and those pictures don't certainly [sic] suggest it" (2006:30). In an interview, one of the prosecutors explained why the information on the website makes the defendants criminally liable:

> The first time I can claim that I didn't know that you were really going to do that. The second and third time I know that you are actually going to do it. And every time I announce the success of the organization. At some point during the continuum, you become complicit. We indicted the people in the leadership roles. [...] If you fight a war, they were generals sitting at their desks, planning. The generals are guiltier than the foot soldiers: they provide information and they were the ones that took the credit. These defendants were on the phone saying: "we did it." These defendants decided that the targets were going to be Deloitte & Touche. That person is to me as guilty as the foot soldier. (Interview US-13)

Without the SHAC website, there would be no campaign, he argued. In the prosecutorial narrative, defendants went on to a next target "knowing that in the past when they had identified targets, violent acts and illegal acts followed" (Case SHAC 7, Summation, 2006:11).

To counter the prosecutorial narrative, the defendants pointed out that the SHAC website not only provided addresses of targets and ideas for tactics, but was primarily geared toward providing information on the vivisection practices at HLS in order to inform the public of the reasons for the campaign and its demand that animal experimentation be stopped. Much of this information was based on investigations done by Michelle Rokke, an activist with People for the Ethical Treatment of Animals (PETA), who was employed as an associate technician at HLS from September 1996 until May 1997. During this period, she secretly videotaped the behavior of her co-workers, took documents from desks, and copied files from computers. Information on practices involving animal cruelty at HLS collected by Rokke became publicly available and was thus later featured on the SHAC website. The defense attorney for the SHAC activists argued that "you can't look at the website without looking at the entire context of the website, including the educational stuff" (Case SHAC 7, hearing, 7 February 2006:11).

While the SHAC website was the centerpiece of the indictment and, for the defendants, providing information on prevailing practices in animal industries formed a key part of its mission, the prosecutor sought to explicitly exclude any information from undercover investigations from the courtroom discussion. He referred to the undercover investigations as "nothing more than trespassing or being on the Huntingdon Life Sciences' property under false pretenses" and "hearsay" (Case SHAC 7, stenographic account, hearing, 7 February 2006:7–8) arguing that "It's our position Huntingdon Life Sciences is not on trial here, and understanding a certain amount of this information is going to leak in, we don't think that the defense should be permitted to open on, or cross-examine on [...] the five undercover investigations" (Case SHAC 7, stenographic account, hearing, 7 February 2006:9).

Thus, the prosecutorial narrative successfully contextualized the defendants' website activities in relation to what "was happening to families all across of America," while rejecting the relevance of information about HLS's vivisection practices. The prosecutor's choice to focus on the people running the website while letting the "foot soldiers" go was supported and legitimized by the terminology proposed and pattern construed by the prosecutorial narrative. After a number of arrests and convictions of SHAC activists, not only in the United States, but also across Europe, activists officially ended the campaign in 2014 (Peachey 2014).

The prosecutorial narrative establishes a line between free speech and (incitement to) intimidation

According to a defense lawyer for one of the activists, "SHAC decided to leave the ranks, to be unpopular, be aggressive, and be offensive." She noted, "They were unaware, though, that what they were doing might be considered illegal" (Interview US-14). Supporters emphasized the "chilling effect" that the SHAC case would have on activism more generally. In a publication titled "Punishing Protest: Government Tactics That Suppress Free Speech," the US National Lawyers Guild argued that the SHAC case "reveals a de facto censorship of the activist communities' First Amendment rights by attempting to criminalize the use of the internet by activists" (Boghosian 2007:17). Cooperating counsel Matthew Strugar claimed that the court's decision gave the government "carte blanche to prosecute organizers of internet-based social justice campaigns that involve any hint of intimidation by rogue third parties. That kind of liability flies in the face of decades of Supreme Court precedent" (CCR 2010a). Due to this concern, even activists uncomfortable with the tactics advocated by SHAC disagreed with the criminal prosecution against them. Thus, the SHAC case raised the question of under what conditions those raising public awareness about a controversial issue could be held criminally liable for illegitimate acts of intimidation carried out by others for the same cause.

Brent McIntosh, Deputy Assistant Attorney General of the US Justice Department, addressed the accusation of a "chilling effect" on free speech in a 2006 hearing before the Subcommittee on Crime, Terrorism, and Homeland Security on the proposed AETA:

> Before I conclude, let me spend a moment on people the Department does not prosecute. The Department is acutely aware of the importance of protecting the first amendment rights of those who lawfully protest the treatment of animals. Let me say this as clearly as I can: The department does not prosecute and does not wish to prosecute those who lawfully seek to persuade others. (McIntosh 2006)

As explained to the jury during the SHAC 7 trial, speech or conduct loses its First Amendment protection if it rises to the level of a "true threat" or "intimidation" (Jury Charge, 27 February 2006:58). In his opening statement, the prosecutor addressed the "line" between permitted political engagement, on the one hand, and illegal action, on the other:

> We all encourage our young people to be involved in the social issues of the day, but always within a framework of what is just and what is fair. What we don't encourage and where we draw the line is that lawless behavior that steps on the rights of others, because we don't want people involved in causing what happened to Sally [D] and her family. In this case, the evidence will show that the defendants went well over the line. They went from having a concern for animal welfare, something that is worthwhile and praiseworthy, to a campaign of thuggery and intimidation. (Case SHAC 7, stenographic account, hearing, 7 February 2006:40)

Throughout the trial, the prosecutorial narrative framed this "line" as a clear-cut boundary that the SHAC defendants clearly crossed: "There is a line between advocating your beliefs, which these defendants, like anyone, have a right to do, and threatening someone to get them to do what you want" (Case SHAC 7, Summation, 2006:85). The prosecutor claimed that other animal rights organizations protesting against HLS "knew about that line, and they stayed on the right side" (Case SHAC 7, Summation, 2006:86). For instance, he mentioned, other animal rights organizations did not list the home addresses of employees on their websites or encourage others to throw bricks through people's windows. The prosecutor was very specific about what the defendants should have done differently to maintain legitimacy: "If this is a campaign about education you might go to the decision makers and want to talk to them about what animal testing is all about" (Case SHAC 7, Summation, 2006:31). He quoted defendant Lauren Gazzola, who described the reason for insurance provider Marsh pulling out of HLS as: "We fucked them up and then they pulled out." The prosecutor emphasized that these were "Her words. Not we educated them. Not we appealed to their conscience" (Case SHAC 7, Summation, 2006:10).

Thus, the prosecutorial narrative responded to and refuted the claims by defendants and their supporters that the role of the SHAC campaigners running the website was well within the bounds of legitimate protest. The prosecutor argued that the personal information published on the SHAC website regarding where employees live, what they look like, where their kids go to school or where they attend church, could only have been obtained by "stalking" someone and its publication could in no way be understood as an attempt to "educate" the employee whose information was publicly exposed. Instead, in combination with the mention of the "top twenty terror tactics" on the SHAC website and knowledge of what happened to other "targets," the prosecutor argued that the purpose of publishing this information could only be understood as a means to threaten the employee. Countering this interpretation, activist and journalist Will Potter pointed out that this list of terror tactics was originally created by the Research Defence Society, a British animal testing lobby group that supported Huntingdon. As he put it: "in typical SHAC style, the group republished the list online with a note about its origins" (2011b:100). Defending the activists' right to free speech, one of the defense lawyers pointed out that the website and tactics, such as copying the "top twenty terror tactics" often constituted "satire" (field notes, conference, November 2007). Thus, the prosecutorial narrative and the narrative of the defendants and their supporters presented fundamentally different understandings of where the boundaries of protected speech and peaceful assembly lie and when speech (educational or satire) turns into a threat.

The SHAC case was not the last prosecutorial attempt to criminalize the publishing of addresses and home visits. In 2009, animal rights activist Kevin Olliff and ALF press officer Linda Greene were indicted for a conspiracy to commit the crime of stalking and threatening two UCLA (University of California Los Angeles) professors and a juice company executive. The prosecutors replicated the use of the stalking statute pioneered in the SHAC case, thus reproducing the same prosecutorial narrative. Among other things, both defendants were alleged to have participated in home visits. Linda Greene was further said to have published an ALF communiqué about a Molotov cocktail that was placed in front of a UCLA professor's doorstep. As the first of the overt acts in the alleged conspiracy, the prosecutor described how "unnamed and/or unidentified co-conspirators" provided information about the professor "as the 'target' on the website uclaprimatefreedom.com, publishing her photograph, date of birth, personal contact information and a statement about her alleged animal experimentation at UCLA" (Indictment Greene and Olliff 2009). The prosecutor even tried to convince the judge that the actions were committed as part of a gang, which would raise the sentence. The judge, however, ruled that "ALF does not meet the legal requirements to be considered a gang. Their primary goal is to save animals, not commit crimes" (IndyBay.org 2010). Olliff was sentenced to three years in prison and Greene to five years probation (Reuters 2010).

In 2010, the first case of home demonstrations charged under the AETA came before a judge. The indictment described the behavior of the four defendants as "criminal trespass, harassment, and intimidation at a bio-medical researcher's residence in the East Bay," which was construed as an overt act in the conspiracy to violate AETA. Defense lawyers claimed that the activists were only "chanting, leafleting and chalking on public sidewalks in front of University of California researchers' homes, and using the Internet to conduct research on the activities of the protested company" (CCR 2010b). Others, however, did not see innocent chanting and leafleting, but threats and intimidation. "Any reasonable person would see it as threats," said J. David Jentsch, a neuroscientist at UCLA who experienced such harassment himself (Miller 2010).

On 12 July 2010, a judge dismissed the indictment, arguing that it did not sufficiently specify the criminal conduct alleged to have been committed by the four defendants. She deemed this important because "the species of behavior in question spans a wide spectrum from criminal conduct to con-stitutionally protected political protest. While 'true threats' enjoy no First Amendment protection, picketing and political protest are at the very core of what is protected by the First Amendment" (Case AETA4, 2010). While the case did not result in a conviction, it demonstrated a continued attempt to prosecute these activities as terrorism. At the same time, the judges were receptive to the narrative proposed by prisoner supporters about the importance of protecting the right to political protest.

Not only the publishing of addresses and home visits, also other public protests have become the focus of prosecutions, not necessarily ending in convictions though. In July 2015, four activists in Oregon were charged with harassment, criminal mischief, and disorderly conduct after using washable chalk to write slogans such as "Save the animals" on a public street as part of the "No New Animal Lab" campaign. Within two weeks the charges were dropped (Potter 2015b). In turn, the activists filed a lawsuit against the police who arrested them for violating their right to free speech (Brown 2017). In a similar case in August 2015, two animal rights activists in Utah were charged with protesting against an amusement park's treatment of animals, for failing to pay a US$50 fee and complet-ing a permit application. The activists occasionally chanted and held signs that said "Stop imprisoning animals" (Potter 2015a). After a countersuit by the activists together with the Utah legal clinic and the American Civil Liberties Union (ACLU) calling the ordinance unconstitutional, the charges were dropped a month later (Jones and Curtis 2015). These cases show the ongoing contestation of the prosecutorial categorization of activist tactics to draw public attention to the treatment of animals.

Another controversial activist practice is undercover investigations. In response to the investigations by Michelle Rokke in the 1990s, Hunting-don filed a civil lawsuit against both Rokke and PETA for stealing trade secrets and trying to put HLS out of business. In another case in 2015, an animal rights activist was sentenced to 45 days jail after photographing and rescuing several ducks from a *foie gras* producer in New York (Potter 2015c). According to the American Society for the Prevention of Cruelty to Animals (ASPCA), during the past decade, the animal-agriculture industry has been behind the introduction of a number of "ag-gag" bills, prohibiting covert investigation on the agricultural industry. Due to the opposition of groups like ASPCA as well as a number of constitutional challenges, not all industry efforts have turned into legislation. Still, in 2019, ag-gag laws existed in eight states (ASPCA 2019; Animal Legal and Historical Center

2019). There have hardly been any prosecutions under these laws yet. In 2014, four activists in Utah were charged for photographing a factory farm (Potter 2014). The agricultural interference charges were later dropped, though, while a count of trespass remained (Whitehurst 2015). As long as these tactics of animal rights activists remain controversial, the battle over the judicial interpretation of whistleblowers who record and distribute photo and video materials on industrial farms will not be over.

The construction of a pattern to impose criminal liability

In order to legitimize the charges and the chosen defendants, one of the prosecutors in the SHAC 7 case specifically distinguished between the (criminal) SHAC campaign and other (legitimate) animal rights activity. Given widespread public support for moderate environmental and animal welfare demands, he made it a point during the trial to emphasize the "glaring difference" between SHAC and other animal rights organizations that did not go to the same "extremes" because "they did not want to break the law." Similarly, the US Justice Department allied with the Humane Society, a prominent animal welfare organization, when deputy assistant Attorney General McIntosh claimed to have met with them and publicly stated that "the Department has found wide common ground with members of the Humane Society. [...] We all agree that any tactic or strategy of involving violence or threats of violence is not to be tolerated" (McIntosh 2006). The prosecutorial narrative thus sought to marginalize SHAC activists from the broader animal rights community, severing links of solidarity and sending a strong message to the more moderate groups and individuals to distance themselves from SHAC's tactics of "nuisance campaigning."

The publication of addresses of potential targets for animal rights and environmental protest has long been controversial. Before activists started publishing home addresses in the SHAC campaign, the Final Nail was a list of targets made by activists for animal "liberation" activities, including laboratory animal suppliers, trappers, slaughterhouses and fur farmers. Contrary to criticism by animal enterprises and the FBI that likened such tactics to making "hit lists" for terrorists, activists like Peter Young openly emphasized the power of such information:

What I believe would see the greatest surge of direct action is providing people with more names and addresses. This is what made The Final

Nail so successful in the 90s, and it's what has made the anti-HLS campaign so successful today. It is something that would make animal abuse no longer an abstraction but something with an exact physical location, erasing most people's excuse for turning away. (Young 2005b)

Despite the SHAC convictions in 2006, activists continued to publish names and addresses of potential targets for animal rights activism. In 2018, the website of the Final Nail was still accessible, with a disclaimer stating that "any names and addresses on FinalNail.com are published solely for educational, research or other lawful purposes. We do not encourage illegal activities." Lawyers have warned activists, however, that such disclaimers may not protect them from future prosecution. One activist reported that this situation has left her careful with public statements and fearful that distributed information might lead to raids by the FBI (Interview US-16).

Within liberal legalist frameworks, people can only be held criminally liable for their own conduct. However, different types of involvement in the commission of an offense, such as aiding and abetting, incitement, conspiracy or membership in an organization, can also lead to criminal liability. Prosecutors in many of the criminal cases examined in this book argued that defendants were supposedly manipulated or following orders, and did not make their own decisions or invent their own actions. In the prosecutorial narrative, young animal rights and environmental activists in the US were incited by the writing of ideologues; Mapuche smallholders manipulated by foreigners; and decision-making in the ETA hierarchy followed a Leninist approach that dictated precise roles, such as the youth cells committing acts of *kale borroka*. These images shifted the attention of prosecutors away from the people who directly engaged in the alleged criminal conduct to those supposed to have ordered or incited the actions in question.

Following that crime image, in the US, prosecutorial narrative – pushed by the mobilization of animal enterprises and the FBI – shifted from a focus on separate events of vandalism toward the construction of a pattern. Prosecutors contextualized the posts on the SHAC website in a broader series of events to impose criminal responsibility on the defendants for the actions of vandalism committed by other activists. A similar narrative device of pattern construction was also employed by Spanish prosecutors against those suspected of involvement in *kale borroka* in the Basque Country and in a number of prosecutions against Mapuche activists in

Chile. By relying on pattern narratives, prosecutors no longer needed to prove that a specific defendant was present or participated in a particular criminal incident. Prosecutorial narrative thus came to rely on a contextualization which was invariably contested.

12

Conclusion: The Prosecutor's Contested Claim to Criminal Justice

The dual challenge for prosecutors in liberal democracies

In the introduction, I wrote that this book can be seen as a long response to a prosecutor in Chile, who assured me that she was "just applying the law" in criminal cases against Mapuche activists. Yet, in the "hot" context of the Chilean–Mapuche territorial conflict, she was certainly aware that prosecutions involved choices with political consequences. The decision to charge Mapuche activists as terrorists, for example, let prosecutors use anonymous witnesses. Landowners believed anonymous witnesses were the only way to secure convictions, while Mapuches firmly believed such witnesses to be bribed and lying, confirming for them the injustice of such prosecutions. Vidal's statement, however, reflects an ideal that is very much alive. Her words reflect the desire of prosecution offices in Chile, Spain and the United States to avoid getting mired in the politics of a case. The refusal to openly acknowledge the complexity of "just applying the law" communicates the prosecutors' commitment to the promise of legitimacy and justice expected from faithful adherence to the rule of law in liberal legalist frameworks.

Criminal law aspires to legitimate, "euphemise and authorise" coercion and the use of state force (Bhuta 2005:245). As Kirchheimer pointed out, to do so effectively, a trial must bring contested events "from the realm of private happenings and partisan constructions into an official, authoritative and quasi-neutral sphere" (1961:422). At stake, then, is nothing less than a battle over the legitimate use of the state's coercive power and the establishment of legal order. The competing voices of "victims" and "prisoner supporters" in the meta-conflict of a contentious episode transform the "official, authoritative and quasi-neutral sphere" of trials, exposing the multiple possible constructions of reality.

Prosecutorial narrative often seems like an objective description of events. However, the examples in this book show that meaning-making is an inherent part of building a criminal case. Making competing narratives visible can reveal how prosecutorial narrative is not a natural statement of fact, but an inevitably particular and partial version of events. The examples from episodes in Chile, Spain, and the United States have shown how changes in prosecutorial narrative can expand criminal responsibility and turn courtrooms into central sites of contentious politics, where prosecutors play a lead role in establishing the accepted vocabulary and hegemonic definition of a situation. Despite liberal legalism's claim to bracket political ideologies, criminal proceedings can become the arena in which political contention is played out.

As a way to think about the many possible modalities of criminalization, this book has sought to unpack the analytical boundary between the political arena and the criminal justice arena, as well as the processes and narratives that constitute, reject, move, and modify this boundary. During the trial against the *Lonkos* of Traiguén in Chile, I approached the assistant prosecutor and asked whether the opening statement of the lead prosecutor – tracing Mapuche–Chilean relations since the "Pacification of the Araucanía" – had not been somewhat political. "Not at all!" he replied. Instead, he argued that the opening statement had "technically" addressed all the elements that would be necessary to prove that the defendants' conduct constituted "terrorist" arson and threats (field notes April 2003). This set me on a path to explore competing meanings of political and technical modalities of criminal prosecution in cases of contentious criminalization, conceptualized as the contested expansion of the criminal justice arena at the expense of the political arena. As an ethnographic analysis, this book sheds light on the micro-encounters and mechanisms behind broad terms like "criminalization" and "rule of law."

This concluding chapter serves to reiterate the main points elaborated throughout the book. It returns to the conceptualization of prosecutorial narrative as part of an ongoing conversation in society and revisits the mobilization by interest groups in the criminal justice arena, including victimhood and prisoner support narratives that aim to influence prosecutors to initiate, change, or drop criminal proceedings. It then summarizes the shifts in discursive choices in prosecutorial narratives in action in Spain, Chile, and the United States. It highlights how contextualization

devices led to expanded criminal liability, how processes of criminalization sidelined political grievances, and how prosecutors differentiated
between groups whose consent they considered necessary versus those
they felt could be marginalized without risking the ability to maintain
order and legitimacy. Finally, this chapter reflects on the limits of what a
criminal justice system can accomplish in a divided and unequal society.

The conversation in the co-production of criminal justice

This book approached criminalization as a process of translation and trans-
formation from everyday reality into the specific legal reality of criminal
law logic, doctrine, and concepts. Every choice a prosecutor makes relies
on and reproduces a certain definition of a situation. It entails choosing
a perpetrator, a victim, a certain act, and a charge. Examples in this book
have shown that using doctrinal devices like charging an "organization"
leads prosecutors to create an image of a group that fits a particular definition of the situation. In Chile, for instance, although Mapuche activists
defended CAM as a legitimate organization engaged in a justified struggle,
prosecutors framed CAM as a well-trained hierarchical organization with
connections to foreign terrorist groups. Similar narratives competed
around the composition and motives of those engaged in *kale borroka*
(street struggle) in Spain or "cells" of animal rights and environmental
activists in the US.

In this analysis of criminal prosecutions as communicative acts, prosecutorial narrative was loosely viewed in relation to criminal law as *"parole"*
stands to *"langue"* á la Saussure (see Barthes 1977:13), that is, criminal law
is that which is codified and not used, whereas prosecutorial narrative is
the application and use of criminal law language. As prosecutors recon-
structed contentious events in Spain, Chile, and the United States, they
subjected these events to the operations of the criminal justice system and
drew boundary lines between the political arena and the criminal justice
arena. This book traced changes in these prosecutorial narratives. At
times, actual changes in protest actions – such as when Mapuche activists
pioneered "productive land occupations" – precipitated a change in prosecutorial narrative. At other times, the emergence of new evidence – such
as seized documents from the ETA leadership – led to a reframing. In many
examples in this book, though, prosecutors did not argue that there were
changes in facts on the ground or that new evidence warranted a different
discursive choice. Instead, narrative shifts were frequently defended as

amended strategies that better fit the "reality" or more effectively yielded convictions.

Interventions in these conversations about crime and justice can present fundamentally different representations of reality and can be deeply morally charged: What is ETA? Who is the real eco-terrorist? Do the defendants really represent the Mapuche people? Prosecutorial answers to these questions are not neutral and objective, but this is not only due to individual prosecutorial bias. Liberal legalism assumes that individuals executing the law are biased, which it accounts for through inbuilt checks and balances, such as the need to argue on the basis of legal provisions and established jurisprudence, and by providing defendants with an opportunity to appeal verdicts. Yet, despite explicit efforts on the part of prosecutors to present criminal trials as objective, in line with the liberal presumption of innocence and the strict use of evidence to reach individualized conclusions, the examples in this book show how prosecutors can perpetuate certain perspectives on and stereotypes of criminality. Moreover, they demonstrate how prosecutorial narrative inevitably tells a story that prioritizes particular voices in a contentious episode, while marginalizing others.

To a certain degree, criminal proceedings are always a site of contestation. Prosecutors and defense lawyers face off in a battle over the interpretation of events and the determination of fact and fiction, legal and illegal. While dispute over the role and conduct of the defendant is the routine material of contestation in the courtroom, the cases in this book have focused on the various voices in these criminal proceedings engaged in discursive struggle over (1) whether the events/conduct in question should be dealt with in the criminal justice arena at all, and (2) what context should be considered relevant for interpreting the disputed events/conduct. The comparison of competing narratives in Chile, Spain, and the US has sought to "de-naturalize" or "de-familiarize" (Chandler 2002:227) the prosecutorial narratives, revealing the choices and assumptions they took for granted. Federal prosecutors in the United States, for example, did not prosecute the Huntingdon Life Sciences laboratory for "animal cruelty" or "murder" for killing 500 animals per day in commercial product testing. The prosecutor told a certain story, in which economic damage and fear were emphasized rather than animal rights. That these choices in prosecutorial narrative are taken for granted as natural betrays an essential feature of the hegemonic discourse being reproduced through prosecutorial narrative and judicial decisions.

In contentious prosecutions, an enormous number of people engage with the language of criminal law. In Chile, for example, the co-production of criminal justice took place in meetings between high-level officials in Santiago, around the fireplace in remote Mapuche community homes, in public demonstrations in Temuco, and in business emails between forestry companies. While the different actors and organizations involved all drew upon (at times by explicitly rejecting) the same basic framework provided by liberal criminal law – including the dichotomy between victim and perpetrator, liberal notions of equality, and the presumption of innocence – how they translated their lived experiences and assigned meaning to them within the same framework often differed greatly. The analysis also showed how, over time, prosecutorial definitions of crime can change. Symbolic land occupations by Mapuche activists that were considered radical criminal acts in the early 1990s would no longer be considered so today.

Polarization

Criminal trials are nerve-wracking. The presence of opposing parties, the potential of jail-time, and the lack of certainty about the truth all come together to make a criminal trial a tense event. The moment in which the verdict is handed down and judgment pronounced is the most serious of all. As I attended politically charged trials in Spain, Chile, and the United States, I often had no neutral place to sit in the courtroom. The benches on one side were generally the province of supporters of the defendant, while the benches on the other were occupied by supporters of the proclaimed victims. This divided visual orchestration of the courtroom is iconic of the polarization and identification split of societal groups through the mutually exclusive roles of victim and defendant. Frequently, witnesses would be divided along the relevant identity groups as well. The few Mapuches who ever testified for the prosecution were considered traitors by Mapuche activists, and thus presented as anonymous witnesses. During trials, they would appear behind a folding screen, while speaking through a voice-changing device, enabling interrogation by defense lawyers, while avoiding repercussions. Commercial landowners in Chile, on the other hand, often cooperated as witnesses for the prosecution. Their statements in the cases of fellow non-Mapuche farmers served to sketch a pattern. In this way, criminal justice dynamics influence interactions outside the courtroom by cementing divisions or even fomenting polarization. The claim that liberal criminal justice systems apply the law equally to everyone loses traction once the roles of victims and perpetrators become systematically allocated to competing actors, namely defenders and challengers of the status quo in divided, unequal societies. Ultimately, the prosecutorial claim to criminal *justice* remains contested.

Two activists from Gesto por la Paz in the Basque country explicitly warned of polarizing dynamics due to criminal proceedings (*El Correo*, 27 January 2008). They recounted a day in which in the morning a demonstration criticized the verdict in macro-trial 18/98 and in the afternoon a demonstration protested an ETA attack causing two deaths. As a testimony of the polarization in the Basque Country, they observed that it had become impossible in the perception of the public to attend both demonstrations and still have a coherent position, even though rejecting the violence of ETA does not mean that one accepts *any* measure taken in the struggle against ETA (such as, in their examples, the 18/98 trial or the closure of newspaper *Egunkaria*). Similarly, criticizing the measures taken by the state does not mean that one accepts ETA violence.

Skepticism toward the judicial system among parts of the population in Spain, Chile, and the US led people to refuse to contribute to criminal investigations. Such refusal to cooperate poses a challenge to prosecutors. Not only do they rely on the public for testimonies and leads to perpetrators, in liberal democracies prosecutors also need to present their charges as legitimate and well-founded. By providing convincing evidence upon which judges and juries can give their verdict "beyond a reasonable doubt," prosecutors can clear away any assumptions or prejudices as to the guilt or innocence of defendants. Providing convincing evidence can be difficult, though, when sympathizers host fugitives and refuse to testify in court and the credibility of evidence is disputed. Allegations of torture in Spain to extract confessions, suspicion of bribes for anonymous witnesses in Chile, and accusations of entrapment by FBI informants in the United States undermined the credibility of the prosecutor's evidence in the eyes of significant portions of the population. These different public perceptions of the evidence presented in the courtroom posed a challenge for prosecutors as they tried to present their cases as unbiased and valid.

Polarization can thus make the criminal justice system incapable of generating a shared truth. For example, landowners in Chile interpreted the high acquittal rate of Mapuche activists as an indication that evidentiary thresholds were too strict to achieve justice. Mapuche activists, on the other hand, read acquittals as a confirmation of the defendants' innocence and the unjust repression of Mapuche activism by prosecutors. Different interpretive communities thus "decode" criminal justice messages, like indictments and verdicts, in different ways, fomenting further polarization. Prisoner supporters and victim mobilizers engage in signifying practices in order to communicate their "preferred reading" of a situation, as when prisoner supporters invert the meaning of the prison sentence from condemnation into heroic resistance.

Interest groups put pressure on prosecutors

In most of the criminal cases in the selected episodes, prosecutors faced criticism from multiple sides. They were often simultaneously accused of being too repressive by some and too lax by others. This pervasive discontent in contentious prosecutions in the criminal justice arena is the most persuasive piece of evidence suggesting that criminal prosecutions and "rule of law" should not be expected to "solve" protracted conflicts. All too often, it is assumed that when both sides of a political conflict are dissatisfied with the performance of the criminal justice system and its proceedings, the system is actually performing as it should. Yet, the opposite is often true. Rather than finding a satisfactory middle ground, the state is failing both sides. Shifting issues over which there is no societal consensus into the logic and language of criminal law can lead to proceedings that are both needlessly oppressive toward defendants *and* ineffective in satisfying victims in their search for truth and protection.

The examples offered in this book show the need for skepticism of the "truth" produced in democratic courtrooms and to critically question the underlying interests and logic of prosecutions: What narrative does the prosecutor present? Who pushes this narrative in society? What other narratives are marginalized as a result?

While this book rejects the notion that law is autonomous, it also does not support the view that law is just an instrument in the hands of the elite and simply politics by other means. Law and its enforcement are more complicated than that. Paradoxically, law can make ruling elites go against their short-term interest in order to maintain long-term legitimacy (Thompson 1975). For Thompson (1975:265), in his study of 18th-century England, the elite seems to be synonymous with the upper-class or political oligarchy. Following a more useful definition by Khan (2012), elites are those who have vastly disproportionate access to or control over social resources, whether economic, political, or cultural, thus providing them with social power and economic rewards.

If elites had it their way entirely, criminal prosecutions in the contexts researched would probably have looked very different. Large transnational companies in Chile, for example, would not have had to complain about the lack of convictions of those encroaching on their estates. Indeed, while indisputably having disproportionate access to economic and political resources – and Mapuche activists thus often speak about forestry companies in Chile as powerful actors – the general manager of CORMA (an association of forestry companies) in the 9th Region has claimed the opposite, insisting "We are weak! If we had power, we would not have been forced to sell lands. Then there would not have been arsons" (Interview 2003, C-35). The chief of public relations from the company Forestal Mininco agreed, noting "they are threatening us with a match," while lamenting that the company did not have much room for maneuver due to market competition (Interview 2003, C-17).

A transnational corporation or a Chilean landowner such as Agustín Figueroa, who was also a member of Chile's Constitutional Court and former Minister of Agriculture, can be classified as elite without much trouble. The same cannot be said, however, of fur farmers in the American Midwest, who had to struggle to build up enough political clout to be seen and heard by the FBI and US prosecutors. Similarly, family members of Spain's Guardia Civil do not necessarily count as the country's elite. Their private interest in criminalizing ETA was not automatically equated with the public interest, and for years they did not enjoy privileged access to decision-makers. Mapuche activists, in contrast, despite not belonging to the country's elite, were clearly able to put significant pressure on Chilean politicians and prosecutors, due to international as well as domestic recognition of the legitimacy of their demands as indigenous people. Thus, instead of viewing the law as a simple instrument in the hands of the elite, this book has described the processes of interest groups attempting to become effective "troublemakers" (Waddington 1998) with the ability to obtain leverage over prosecutorial narratives – either mobilizing as victims or as prisoner supporters.

While elites may indeed have an easier time being recognized as effective troublemakers and thus getting their accounts of victimhood honored in criminal proceedings, this does not necessarily lead to swift and harsh prosecutions on their behalf. A practical explanation is that the state is not a monolithic entity. Many different actors are involved in criminal policy and proceedings. Prosecutors are obviously key actors, but others can include members of investigative agencies like the police or FBI, functionaries in military justice systems, or bureaucrats from ministries in charge of internal affairs or homeland security. In Spain, instruction judges were important players in deciding on prosecutions against the ETA network, while in Chile, regional governors and representatives from the Ministry for Development and Planning were involved in decisions about the criminal policy vis-à-vis Mapuche activists.

As the analysis of the contentious episodes in this book has demonstrated, different state agents do not necessarily have the same priorities or interests. In Spain, centralization of ETA cases at the Audiencia Nacional in Madrid streamlined the prosecutorial approach. In Chile, however, there was an obvious tension between regional priorities and the politics of "Santiago." For example, former Regional Governor Belmar claimed she never filed complaints using the qualification of terrorism (Comisión de Constitución 2006:11). Yet the Ministry of Internal Affairs in Santiago pushed for terrorism qualifications, due to pressures from the parliament and senate, despite the regional authorities assessing the situation differently. In Chile, the liberal ideology of the "separation of powers" sometimes turned into a "denial of responsibility," as the Mapuche conflict seemed to be tossed around like a hot potato between the various governmental powers involved. In the United States, the Department of Homeland Security criticized the FBI for its focus on animal rights and environmental groups at the expense of mass-casualty terrorism.

Another explanation for elite interest groups not always getting their way is that, at times, judges refuse to accept innovative prosecutorial narratives without solid legislative or evidentiary basis. For example, judges in Chile blocked efforts by prosecutors to get CAM convicted as a terrorist organization. Similarly, in the United States, a judge ruled that the ALF did not qualify as a gang, as their primary goal was to save animals, not commit crimes. In Spain, prosecutions of public expressions in support of ETA only took off after a new law criminalized the glorification of ETA and humiliation of its victims. Prior to this law, attempts to frame expressions of support for ETA prisoners as crimes were not easily accepted by Spanish judges, as it touched upon a core tenet of liberal legalism, that ideas cannot be punished. Arguably, unsuccessful prior prosecutions were a key step toward the enactment of the new law. Similarly, in the United States, the passage of the Animal Enterprise Terrorism Act (AETA) was preceded by prosecutions in which new images (for example, stalking) and interpretations were already tested, and in which legal boundaries were pushed. Even after interest groups succeeded in enacting new legislation, continued filing of criminal complaints was often necessary to push for the initiation of prosecutions. Thus, criminalization is an interactive process rather than a one-way street – even for interest groups belonging to a country's elite.

Prosecutorial narratives in action

Drawing on empirical examples, Part II of this book showed how criminal proceedings became the site of political mobilization and how prosecutorial narratives and charging choices changed as a consequence – responding to appeals by victim alliances or critiques leveled by prisoner support groups. During the 1970s and 1980s, prosecutors in Spain described ETA as an "enemy" in a "war" and the criminal justice arena was not viewed as an adequate venue in which to address ETA violence. Throughout the 1990s, however, the criminal justice arena became dominant in the state's dealings with ETA. This change was due to a combination of factors, including an increased transfer of autonomous competences to the Basque Country's government, ETA's qualitative leap toward killing politicians, lobbying by associations of victims of ETA violence, France overcoming its earlier refusal to extradite ETA members, as well as a decline in sympathizers' support for ETA's armed struggle.

At the same time, prosecutorial narrative cast a wider net by newly conceptualizing ETA as a network encompassing a number of Basque left-nationalist socio-political organizations as well as a newspaper. From the late 1990s onwards, this narrative shift led to so-called "macro-trials" against more than 200 alleged members of the ETA network, claiming that their socio-political work fulfilled "functions" within ETA's overarching strategy. A second narrative shift occurred when Spanish prosecutors began to interpret speech and expressions in support of "Basque political prisoners" as humiliation of victims of ETA violence or glorification of terrorism. Until a new law was enacted in 2000, such prosecutions led nowhere, as judges required prosecutors to prove that the contentious speech acts would incite crime. In a contrasting "state of exception" narrative, supporters of those imprisoned for alleged street violence or ETA membership felt their public expressions should be viewed in the context of disproportionate Spanish repression and police violence against Basque left-nationalists.

In Chile, instances of Mapuche activists physically occupying contested lands and taking wood from commercial tree plantations often went without prosecution, but at other times, protest actions led to entire organizations being charged as criminal or even terrorist. Private landowners and forestry companies were able to build a strong victim narrative to decontextualize alleged crimes by Mapuche leaders from their legitimate claims for land restitution. At the same time, the "criminalization of social protest" narrative of the Mapuche movement in Chile received substantial backing from the Inter-American Commission on Human Rights and UN Special Rapporteurs. As a result, prosecutorial efforts to appease alliances of commercial landowners through harsh convictions of Mapuche activists were often followed up by state efforts to appease Mapuche communities' underlying land claims. Some Mapuche activists spent months in pre-trial detention or years in prison for "terrorism" charges, yet many communities of Mapuche convicts were offered land deals in subsequent negotiations with state agents. Threat assessments by government actors and prosecutors over the years meandered between the specter of a "little Chiapas" and downplaying the problem entirely as merely private land disputes.

Prosecutorial narrative in Chile responded to the widespread societal recognition of legitimate land claims by insisting that "the Mapuche people" were not on trial. At the same time, however, Mapuche prisoners claimed to be political prisoners and, together with their supporters, often accused prosecutors of racism and repression against the entire Mapuche people. In response to such allegations, Chilean prosecutors frequently went to great lengths to create an image of "good" or "true" Mapuches, as a contrast to the activists standing trial. A prosecutor once argued, for example, that the traditional chiefs on trial did not represent their communities because "real Mapuches are peaceful," whereas the defendants were just "abusing their Mapuche identity" to get away with crime. Thus, prosecutorial narrative created and reproduced certain "ethnic images" (Terwindt 2009). At the same time, the purposive selection of a few defendants from a larger group of protest participants reproduced the image of a radical minority of "activists."

From the late 1990s onwards, prosecutorial narrative in the United States developed the concept of "eco-terror" to describe contentious environmental and animal rights protest. The alliance-formation, and mobilization of a victimhood discourse by so-called "animal enterprises" (universities, testing companies, etc.) managed to get the attention of the FBI and elevate "eco-terrorism" to the government's agenda. This narrative emphasized the need to prevent acts of "terrorism," thus precipitating a shift toward proactive investigations and conspiracy charges, as well as harsher sentences meant to deter similar acts. In response, activists, prisoner support groups as well as critical lawyers raised concerns about what was dubbed the "Green Scare": high sentences for some were thought to produce a chilling effect among larger groups of activists.

When law enforcement officials were unable to find the direct perpetrators of vandalism and intimidation linked to the Stop Huntingdon Animal Cruelty (SHAC) campaign against vivisection company Huntingdon Life Sciences, prosecutorial narrative shifted to criminalizing the publication of targets and tactics for animal rights campaigning. In the "SHAC 7" case, prosecutors held the SHAC website administrators criminally liable for property damage committed by any supporter of the campaign, while the defendants and their supporters criticized the criminalization of free speech and the right to associate for legitimate political goals. Prosecutorial narrative in this case used a technique common across the three episodes: narrating a pattern in order to hold a known defendant responsible for criminal acts committed by unknown others.

Sidelining political demands

When the criminal justice arena becomes the state's main forum for interacting with both challengers and defenders of the status quo, the state's approach to the matter shifts the debate from questions of the legitimacy and viability of groups' political demands to incarceration and the legality and legitimacy of criminal proceedings. Criminal justice issues can even come to replace, overshadow, or complement the original political claims (Starr et al. 2008:265). Some challengers of the status quo claim that this diversion is precisely the aim of such prosecutions. In Chile, for example, Mapuche activists all too often expended their energy on endless debates about traitors and mutual suspicion within Mapuche communities, thus weakening the movement. The displacement of political grievances to an arena and operating logic fundamentally incapable of addressing them explains the widespread impotence experienced by all actors in the Chilean–Mapuche territorial conflict. Placing conduct in the political arena (versus criminal justice arena) does not mean that such conduct is necessarily appropriate, good, or legitimate. Indeed, it can still be labeled as offensive, unpopular, and unwise. The division between these arenas is not a matter of "good" versus "bad," but a matter of different rules, understandings, consequences, and criteria guiding their operation.

During trials, prosecutors often addressed and erected the boundary between the different arenas by indicating what "belongs" where and employing a visual metaphor of "crossing the line" to describe when particular conduct might move from one arena into the other. Liberal democracies are premised on the notion that the criminal justice system should remain politically neutral by formalizing categories and excluding context. Debates about the legitimacy of the political claims underlying alleged criminal conduct were thus deliberately excluded from trials, in order to explicitly relegate the political issues to the arena where they "belong."

The transfer of political contestation to the criminal justice arena means that the relevant issues change. In the transfer process, political dynamics are reframed and defined according to the logic and language of criminal law and the roles built into the criminal justice system. By addressing the burning down of a commercial tree plantation by Mapuche activists in the criminal justice arena, the conversation shifts from a debate about how pine and eucalyptus tree plantations affect the soil quality and water availability, and hence the livelihoods of neighboring communities, to a question of whether or not the Chilean state can use anti-terrorism laws in cases of property destruction, or whether or not prisoners should have the right to perform Mapuche religious ceremonies in prison. When criminal prosecutions lead to the stigmatization of activists as criminals and statements by present-day landowners like "we don't negotiate with terrorists," the transfer of contentious protest action from the political to the criminal justice arena can be difficult to reverse, making a shift back to the negotiation table harder to sell (Della Porta and Reiter 1998:28; Zulaika and Douglass 1996:x).

Transfer of a socio-political conflict to the criminal justice arena also means, very concretely, that news coverage of the conflict changes too. Reporting inevitably shifts to reflect police and prosecutorial accounts, thus adopting certain dominant views and voices, while marginalizing others. Interestingly, in Del Valle's analysis of the sources of newspaper articles in relation to the "Mapuche conflict," it turned out that prosecutors were the most important voice represented, figuring in 26.7 percent of the articles as a source. In comparison, "victims" were only relied upon in 3.3 percent of the articles and "indigenous people" in none of the articles (2005:88). Del Valle further points to the dominance of police reports and their hierarchical superiority in the construction and establishment of "facts" in comparison to other sources of evidence.

In the divided societies analyzed in this book, radically different images existed regarding the status quo that protesters confronted. Challengers of the status quo in the United States saw animal testing as torture rather than a necessary product safety measure; producing and eating meat as murder rather than a profitable and necessary food industry; or the industrial exploitation of nature as destructive and unnecessary rather than valuable for advancing human and economic development. The images proposed by activists challenging status quo perceptions were generally ignored or actively sidelined in criminal prosecutions due to an understanding that such claims belong in the political rather than criminal justice arena. The US prosecutor in the case against SHAC campaigners argued before the jury that animal testing was a "wholly lawful activity" and not "the issue in this case [...] because the FDA [Food and Drugs Administration] requires the testing be done" (Case SHAC 7, hearing, 7 February 2006).

Instead of addressing the underlying competing interests of challengers and defenders of the status quo, a veritable cycle of criminal prosecutions emerged when defendants and their supporters were convicted for undermining the legitimacy of proceedings and state authority, in addition to their convictions for the allegedly criminal conduct of their contentious protest activity. For example, in the United States, several activists and their supporters, as well as a researcher, were jailed for contempt of court for refusing to provide information during Grand Jury hearings. In Chile, some Mapuche activists were additionally prosecuted for their disrespect of judges and aggressive behavior toward prosecutors during their trials, such as when one activist stood with his back to the judge. In such "secondary" convictions, the state communicates norms about the proper process of criminal investigation and prosecution, and attempts to enforce respect for the state's authority and legitimacy in carrying out such prosecutions. This conversation about the legitimacy of criminal proceedings can also take place outside the courtrooms, for example, when street violence was motivated by outrage about criminal justice issues, such as the detention or alleged torture of ETA militants (MA 1994:474; Van den Broek 2004:719). Once such dynamics are at play, the underlying political demands become sidelined even more.

Contextualizing devices depart from the default mode of liberal legalism

In each of the episodes, prosecutorial narrative changed significantly over time. The common patterns identified over time and across cases strengthen the claim that these changes in criminal prosecution cannot be dismissed as the result of one rogue prosecutor or a dysfunctional justice system. Instead, the observations point to the significance of the role played by interest groups and their discursive mobilization in the criminal justice arena in all liberal democracies. On more than one occasion, prosecutors in Spain, Chile, and the United States departed from a narrow focus on the protection of certain property or a specific individual, which can be defined by indicating a concrete time and place, to a broader legal interest, such as national security or democracy, which is not necessarily located in a specific time, place, or person. Difficulties in obtaining arrests or convictions of direct perpetrators spurred prosecutorial efforts to hold the "organizers" or "inciters" of criminal actions accountable. Patterns were constructed and public speeches or web entries were linked to underground acts of sabotage or vandalism. Acts that were not previously regarded as illegal came to be considered within the purview of the criminal justice arena, such as displaying pictures of imprisoned ETA militants in the streets of the Basque Country. In each of the episodes, historical accounts or previous events beyond the concrete times and places of the specific and isolated criminal conduct on trial were drawn into the courtroom.

Prosecutorial narratives thus shifted discursively from the individual to the collective, from isolated incidents to a pattern, and from a narrow legal interest to a broader legal interest, expanding the time-frame, geographical reach and number of eligible defendants in a criminal case. The narration of a pattern (of incidents) is what I call a "contextualizing device" as it allows a prosecutor to put a single incident in a broader context. In a number of proceedings, this enabled the prosecution to argue that multiple defendants should be held liable for a series of events, even though they were not present during all of those events. Such patterns were created in Spanish prosecutorial narratives against so-called "Y-groups" in cases of *kale borroka* and in US prosecutorial narratives against presumed "cells" related to the Earth Liberation Front. The examples showed how prosecutors can shift their focus from charging single individuals to the prosecution of groups and organizations, and in the process, foreground, create or draw upon collective identities. When prosecutorial narrative attempted to demonstrate connections between single events by framing them as part of a larger picture, it expanded the legally relevant context of a criminal prosecution, while simultaneously denying any political implications of doing so. A prosecutor choosing a doctrinal device for opportunistic purposes, like drawing on provisions against "stalking" or "criminal organizations" to have more investigative tools and flexibility, can inadvertently be drawn into the morass of competing contextual narratives.

In each of the contentious episodes, property destruction was redefined as an act of terrorism thus shifting the legal interest at stake. This was so, for example, with the use of Molotov cocktails by youth in Spain, animal releases in the United States, and arson of plantations in Chile. Such broadening of the terrorism label beyond incidents of personal injury was invariably contested and thus prosecutors were faced with the challenge of justifying the framing that transformed a single incident into a public emergency. Such reframing was supported by victimhood narratives emphasizing fear and danger to human lives. The concept of "terrorism" comes with existing associated images of events like the 9/11 attacks in the US. One prosecutor in the United States argued that existing preconceptions or images of terrorism raised the bar for making a convincing case: "I never thought that it was going to help me to call them [a group of animal rights activists] terrorist: white, male and female, fairly well dressed, 20-something, no one thinks they are terrorists" (Interview US-13). He argued, "they are not terrorists, but their victims are indeed terrorized." These words were remarkably similar to those of prosecutors in Chile, who made a distinction between calling the Mapuche activists "terrorists" and describing their actions as "terrorist." One prosecutor stated, "even if it is not like 'Bloody Sunday' in Northern Ireland, it is the same underlying logic" (Interview C-13).

In each of the episodes analyzed in this book, prosecutorial narrative drew upon and reproduced social identities of defendants and victims. Given that people always have multiple identities, contextualization happens when the prosecutor chooses to prioritize a political identity ("Mapuche" or "anarchist") or to identify a defendant as a member of a particular group ("ETA network"). In the US prosecutorial narrative, anarchist references were cited as part of the defendant's motive. In Chile, when prosecutors addressed Mapuche activists as "Chilean citizens", they asserted their equality before the law and, at the same time, negated their claims based on their Mapuche identity. This notwithstanding, the prosecutorial narrative also created the image of a "true" Mapuche and contributed to conceptualizing the categories "Mapuche" and "Chilean" as binary and exclusive, denying the possibility of being both and thus reproducing the polarization of Mapuches and Chileans.

Criminal law legitimizes the state's application of force, meaning prosecutorial narratives have real consequences. The examples in this book showed how prosecutorial narratives expanded the boundaries of what was considered criminal in society. This was done in three distinct ways. Some prosecutorial narratives intervened earlier in the criminalization process, by focusing on preparatory or conspiratorial activities. Others broadened the pool of potentially eligible subjects of punishment by connecting those engaged in public speeches, websites, or socio-political organizing to certain criminal events conducted by unknown perpetrators (for example, by charges of incitement, glorification, or membership in a terrorist organization). Lastly, certain prosecutorial narratives pushed understandings regarding the gravity of conduct and the harm it inflicts, thus legitimizing higher sentences. For instance, conduct that used to be considered public disorder came to be charged as terrorism.

With whom does the prosecutor speak?

To different degrees in each of the contentious episodes examined in this book, state control was weakened, challengers or defenders of the status quo followed alternative rules or authorities, and the legitimacy of the state's monopoly on the use of force was no longer recognized by all of society. In each contentious context, prosecutors sought legitimacy for their criminal proceedings by choosing which audiences to appease and which to ignore in their prosecutorial narratives. An image mobilized by prosecutors in each episode was that of a pyramid, whereby groups using violence or property destruction for a political cause were viewed as sitting on top of a broader base of sympathizers and supporters. According to this image, the state must respond to the lawbreakers without alienating the lower parts of the pyramid. Not only prosecutors, but also judges, clearly took societal approval into account in their sentencing decisions. For example, a common tactic to avoid additional outcry from prisoner supporters was the practice of sentencing convicted defendants to the time already served awaiting trial (for a similar observation, see Balbus 1973:237). In other cases, judges preferred to limit sentences to the amount of time that could be served on probation, that is, without entering prison.

Roughly, three different tendencies could be observed in the prosecutorial narratives in the contentious episodes in Spain, Chile, and the United States (adapted from Van Reenen 1979). First, an "individualized narrative" communicated to the defendant that he or she would be punished, and then allowed back into society. At the same time, this narrative communicated to the rest of society that the state takes care of maintaining norms, protecting law-abiding citizens, and punishing deviation. This "individualized narrative" is generally decontextualized and considered to be "normal" criminal justice, in line with the values of liberal legalism. The government communicates to the "extremist" that she should not continue on her present path, but should rather accept democracy and "common" values (reflecting the assumption of a society in consensus), regret her action, and society will take her back.

This approach was employed in each of the episodes and often included attempts to prohibit defendants from interacting with activist friends, or forcing them to publicly reject illegal protest methods. For example, a US judge reduced the sentence of animal rights activist Viehl after he showed remorse (Young 2010). In their plea deals and sentencing, activists Rod Coronado and Jonathan Paul were pressured into leaving activist circles and denouncing the use of "violence" by animal rights and environmental protesters. In Chile, a former CAM member told me that during a hunger strike in 2005, prisoners were pressured to stop their strike and sign a paper that would confirm that they repented for having caused harm, but they rejected the offer (Interview C-46). In Spain, the government launched a project to motivate ETA prisoners to accept the rules for a "repenting prisoner" (*arrepentido*). Even though in the early 1980s various prisoners did accept the proposal, the policy resulted in failure. ETA reacted harshly against some of the prisoners who accepted the deal with the state. Thus, governments may attempt to individualize, but defendants and their supporters may resist this strategy by collectively refusing to legitimize a prosecution, conviction or repentance.

Second, a "marginalization narrative" communicated to specific defendants that they were excluded from society. In this narrative, detention is more about incapacitation and setting an example than punishment. It communicates to sympathizers: "Don't go there." This tendency could be observed in some of the cases against animal rights and environmental activists in the US during the 2000s, in which prosecutors made it a point to separate "extremists" from "moderates." This approach assumes that there is a contingent of sympathizers among the public that must be pacified and kept from engaging in the unlawful behavior being put on trial.

To a large extent, the intended audience of the prosecutorial narrative in cases against SHAC campaigners and other animal rights or environmental activists in the United States consisted of potential future lawbreakers, "kids" who might get carried away by ideologues or the encouragement of "role models" and "heroes." The narrative isolated the "bad apples" from a larger peer group and set them apart as an example. A distinction was made, for example, between "good ways" to work for a political cause and "bad ways" to work for a political cause (or, in Chile, between a "true" Mapuche and "abuse" of identity). The US prosecutorial narrative also encouraged "moderate" and "mainstream" organizations to distance themselves from all actions and actors that had been labeled as "eco-terrorism" or "terrorist." In return, the prosecutorial narrative ensured that moderate ("welfare") demands were squarely located in the political arena. As one of the prosecutors in the SHAC 7 case emphasized, out of thousands of people who were involved in animal rights activism, only six had been indicted.

Third, a "lump narrative" communicated to sympathizers of defendants, that their support was as bad as pulling the trigger, because it enabled the crimes. This communicates to a wide range of people that their conduct may fall under the net cast by criminalization. The Spanish prosecutorial narrative from the late 1990s onwards seemed to follow this approach. It reinforced the notion that actions of support and approval, and speech acts that were previously considered to be less harmful should be *equated* with the criminal activities originally put on trial. As the counter-narrative put forward by the left-nationalist movement lost its traction in the prosecutor's offices in Madrid, the prosecutors chose to send the message that organizing and speech acts in support of ETA would not be tolerated.

The production of prosecutorial narrative can thus be interpreted as a balancing act, as it navigates between fringe and mainstream, between extremists and moderates, between radicals and compromisers – and actively co-produces the labels of these groups. As prosecutors choose their primary and secondary audiences, their narrative actively contributes to (re)producing boundaries between societal groups and pressures actors to take a stand. For example, moderate environmental organizations in the United States distanced themselves from "eco-terrorists" in what seemed to be a mutually reinforcing process: the mainstream rejection of certain activist groups provided more leeway for harsher prosecutions while, at the same time, the distance sought by moderate organizations was a consequence of these prosecutions. Prosecutors thus employ different narratives depending on their primary audience to secure public legitimacy for their criminal prosecutions.

Limits of the criminal justice system in a divided and unequal society

The bigger issue addressed in this book concerned the question of how competing definitions of crime, harm, and protest feed into the struggle of interpretation that is part and parcel of initiating and building criminal prosecutions in liberal democracies. It dug into the multiple layers constituting the shift from political contention to criminal treatment of an issue, activists, and movements. It examined the process in which prosecutors (and victim alliances) sorted out "criminalizable events" in the relations between commercial landowners and Mapuche communities in Chile, or between animal rights activists and animal enterprises in the United States. This book has shown what the criminalization of social protest means beyond people ending up in prison and the diversion of movements' resources and focus. It has shown that the process of contentious criminalization is characterized by constant mobilization inside and outside the courtroom in relation to charges, sentences, the use of anti-terrorism legislation, and narratives that claim harm and place blame on specific individuals or organizations.

So, what is the takeaway of this comparison of the contestation around and development of prosecutorial narratives in three contentious episodes? As it turns out, a lot happens outside the courtroom in contentious prosecutions that will influence what happens inside too – and vice versa. Even in liberal democracies power politics permeate criminal proceedings. Over time, discourses shifted, sometimes significantly. Groups on all sides deliberately used and produced narratives to persuade prosecutors and the broader public of their views and definitions of harm and justice. The examples in this book have shown that public support for a particular narrative is likely to influence prosecutorial decision-making. Prosecutors in liberal democracies are easily drawn into contextualizing narratives; this is also evident in episodes not studied here. For example, during what were labeled as "riots" in London in August 2011, judges sentenced a man to 18 months in custody for handling a stolen television due to the "widespread fear caused by the riots as an aggravating factor," while in ordinary circumstances this probably would have led to a community sentence (*Economist* 27 August 2011: 30). Such severe punishment was supported by the general public according to a survey that stated that 70 percent of voters thought that sentences should be more severe for crimes committed during the riots (ICM Poll, in *Economist* 27 August 2011).

Criminal proceedings function as a site of political struggle in contentious episodes beyond those selected in this book. For example, in 2016, several European politicians called for the criminalization of people who supported refugees along the Balkan route to Europe. When prosecutors responded to such calls by initiating criminal investigations, their prosecutorial narratives often built on specific protectionist discourses about the right to asylum and the role of smugglers, in contrast to the narrative of open borders proclaimed by the refugee supporters themselves. The examples and analysis offered in this book highlight common features in how discursive mobilization influences prosecutorial narrative, shaping criminal investigations, driving prosecutorial choices and feeding back into political contention. Furthermore, I have argued that the contentious processes described in the construction and functioning of prosecutorial narrative are built into the very premise of the rule of law.

Targets of protest activity in each of the episodes have frequently appealed to the state for protection. At times this was granted, such as when forestry companies in Chile were offered police protection against arson and theft during the felling of woods (Informe Especial 2016). In other instances, targets were unprotected by the state. While this should be taken seriously, under pressure of powerful "victims," prosecutors should not inflate charges to come under anti-terrorism legislation in a desperate bid for effective deterrence. Nor should they prosecute just anyone who seems remotely connected to the offense. In many of the criminal cases discussed in this book, the defendants were not direct perpetrators, but related in some form to illegal activity – often not closely enough to justify a criminal conviction. In response, prosecutors frequently resorted to charges of conspiracy, of belonging to a terrorist organization, or glorification of terrorism in order to argue for convictions.

These prosecutions were often on an uneasy footing in relation to basic liberal principles, such as freedom of speech, freedom of association, a concrete and narrowly defined legal interest, individual responsibility, guilt for past harm instead of future danger, strict protection of the defendant as potentially innocent (instead of long pre-trial detention), criminal justice as a last resort, and fair individual retribution (instead of example-setting deterrent sentences). Moreover, the legislative basis for these prosecutions often shifted from the use of the ordinary, routine instrumentarium of criminal laws toward the use of special measures, special laws, and special courts, as well as an increased reliance on confidentiality and secrecy surrounding proceedings. Such illiberal moves rightly led to debates in and outside the courtroom about the perceived need for these measures versus the protection of liberal principles. While victim alliances pressed the state for action against perceived impunity and lack of protection, defendants and their supporters often disputed proclaimed law enforcement concerns. For example, activists in Chile and the US routinely downplayed the fear that targets of their protests were said to have, thus denying a key justification of the anti-terrorism measures.

Beyond debates about the state's adherence to the rule of law, protesters routinely accused the state of criminalizing their issue, meaning that their protest actions were prosecuted "*not* because they fail[ed] to respect freedom and equality, but because they threaten[ed] the vested interests of those with unjust social power" (Duff 2017:488). The challengers of the status quo in this book questioned the fundaments of the existing liberal order, be it sovereignty, property distribution, or the separation between humans and animals. Regardless of the law enforcement motives behind the initiation of criminal proceedings, my research has shown how criminal prosecutions tended to effectively sideline the political issues. They concentrated the government's intervention on the criminal aspects, at the expense of the activists' political demands. This is problematic as activity thus viewed as illegal was often the expression of a more widely shared grievance. Moreover, in many cases the disruptive actions were more effective in calling attention to or even achieving political demands than the legal activities undertaken for the same political cause. For example, the animal-testing company Huntingdon Life Sciences was weakened due to the controversial SHAC protests in the United States, and land occupations and arson in Chile led to a number of communities obtaining access to disputed lands.

Awareness of political demands behind illegal activity does not mean that society simply has to bow to controversial protest actions and acquiesce to any demands raised. Still, criminal justice does not solve political conflicts. It was never designed to do so. While a high number of ETA militants and their supporters have been imprisoned and ETA has decided to lay down its arms, the question of Basque autonomy (or Catalan autonomy for that matter) remains. What is more, criminal proceedings may actually complicate political conflicts. As laid out before, protracted conflicts can become even more difficult to disentangle due to polarization in the courtroom. Also, defendants as well as victims – frequently both – can feel resentment about perceived unjust procedures or outcomes. As prosecutorial choices and narratives are at the heart of such dynamics, prosecutors should tread carefully when choosing their narratives – even if a criminal case is entirely in line with liberal principles.

Prosecutors are expected to act in the public interest. They should avoid representing – or seeming to represent – the interests of a particular group or category of victims at the expense of others. As Duff (2017) points out, not *all* dissent should be tolerated. In typical liberal fashion, she posits that restrictions on protest activity should be based on an appeal to universal values such as freedom and equality for all, instead of particular interests like those of the wealthy and powerful (Duff 2017:491). This book has shown, however, how values like freedom and equality are often appropriated by competing narratives, concealing the particularistic interests they may serve. Moreover, prosecutors should be careful about the narratives they institutionalize and marginalize in criminal proceedings. For example, Chilean prosecutors should not rely on a simplistic juxtaposition of good and bad Mapuches or accuse Mapuche leaders of not being "real." Reproducing discriminatory ethnic images in the courtroom is not just plainly wrong. As the identity, autonomy, and integration of Mapuches in Chilean society are in the process of being renegotiated, doing so to justify imprisonment also adds poison to an already complex mix of identity politics.

As the language and structure of the criminal law fundamentally simplifies questions of guilt, such law is hardly suitable to address more complex political questions around ethnic discrimination, land rights, regional independence, or animal rights. The allocation of individual responsibility and punishment is the dominating logic in the criminal justice arena. To avoid being trapped in this grammar and vocabulary, defendants and their supporters often tried to draw attention to their political grievances. Furthermore, they frequently scrutinized victim narratives, attempting to reveal the interests and actors served by such narratives. At times, they managed to expose how necessary debates about identity, democracy, sovereignty, and economic interests were deformed in prosecutorial narratives. For example, when a Chilean prosecutor defined the loss of a plantation in an arson incident in terms of the financial profit that could have come from each pine tree, activists pointed out that in the criminal court there was no room for debate about the desirability of this economic model for the development of the rural south where most Mapuche communities live. Sometimes, though, defendants and their lawyers deemed it more expedient simply to focus on a technical defense (for example,

by contesting the available evidence). Beyond such individual trial strategies (that is, either sticking to a technical defense or bringing the political
grievances back to the table and pointing out particular interests served by
specific criminal prosecutions), defendants and their supporters should
push society to critically assess what is framed as being properly dealt with
in the criminal justice and what in the political arena, and how this may
have changed over time.

A key question is how much weight *should* context be given in prosecutorial narratives? Similar questions have also divided scholars on
the effect and desirability of hate crime legislation, which differentiates
between otherwise identical offenses on the basis of the motive of the
offender and the suggested greater harm to society as a consequence.
Franklin (2002) points out that because of the existing social power
structure, these laws may paradoxically be used more against tradition-
ally victimized minorities whom the legislation was supposed to protect.
Along the same lines, my research made me understand how groups
sought to exert power in and through criminal proceedings. Both victim
groups and prisoner supporters boosted their strength through strategic
movement building and outreach. Due to strong alliances, widespread
public approval, or well-known international supporters such groups were
able to gain leverage over prosecutorial discourses and decision-making.
My book shows the importance of these competing narratives and of the
ways in which a certain type of contextualization often serves the interests
of particular groups. The choice of a particular prosecutorial narrative is
a political choice. In conclusion, then, rather than accepting the common
justification that prosecutors are simply applying the law, this book shows
how criminal cases are narrated and calls for a heightened sensitivity to
the role of discursive mobilization in shaping criminal justice decisions
and for a critical attitude toward contextualizing moves by prosecutors.

References

Aaronson, Trevor and Katie Galloway (2015) Manufacturing terror. *The Intercept*, 19 November.

Abel, C.F. and F.H. Marsh (1994) *In Defense of Political Trials*. Westport, CT: Greenwood Press.

Acevedo, Paulina (2014) CIDH condena al estado de chile por aplicación de ley antiterrorista a dirigentes mapuche. LeMondeDiplomatique.cl, 31 July.

Agamben, Giorgio (2005) *State of Exception*. Chicago: University of Chicago Press.

Águeda, Pedro (2013) Quién es quién en el mundo de las víctimas del terrorismo. *El Diario*, 28 October.

Aizpeolea, Luis R. (2011) Batasuna toma velocidad. *El País*, 6 February, https://elpais.com/diario/2011/02/06/espana/1296946807_850215.html

Alcedo Moneo, M. (1996) *Militar en ETA: Historias de vida y muerte*. Donostia-San Sebastián: Haranburu Editor.

ALF (2011a) The ALF credo and guidelines, www.animalliberationfront.com/ALFront/alf_credo.htm (accessed September 2011).

——(2011b) Monumental Animal Liberation Front actions in the United States, www.animalliberationfront.com/ALFront/Actions-USA/alfusa.htm (accessed August 2011).

Alonso, Rogelio and Fernando Reinares (2005) Terrorism, human rights and law enforcement in Spain. *Terrorism and Political Violence*, 17(1): 265–78.

Alonso, C., R. Lago and I. Barcena (2008) El tren de alta velocidad y la brunete judicial. *Gara*, 3 February.

Alonso, Rogelio (2016) Victims of ETA's terrorism as an interest group: Evolution, influence, and impact on the political agenda of Spain. *Terrorism and Political Violence*, 29(6): 1–21.

Amnesty International (2017) *Informe 2016/2017*, www.amnesty.org/download/Documents/POL1048002017SPANISH.PDF (accessed January 2019).

Amnesty International (2018) *Pre-juicios injustos: Criminalización del Pueblo Mapuche a través de la ley "antiterrorista" en Chile*, www.amnesty.org/download/Documents/AMR2288622018SPANISH.PDF (accessed January 2019).

Animal Legal and Historical Center (2019) Ecoterrorism or agroterrorism: Related statutes. Michigan State University, www.animallaw.info/statutes/topic/ecoterrorism-or-agroterrorism?order=title&sort=desc (accessed January 2019).

Ansa (2001) Denuncian relación de sitio web Mapuche con Osama Bin Laden. *Emol*, 28 September.

Apter, D. (ed.) (1997) *Legitimization of Violence*. New York: New York University Press.

Arzuaga, Julen (2010) *La maza y la cantera: Juventud vasca, represión y solidaridad*. Navarre-Nafarroa: Editorial Txalaparta.

Asamblea Mapuche de Izquierda (Chile) (2008) ¿Por qué nunca se aclaran los incendios en territorio mapuche? 23 August, http://piensachile.com/2008/08/aipor-que-nunca-se-aclaran-los-incendios-en-territorio-mapuche/ (accessed January 2019).

Asociación Dignidad y Justicia (2007) Nota de prensa Asociación Dignidad y Justicia. Press release, 19 September, www.macrojuicio.com/index_noticia.asp?id=751 (accessed February 2008).

——(2009) Investigaciones sobre las actividades de la organización terrorista Segi y su influencia en los jóvenes vascos. Boletín 12 (December), www.macrojuicio.com/Boletines/2009-12%20Diciembre.pdf (accessed September 2011).

ASPCA (2018) What is ag-gag legislation? Website of the American Society for the Prevention of Cruelty to Animals, www.aspca.org/animal-protection/public-policy/what-ag-gag-legislation (accessed January 2019).

Aukiñ (1992a) Editorial: Integracionismo o autodeterminacion: 1991, cada cual mostro su verdadero rostro. Aukiñ, 19 (November–December): 2.

—— (1992b) Ministro en visita: Acusa a 144 Mapuche de asociación ilícita y usurpación de tierras. Aukiñ, 19 (November–December): 3.

—— (1992c) En Temuco: Los Mapuche no hemos cometido ningún delito. Aukiñ, 19 (November–December): 3.

—— (1993a) Fortalecimiento de la institucionalidad Mapuche: Wallmapu Norngulamtuwun: Tribunal Mapuche. Aukiñ, 20 (January–February): 2.

——(1993b) Editorial: Acusacion a Mapuche. Aukiñ, 20 (January–February).

Austral (2002) Fiscal investiga al "Comando Trizano." Austral, 3 April.

AVT (Asociación de Víctimas del Terrorismo) (2008) Homepage, www.avt.org/ (accessed October 2008).

Baeza Palavecino, Angélica (2013) Denuncias por delitos asociados a conflicto Mapuche aumentaron un 77% en los últimos 12 meses. La Tercera, 14 January.

Balbus, I. (1973) The Dialectics of Legal Repression: Black Rebels before American Criminal Courts. New York: Russell Sage Foundation.

Bake hitzak (2008) Bake hitzak 68. www.gesto.org/es/gesto/bake-hitzak-palabras 75-64.html (accessed 30 July 2019).

Barrera, Aníbal (1999) El grito Mapuche (Una historia inconclusa). Santiago: Grijalbo.

Barria Reyes, Rodrigo (2001) La intifada Mapuche: Se agrava el levantamiento indígena. El Mercurio, 4 February.

Barrio, Carlos (2017) Alberto Muñagorri, víctima de ETA: "Decían que yo era un daño colateral." Interviu, 14 July. www.interviu.es/reportajes/articulos/alberto-munagorri-victima-de-eta-decian-que-yo-era-un-dano-colateral (accessed 30 July 2019).

Barriuso, Olatz (2008) ETA ensancha su diana. El Correo, 9 June, www.elcorreo.com/vizcaya/20080609/politica/ensancha-diana-20080609.html

Barthes, Roland (1977) Elements of Semiology. New York: Hill and Wang.

Bateson, Gregory (2000) Steps to an Ecology of Mind. Chicago: University of Chicago Press.

Becker, Howard (1967) Whose side are we on? Social Problems, 14(3): 239–47.

Beetham, D. (1991) The Legitimation of Power. London: Macmillan Education.

Behatokia, Observatory of Human Rights (2003) *Medidas antiterroristas: panorama internacional y Euskal Herria*. Hernani: Behatokia.

Belloch, Juan Alberto (2000) La apología del terrorismo como delito. *Bake hitzak*, 41 (November): 36–7.

Bengoa, José (2002 [1999]) *Historia de un conflicto: El estado y los Mapuches en el siglo XX*, 2nd edn. Santiago de Chile: Planeta/ Ariel.

Bennett, W.L. and M.S. Feldman (1981) *Reconstructing Reality in the Courtroom: Justice and Judgement in American Culture*. New Brunswick, NJ: Rutgers University Press.

Berger, Peter L. and Thomas Luckmann (1967) *The Social Construction of Reality: A Treatise in the Sociology of Knowledge*. New York: Anchor Books.

Bhuta, Nehal (2005) Between liberal legal didactics and political Manichaeism: The politics and law of the Iraqi Special Tribunal. *Melbourne Journal of International Law*, 6(2): 245–71.

Biurrun, Garbiñe (2000) Penalización de la apología del terrorismo y libertad de expresión. *Bake Hitzak*, 41 (November): 33–5.

Bloom, Jeremy (2011) Eco-terrorism: FBI spends millions harassing artists and activists. *Red, Green and Blue*, 17 May.

Boghosian, Heidi (2007) *Punishing Protest: Government Tactics that Suppress Free Speech*. New York: National Lawyers Guild.

Brass, P.R. (1996) Introduction: Discourses of ethnicity, communalism, and violence. In P. Brass (ed.) *Riots and Pogroms*. New York: New York University Press.

Briggs, Charles (1996) Introduction. In Charles Briggs (ed.) *Disorderly Discourse: Narrative, Conflict and Inequality*. Oxford: Oxford University Press.

Brown, J.M. (2008) Authorities tracking leads in weekend firebombings: Lawmakers says incidents will help get protective measure passed. *Santa Cruz Sentinel*, 4 August.

Brown, Doug (2017) Animal rights activists Sue Beaverton, cops for 2015 arrests. Blogtown, *Portland Mercury*, 13 July.

Calleja, José and Ignacio Sánchez-Cuenca (2006) *La derrota de ETA: De la primera a la última víctima*. Madrid: Adhara Publicaciones.

CAM (2009) Comunicado Público Coordinadora Mapuche Arauco Malleco (Órganos de Resistencia Territorial [ORT] pewenche de la CAM). 14 August, http://werkenkvrvf.blogspot.de/2009/08/comunicado-publico-coordinadora-mapuche_14.html in 2009 (accessed September 2011).

CAM (2018) CAM se adjudica sabotaje en Curanilahue y llama a seguir en el camino de la resistencia y recontruccion nacional Mapuche. Comunicado, 23 November, http://werken.cl/cam-se-adjudica-sabotaje-en-curanilahue-y-llama-a-seguir-en-nel-camino-de-la-resistencia-y-recontruccion-nacional-mapuche/

Camhi, Rosita and Maria de la Luz Domper (2003) *Análisis de la situación económica y social de los pueblos indígenas: Reformas pendientes*. Serie Informe Social 72. Santiago de Chile: Libertad y Desarrollo.

Casquete, Jesús (2017) Epic, memory and the making of an uncivil community. In Rafael Leonisio, Fernando Molina and Diego Muro (eds) *ETA's Terrorist Campaign: From Violence to Politics, 1968–2015*. London: Routledge.

Cayuqueo, Pedro (2003) Paramilitares en La Araucanía, el Far West de Agustín Figueroa. *Kolectivo Lientur*, 27 April, www.nodo50.org/kolectivolientur/paramilitares_malleco.htm (accessed November 2005).

—— (2005a) Paramilitares en el conflicto Mapuche: El regreso de los Trizano. *Azkintuwe Noticias*, June/July: 7–10.

——(2005b) "El Mapuche es depredador … torcido, desleal y abusador." *Azkintuwe Noticias*, 21 June. www.rebelion.org/noticia.php?id=16810

——(2005c) No title. *Azkintuwe Noticias*, 22 July. www.escaner.cl/escaner75/origen. htm (accessed 30 July 2019).

—— (2009) Alianza territorial Mapuche: Renacer de los lonkos. *Punto Final*, 4 September.

—— (2016) Héctor Llaitul, líder de la Coordinadora Arauco Malleco (CAM): "Estamos disponibles para una tregua con el Estado." *La Tercera*, 24 July, www. latercera.com/noticia/hector-llaitul-lider-de-la-coordinadora-arauco-malleco-cam-estamos-disponibles-para-una-tregua-con-el-estado/ (accessed July 2019).

CCR (Center for Constitutional Rights) (2010a) CCR calls on Supreme Court to hear case of SHAC 7. Press release, 16 November.

—— (2010b) U.S.A. v. Buddenberg. www.ccrjustice.org/ourcases/current-cases/usa-v-buddenberg (accessed October 2010).

CEP (Centro de Estudios Públicos) (2006) Los Mapuches rurales y urbanos hoy: Datos de una encuesta. www.cepchile.cl (accessed November 2010).

CERC (Centro de Estudios de la Realidad Contemporánea) (1999) Encuesta nacional CERC abril de 1999. On file with author.

Chambliss, William and Robert Seidman (1982) *Law, Order, and Power*, 2nd edn. Reading, MA: Addison-Wesley Publishing.

Chandler, Daniel (2002) *Semiotics: The Basics*. Abingdon: Routledge.

Christenson, R. (1999) *Political Trials: Gordian Knots in the Law*. New Brunswick, NJ: Transaction Publishers.

CIA (2010) The World Factbook. www.cia.gov/library/publications/the-world-factbook/fields/2172.html (accessed November 2010).

Cole, David (2008) Terror financing, guilt by association and the paradigm of prevention in the "War on Terror." In Andrea Bianchi and Alexis Keller (eds) *Counterterrorism: Democracy's Challenge*. London: Hart Publishing.

Colli, Nieves (2006) Marlaska deja en libertad a los empresarios pero cree que pagaron a ETA voluntariamente. *ABC*, 27 June.

Comisión de Constitución (2003) Informe de la Comisión de Constitución, legislación, justicia y reglamento. Boletín S 680-12 (9 July).

—— (2006) Informe de la Comisión de Constitución, legislación, justicia y reglamento. Valparaíso, Boletín 4.188-07 (14 August).

Comisión de Derechos Humanos (2006) Informe de la Comisión de Derechos Humanos, Nacionalidad y Ciudadanía, recaído en el proyecto de ley, en primer trámite constitucional, que permite conceder la libertad condicional a condenados por conductas terroristas y otros delitos, en causas relacionadas con reivindicaciones violentas de derechos consagrados en la ley No. 19.253. Valparaíso, Boletín 4.188-07 (23 May).

Comisión Especial (2000) Informe de la Comisión Especial constituida para investigar los graves hechos relacionados con los incendios forestales ocurridos en la Sexta, Séptima, Octava y Novena Regiones del país. Parliamentary Commission, Project No. 225 (26 January).

Comisión Seguridad Ciudadana (2009) Session on 30 March 2009 (video online). www.camara.cl/trabajamos/comision_resultadodet.aspx?prmID=2009-14&prmT=Semana%20del%2030%20al%2030%20de%20marzo%20de%20 2009 (accessed November 2010).

Conspiracy (2011) The Age of Conspiracy, http://zinelibrary.info/files/ageof conspiracyPRINT.pdf (accessed August 2011).

Comunicaciones Mapuche Xeg-Xeg (1999) Detienen a 34 Mapuches en la Comunca de los Alamos: Consecuencia del estado de excepción para la cuestión Mapuche. *Equipo Nizkor*, 23 August, www.derechos.org/nizkor/espana/doc/ endesa/detenidos.html (accessed September 2011).

Cook, John (2006) Thugs for puppies. Salon.com, 7 February.

Cooperativa (2006a) Senador Navarro presentó querella por muerte de Mapuche en Nueva Imperial. Cooperativa.cl, 31 August.

——(2006b) Bachelet reafirmó que no se volverá a aplicar ley antiterrorista contra Mapuches. Cooperativa.cl, 13 May.

—— (2010) Fiscal nacional: Cerrar causas contra comuneros Mapuche podría constituir un delito. Cooperativa.cl, 5 October.

——(2018) Coordinadora Arauco Malleco se adjudicó tres atentados incendiarios en La Araucanía. Cooperativa.cl, 3 July.

CORMA (1999a) Mailing ejecutivo. Santiago, Year 3, No. 1 (March). On file with author.

——(1999b) Letter to newspaper *El Diario Austral*, 6 December. On file with author.

—— (2002) Discurso del presidente de CORMA. Araucanía region, document from the CORMA archive in Temuco. On file with author.

Correa, Martín, Raúl Molina and Nancy Yáñez (2005) *La Reforma Agraria y las tierras Mapuches: Chile 1962–1975*. Santiago: LOM Ediciones.

Correa, Martín and Eduardo Mella (2010) *Las razones del illkun/ enojo. Memoria, despojo y criminalización en el territorio Mapuche de Malleco*. Santiago: LOM Ediciones.

Cover, R.M. (1983) Foreword: *Nomos* and narrative. *Harvard Law Review*, 97: 4–68.

CPC (Confederación de la Producción y el Comercio) (2008) Comunicado Prensa CPC en la Araucanía. Temuco, October.

CrimethInc (2011) The SHAC model: A critical assessment. www.crimethinc.com/ texts/rollingthunder/shac.php (accessed September 2011).

Daily Mail Reporter (2010) Animal rights activists send "HIV-contaminated" razor blades to top research scientist. *Daily Mail*, 24 November.

de la Luz Domper, M. and M. de los Ángeles Santander (1998) *Problemas y programas indígenas: Reformas pendientes*. Serie informe social No. 49, July. Santiago de Chile: Libertad y Desarrollo.

De Roos, Th. A. (1987) *Strafbaarstelling van economische delicten*. Arnhem: Gouda Quint bv.

Del Valle Rojas, Carlos (2001) El uso de descripciones factuales como estrategias comunicativas de legitimación discursiva: El "recurso de ley de seguridad del estado" en el proceso judicial de 12 Mapuches en la IX Región (Diciembre de 1997–Abril de 1999). *Revista de Estudios Criminológicos y Penitenciarios*, 3 (November, Santiago de Chile): 117–30.

—— (2005) Interculturalidad e intraculturalidad en el discurso de la prensa: Cobertura y tratamiento del discurso de las fuentes en el "conflicto indígena Mapuche", desde el discurso político. *Revista Redes*, 2: 83–111, http://revista-redes.com/ojs/index.php/Redes-com/article/view/96 (accessed September 2011).

Della Porta, D. and H. Reiter (1998) *Policing Protest: The Control of Mass Demonstrations in Western Democracies*. Minneapolis: University of Minnesota Press.

Department of Homeland Security (2006) Preventing attacks by animal rights extremists and eco-terrorists: fundamentals of corporate security. Memorandum from the Office of Intelligence and Analysis, Dept of Homeland Security, to Federal Departments and Agencies, State Homeland Security Advisors, Security Managers, et al., 13 April, www.greenisthenewred.com/blog/dhs-flyer-distribution/14/ (accessed 2 September 2011).

Department of Homeland Security (2008) *Ecoterrorism: Environmental and Animal-Rights Militants in the United States: Universal Adversary Dynamic Threat Assessment*. 7 May, http://humanewatch.org/images/uploads/2008_DHS_ecoterrorism_threat_assessment.pdf (accessed September 2011).

Diagonal (2015) La Audiencia Nacional pide 14.400 euros a un activista anti TAV para evitar la cárcel, 16 July, www.diagonalperiodico.net/libertades/27371-la-audiencia-nacional-pide-14400-activista-anti-tav-para-evitar-la-carcel.html

Díaz Lombardo, Cristóbal (2007) Podemos caer en la víctimización. *Bake hitzak*, 67.

Douglass, William A. and Joseba Zulaika (1990) On the interpretation of terrorist violence: ETA and the Basque political process. *Comparative Studies in Society and History*, 32(2): 238–57.

Duff, Koshka (2017) The criminal is political: Policing politics in real existing liberalism. *Journal of the American Philosophical Association*, 3(4): 485–502.

Economist (2010) Obituary. *Economist*, 25 September: 91.

EFE (2003) Aznar defiende la lucha contra las "banderas de conveniencia" de ETA. *EL Mundo*, 21 February, www.elmundo.es/elmundo/2003/02/21/espana/1045809316.html

—— (2009) La alcaldesa de Hernani pidió un aplauso para los etarras de la T-4 como "una expresión de cariño." *Público*, 21 May.

—— (2011) Primera condena de la Audiencia Nacional por pagar el "impuesto revolucionario" a ETA. *Diario Vasco*, 30 June.

El Mercurio (2003) Senadores piden sanciones a líderes de tomas Mapuches. *El Mercurio*, 5 December.

—— (2008) Abogado de Luchsinger entrega a Pérez Yoma antecedentes de ataques en la Araucanía. *El Mercurio*, 22 August.

El País (2009) El Tribunal Supremo rebaja las penas a los dirigentes de Ekin. *El País*, 26 May.

ELF Supporter (2008) Well. 1 November, http://seattle.indymedia.org/en/2008/11/269772.shtml (accessed August 2009, no longer available).

Elias, Norbert (1982) *Het civilisatieproces: Sociogenetische en psychologische onderzoekingen*, Utrecht: Het Spectrum.

Engle, Eric (2008) The social contract: A basic contradiction in western liberal democracy. https://ssrn.com/abstract=1268335 (accessed August 2018).

Europa Press (2008) Miles de personas se manifiestan contra "el caso Atutxa." 27 January, www.rioja2.com/n-20853-501-Miles_personas_manifiestan_contra_caso_Atutxa/ (accessed August 2010).

——(2009) Los hijos de Luis Portero confirman ante Marlaska que la txosna de Txori Barrote mostró fotos del asesino de su padre. *El Correo*, 17 September.

——(2017) El entorno de ETA cambia de estrategia: Renuncia a la violencia para evitar la cárcel. Europa Press, 1 January.

FBI (2005) When talk turns to terror: Homegrown extremism in the U.S. 23 May, www.fbi.gov/news/stories/2005/may/jlewis_052305 (accessed September 2011).

——(2006) Incidents and offenses. 2006 Hate Crime Statistics, www2.fbi.gov/ucr/hc2006/incidents.html (accessed August 2011).

——(2008) Putting intel to work: Against ELF and ALF terrorists. 30 June, www.fbi.gov/news/stories/2008/june/ecoterror_063008 (accessed July 2011).

——(2009) Crime in the United States. https://ucr.fbi.gov/crime-in-the-u.s/2009 (accessed September 2018).

Feeley, M. (1979) *The Process Is the Punishment: Handling Cases in a Lower Criminal Court*. New York: Russell Sage Foundation.

FIDH (2006) *La otra transición chilena: Derechos del pueblo Mapuche, política penal y protesta social en un estado democrático*. No. 445/3, April, www.fidh.org/es/region/americas/chile/La-otra-transicion-chilena

Fletcher, G.P. (2000 [1978]) *Rethinking Criminal Law*. Oxford: Oxford University Press.

——(2007) *The Grammar of Criminal Law*. Oxford: Oxford University Press.

Flies on the Wall (2007) Notes from Jonathan Paul's sentencing hearing, 6/5/07. 8 June. http://breakallchains.blogspot.com/2007/06/notes-from-jonathan-pauls-sentencing.html (accessed August 2011).

Foreman, Dave (1991) *Confessions of an Eco-Warrior*. New York: Crown Trade Paperbacks.

Foucault, M. (2001) *Discipline, toezicht en straf: De geboorte van de gevangenis*. Groningen: Historische uitgeverij.

Foundation for Biomedical Research (2006) *Illegal Incidents Report: A 25-year History of Illegal Activities by Eco and Animal Extremists*. February, Washington, DC.

Franklin, Karen (2002) Good intentions: The enforcement of hate crime penalty-enhancement statutes. *American Behavioral Scientist*, 46(1): 154–72.

Fredes, Iván and Patricio Gómez (2002) Vinculaciones indígenas la red internacional de apoyo: El lobby de los Mapuches viajeros. *El Mercurio*, 15 October.

Fuenzalida, Sergio (no date) Aplicación de la legislación antiterrorista en contra de personas Mapuches en Chile. http://ejp.icj.org/IMG/ExposicionSergioFuenzalida.pdf (accessed September 2010).

Fur Commission (1998) Utah bomber Ellerman sentenced. Press release, 10 September, www.furcommission.com/news/newsB6.htm (accessed 7 September 2011, no longer available).

Fur Commission (2009) Special feature: Peter Young resources. November, www.furcommission.com/resource/pressYoung.htm#Anchor-1997-47857 (accessed November 2010).

Galindo, E.R. (2006) *Mi vida contra ETA: La lucha antiterrorista desde el cuartel de inchaurrondo*. Barcelona: Editorial Planeta.

Gallego-Díaz, Soledad (2010) Estados Unidos descarta en cables secretos existencia de "terrorismo Mapuche" en Chile. *Azkintuwe*, 14 December.

Gara (2007) Interview with ETA. 8 April.

——(2009) Comunicado de los presos políticos vascos en el 20 aniversario de la dispersión, 26 April.

García, Pedro (2002) *Exposición: Reforma procesal penal y problema Mapuche*. FORJA-IEI.

Garfinkel, Harold (1956) Conditions of successful degradation ceremonies. *American Journal of Sociology*, 61(5): 420–24.

Gargarella, Roberto (2011) Penal coercion in contexts of social injustice. *Criminal Law and Philosophy*, 5(1): 21–38.

Garland, D. (1990) *Punishment and Modern Society: A Study in Social Theory*, Oxford University Press.

Garzón, Baltasar (2005) *Un mundo sin miedo*, 2nd edn, Barcelona: De Bols!llo.

——(2006) *La lucha contra el terrorismo y sus límites*. Madrid: Adhara Publicaciones.

Geertz, Clifford (1983) Fact and law in comparative perspective. In *Local Knowledge. Further Essays in Interpretive Anthropology*. New York: Basic Books.

Gesto por la Paz (2008) Ante el atentado contra Ignacio Uria Mendizabal. Press release, 3 December, www.gesto.org/es/gesto/sala-prensa.html (accessed July 2019).

Guenaga, Aitor (2017) Los presos de ETA aceptan mayoritariamente la legalidad penitenciaria. *El Diario Norte*, 30 June.

Guerra, Marta M. (2010) Absuelven a ex huelguista tras 14 meses en prisión preventiva. Liberar.cl, 5 November.

Guither, H. (1998) *Animal Rights: History and Scope of a Radical Social Movement*. Carbondale: Southern Illinois University Press.

Gurruchaga, Carmen (2006) *Los jefes de ETA*. Madrid: La Esfera de los Libros.

Gusterson, Hugh (1997) Studying up revisited. *PoLAR*, 20(1).

Habermas, Jürgen (1998) *Between Facts and Norms: Contributions to a Discourse Theory of Law and Democracy*. Cambridge, MA: Massachusetts Institute of Technology.

Hall, S. (1978) *Policing the Crisis: Mugging, the State, and Law and Order*. London: Macmillan.

Harper, Josh (2002) In honor of Jeff Luers. *No Compromise*, 18.

Harrison, Michael M. (1994) France and international terrorism: Problem and response. In David A. Charters (ed.) *The deadly sin of terrorism: Its effect on democracy and civil liberty in six countries*. Westport, CT: Greenwood Press.

Held, David (1996) *Models of Democracy*, 2nd edn. Stanford, CA: Stanford University Press.

Holden Jr., Matthew (2006) *Mechanisms and Processes of Legal Initiation*. Working Paper on the Executive-Bureaucratic Role in Law. On file with author.

Hollenbeck, Carol (1999) Stiffer laws for releasing animals sought. *Daily Press* (Escanaba, Michigan), 20 July.

HRW (Human Rights Watch) (2004) *Indebido proceso: Juicios anti-terroristas, los tribunales militares y los Mapuche en el sur de Chile*. 26 October, www.hrw.org/sites/default/files/reports/chile1004sp.pdf (accessed July 2019).

——(2005) *Setting an example? Counter-terrorism measures in Spain*. 17(1): 1–65. www.hrw.org/report/2005/01/26/setting-example/counter-terrorism-measures-spain (accessed July 2019).

Hulsman, Louk (1986) *Afscheid van het strafrecht: Een pleidooi voor zelfregulering*. Houten: Het Wereldvenster.

Humane Society (2005) Letter to Senator Inhofe. 19 May, www.humanesociety.org/assets/pdfs/letter_to_sen_inhofe-_5_18_05.pdf (accessed September 2011).

—— (2009) About us: Overview. 30 September 2009, www.humanesociety.org/about/overview/ (accessed September 2011).

IndyBay.org (2010) Judge rules that Animal Liberation Front is not a gang: Activist Kevin Olliff remains jailed anyway on $460,000 bail. Animal Liberation Press Office, 26 January.

Informe Especial (2016) Reportaje sobre la CAM lidera sintonía. 24horas.cl, 29 May, www.24horas.cl/programas/informeespecial/informe-especial-reportaje-sobre-la-cam-lidera-sintonia--2029139 (accessed July 2019).

Instituto Nacional de Derechos Humanos (2017) *Informe programa de derechos humanos: función policial y orden público*, Santiago de Chile, Diciembre, https://indh.us13.list-manage.com/track/click?u=89ffae7a941c0b05240d208a3&id=babc828e75&e=3ead140d6f)

Instituto Nacional de Estadística (INE-Chile) (2002) Estadísticas Sociales de los Pueblos Indígenas en Chile. Censo 2002, www.ine.cl/canales/chile_estadistico/estadisticas_sociales_culturales/etnias/pdf/estadisticas_indigenas_2002_11_09_09.pdf (accessed September 2011).

Jack, Andrew (2007) Call to resist animal rights threats. *Financial Times*, 16 September.

Jakobs, G. and M. Cancio Meliá (2006) *Derecho penal del enemigo*, 2nd edn. Navarra: Editorial Aranzadi.

Jaramillo, Betzie (2005) La guerra de Aucán Huilcamán. *La Nacion*, 14 August.

Jarboe, James F. (2002) The threat of eco-terrorism: Testimony before the House Resources Committee, Subcommittee on Forests and Forest Health. 12 February, www2.fbi.gov/congress/congress02/jarboe021202.htm (accessed May 2011).

Jasper, James M. and Dorothy Nelkin (1992) *The Animal Rights Crusade: The Growth of a Moral Protest*. New York: The Free Press.

Jones, Chris and Larry Curtis (2015) Farmington will no longer enforce ordinance. 15 September, https://kutv.com/news/local/farmington-will-no-longer-enforce-ordinance (accessed January 2019).

Jones, Sam (2018) Basque separatist group ETA announces dissolution. *The Guardian*, 2 May.

Kelman, M. (1981) Interpretive construction in the substantive criminal law. *Stanford Law Review*, 33: 591–673.

Khan, Shamus (2012) The sociology of elites. *Annual Review of Sociology*, 38: 361–77.

Kirchheimer, Otto (1961) *Political Justice: The Use of Legal Procedure for Political Ends*. Princeton, NJ: Princeton University Press.

Kirchner, Lauren (2015) Whatever happened to "eco-terrorism?" *Pacific Standard*, https://psmag.com/environment/whatever-happened-to-eco-terrorism (accessed January 2019).

Kyprianou, Despina (2008) Comparative analysis of prosecution systems (Part II): The role of prosecution services in investigation and prosecution principles and policies. *Cyprus European Law Review*, 7.

Landáburu, José Ruiz (2002) *Provocación y Apología: Delitos de Terrorismo*. Madrid: Editorial Colex.

Lacey, N. and C. Wells (1998) *Reconstructing Criminal Law: Text and Materials*, 2nd edn. London: Butterworths.

La Tercera (2010) Familia de Matías Catrileo apelará a condena de tribunal militar. La Tercera.com, 15 January.

Lavanchy, Javier (2003) El Pueblo Mapuche y la globalización: Apuntes para una propuesta de comprensión, de la cuestión Mapuche en una era global. Paper prepared for the seminar "Desarrollo hacia fuera y globalización en Chile siglos XIX y XX," www.xs4all.nl/~rehue/art/lava4.pdf (accessed November 2010).

Le Bonniec, Fabien (2004) Las cárceles de la etnicidad: Implicancias prácticas y sociales de una etnografía de la transgresión en el sur de Chile. Colegio de Antropólogos de Chile, 5th Congreso Chileno de Antropología, 2004, San Felipe, Chile: Lom Ediciones, II, pp. 759–67.

—— (2008) Crónico de un juicio antiterrorista contra los dirigentes Mapuches: Imposición y uso del derecho entre los Mapuche de Chile. In Ángela Santamaría, Bastien Bosa, Eric Wittersheim (eds) *Luchas indígenas y trayectorias poscoloniales*. Bogotá, DC: Editorial Universidad del Rosario.

Leiva, Claudio (2008) Fiscales del conflicto Mapuche acumulan más de 60 causas. *La Nación*, 22 December.

Lewis, John E. (2004) Statement in the hearing before the Senate Judiciary Committee, 108th Congress, 2nd session, Animal Rights: Activism vs. Criminality, 18 May.

Loadenthal, Michael (2013) "The green scare" and "eco-terrorism": The development of US counter-terrorism strategy targeting direct action activists. www.researchgate.net/publication/319619548_%27The_Green_Scare%27_%27Eco-Terrorism%27_The_Development_of_US_Counter-Terrorism_Strategy_Targeting_Direct_Action_Activists (accessed August 2018).

Luers, Jeffrey (2011) Jeffrey Luers' sentence: Comparison to other Oregon State Cases. http://freefreenow.org/res_sentence.html (accessed September 2011).

MA (Memoria Annual), Fiscalía General del Estado (Office of the Director of Public Prosecutions), archived in the library of the Institute for Criminology of the Basque Country in Donostia/ San Sebastián. I had access to the Memoria Annual from the following years: 1978, 1979, 1980, 1981, 1982, 1983, 1984, 1985, 1986, 1987, 1989, 1990, 1991, 1993, 1994, 1995, 1996, 1999, 2000, 2001, 2002, 2004, 2005, 2006, 2007, 2008. Since 2005 online: www.fiscal.

es/cs/Satellite?cid=1240559967921&language=es&pagename=PFiscal%2F-Page%2FFGE_contenidoFinal (accessed September 2011).

Machiavelli, N. (1994) *Selected Political Writings*. Indianapolis: Hackett Publishing Co., Inc.

Mapuche community "José Millacheo Levío" (from the sector Chequenco from the comuna of Ercilla) (2003) Public Declaration, 14 January.

Martín, José Miguel (2003) Declaraciones de Martxelo Otamendi, director de *Euskaldunon Egunkaria. Disenso* 41 (October), www.pensamientocritico.org/josmar1103.htm (accessed September 2011).

McConville, M., A. Sanders and R. Leng (1991) *The Case for the Prosecution*. London: Routledge.

McIntosh, Brent J. (2006) Testimony: Legislative Hearing on H.R. 4239, "The Animal Enterprise Terrorism Act" before the Subcommittee on Crime, Terrorism and Homeland Security U.S. House of Representatives, 23 May.

McLoughlin, James P. Jr. (2010) Deconstructing United States sentencing guidelines section 3A1.4: Sentencing failure in cases of financial support for foreign terrorist organizations. *Law & Inequality: A Journal of Theory and Practice* 28(1), https://scholarship.law.umn.edu/cgi/viewcontent.cgi?article=1132&context=lawineq (accessed July 2019).

Mella Seguel, Eduardo and Fabien Le Bonniec (2004) Administración de la justicia Chilena e interculturalidad. Negación y criminalización del conflicto sociopolitico de las comunidades Mapuche de Malleko: el caso poluco-pidenco. Meli Wixan Mapu, 15 Feb., http://meli.mapuches.org/spip.php?article6.

Meli Witran Mapu (2011) Prisión política Mapuche. 10 August, http://meli.mapuches.org/spip.php?rubrique10 (accessed September 2011).

Melossi, Dario (2008) *Controlling Crime, Controlling Society*. Cambridge: Polity Press.

Mertz, Elizabeth (2008 [2000]) Teaching lawyers the language of law: Legal and anthropological translations. In: Elizabeth Mertz (ed.) *The Role of Social Science in Law*, Aldershot: Ashgate.

Migdal, Joel (2001) *State in Society: Studying How States and Societies Transform and Constitute One Another*. New York: Cambridge University Press.

Millás, Juan José (2010) Entrevista: Felipe González, "Tuve que decidir si se volaba a la cúpula de ETA. Dije no. Y no sé si hice lo correcto." *El País*, 7 November.

Miller, Greg (2010) A tricky balance between activists' and researchers' rights. *Science* 329(5999): 1589–90.

Mininco (1999) Forestal Mininco S.A. a la Opinión Pública. Public declaration after the land occupation of estate Santa Rosa de Colpi, Santiago, 9 March.

Ministerio Público Chile (2002) Boletin de Jurisprudencia: Ministerio Público No. 10, May, www.ministeriopublico.cl/RepositorioMinpu/Archivos/minpu/Boletín%20N10.pdf (accessed September 2011).

Morgan, Emiley (2010) Layton man sentenced to 2 years in prison for mink-farm raid. *Deseret News* (Utah), 5 February.

Murray-West, Rosie (2001) Shares leap as Huntingdon finds banker. *The Telegraph*, 3 July.

Nawrocki, Jill (2004) Animal rights activists arrested. *Daily Local News*, 14 June, www.animalrights.net/2004/11-activists-arrested-in-may-29-home-demonstration/ (accessed August 2011).

Neira Tonk, Roberto (2009) La CAM se atribuye ataque a bus y exige compra de fundo donde murió Catrileo. *Austral Temuco*, 29 July.

Nicolas, Tomás and Carlota Camps (2018) Strasbourg against Madrid: The red cards received by Spain from European justice. ElNacional.cat, 18 February.

Nieburg, H.L. (1968) Violence, law, and the social process. *American Behavioral Scientist*, 2(4): 17.

Nonet, P. and P. Selznick (2005) *Law and Society in Transition: Towards Responsive Law*. New Brunswick, NJ: Transaction Publishers.

Norrie, A. (1993) *Crime, Reason and History: A Critical Introduction to Criminal Law*, 2nd edn. London: Butterworths.

Notimex (2009) Líderes Mapuches se vincularon a las FARC: El Mercurio. Terra. cl, 12 August.

Novartis Global Week of Action (2008) 28 May, www.veganfitness.net/viewtopic.php?t=14502 (accessed September 2018).

Observatorio Ciudadano (2008) La violencia policial en Chile! Documento de Trabajo No. 7, December, https://observatorio.cl/documento-de-trabajo-n-7-la-violencia-policial-en-chile/ (accessed July 2019).

Office of the Inspector General (2003) Audit Report 04-10, U.S. Department of Justice, December, https://fas.org/irp/agency/doj/oig/fbi-info.pdf (accessed August 2011).

Opp, K.-D. and W. Roehl (1990) Repression, micromobilization, and political protest. *Social Forces*, 69(2): 521–47.

ORBE (2002) Mapuches piden renuncia de fiscal de Traiguén por considerarlo racista, 11 January, www.emol.com/noticias/nacional/2002/01/11/75979/mapuches-piden-renuncia-de-fiscal-de-traiguen-por-considerarlo-racista.html (accessed August 2011).

Orellana, Marcos A. (2005) Indigenous peoples, energy and environmental justice: The Pangue/Ralco hydroelectric project in Chile's Alto BioBio. *Journal of Energy & Natural Resources Law*, 23: 511.

P.A.S. (2009) Comando Hernán Trizano y el conflicto Mapuche. *El Incendio* (online), 9 August.

Packer, H.L. (1964) Two models of the criminal process. *University of Pennsylvania Law Review*, 113(1).

Palma, Víctor Hugo (2002) Denuncian comando anti-Mapuches. *Austral*, 13 March.

Peachey, Paul (2014) Animal rights group ends 15-year campaign against experiments at Huntingdon. *The Independent*, 24 August.

Platt, Teresa (1999) Engaging political will. FCUSA Commentary, 4 March, www.furcommission.com/news/newsD9.htm (accessed November 2010).

Portero, Daniel (2007a) *La Trama Civil de ETA: El fin está muy cerca*. Arcopress.

——(2007b) La trama de extorsión de ETA. *Fundación de Víctimas de Terrorismo*, September, pp. 13–19.

Potomac Earth First! (2007) Honor the fallen, remember the snitches, resist the Greenscare! 6 December 2007, www.phillyimc.org/en/node/65283 (accessed September 2011).

Potter, Will (2007) Analysis of the Animal Enterprise Terrorism Act: Using "terrorism" rhetoric to chill free speech and protect corporate profits. July, www.greenisthenewred.com/blog/wp-content/Images/aeta-analysis-109th.pdf (accessed July 2011).

—— (2011a) What is the "Green Scare"? No date, www.greenisthenewred.com/blog/green-scare/ (accessed September 2011).

——(2011b) *Green Is the New Red: An Insider's Account of a Social Movement Under Siege*. San Francisco: City Lights Books.

——(2014) BREAKING: 4 people prosecuted under #AgGag law for photographing factory farm from the road. 27 September, www.greenisthenewred.com/blog/ag-gag-case-utah-circle-four-farms/8073/ (accessed January 2019).

——(2015a) BREAKING: 2 animal activists facing 6 months in jail for protesting on the sidewalk. 20 August, www.greenisthenewred.com/blog/utah-protest-prosecution/8521/ (accessed January 2019).

——(2015b) Animal activists' chalking charges have been dropped! 6 August, www.greenisthenewred.com/blog/animal-activists-chalking-charges-have-been-dropped/8492/ (accessed January 2019).

—— (2015c) Investigator speaks as she heads to jail for exposing factory farm cruelty. 5 July, www.greenisthenewred.com/blog/amber-canavan-interview-investigator/8419/ (accessed January 2019).

Quinney, R. (1964) Crime in political perspective. *American Behavioral Scientist*, 8(4): 4.

Reuters (2006) La Audiencia Nacional condena a Otegi a 15 meses de cárcel. 20minutos.es, 28 April.

—— (2010) California animal rights activist jailed for stalking. Reuters, 10 November.

Richards, Patricia (2010) Of Indians and terrorists: How the state and local elites construct the Mapuche in neoliberal multicultural Chile. *Journal of Latin American Studies*, 42: 59–90.

——(2013) *Race and the Chilean Miracle: Neoliberalism, Democracy, and Indigenous Rights*, Pittsburgh, PA: University of Pittsburgh Press.

Ron, J. (1997) Varying methods of state violence. *International Organization*, 51(2): 275–300.

Saavedra Peláez, Alejandro (2002) *Los Mapuche en la sociedad chilena actual*. Santiago: LOM Ediciones.

Sáiz-Pardo, Melchor (2010) El TS absuelve a la alcalde de Hernani de enaltecimiento a los terroristas. *El Diario de León*, 19 March.

Santos Diego, Doroteo (2008) Acosados. *Fundación Víctimas de Terrorismo*.

Scarce, Rik (2006) *Eco-warriors: Understanding the Radical Environmental Movement*, updated edn. Walnut Creek, CA: Left Coast Press Inc.

Schuster, Henry (2005) Domestic terror: Who's most dangerous? Eco-terrorists are now above ultra-right extremists on the FBI charts. *CNN*, 24 August.

Scott, Marvin B. and Stanford Lyman (1968) Accounts. *American Sociological Review*, 33(1):46–62.

Seguel, Alfredo (2002) El conflicto forestal de las empresas madereras en territorio Mapuche y su poder fáctico en el estado chileno. www.mapuexpress. net (accessed November 2002).

Sellers, Mortimer (2014) What is the rule of law and why is it so important?' In James R. Silkenat, James E. Hickey Jr., Peter D. Barenboim (eds) *The Legal Doctrines of the Rule of Law and the Legal State (Rechtsstaat)*. Dordrecht: Springer International, pp. 3–13.

Senate Report (2006) *Activities report of the Senate Committee on the Judiciary 2005–2006*. Senate Report 109-369, 22 December, www.gpo.gov/fdsys/pkg/CRPT-109srpt369/html/CRPT-109srpt369.htm (accessed September 2011).

Sepúlveda, Lucia (2011) Debilidad en las pruebas marcan juicios por terrorismo contra Mapuches. *Azkintuwe*, 9 September.

SHAC 7 (2008) Homepage SHAC 7, www.shac7.com/ (accessed November 2008).

Shapiro, Ian (2007) *Containment: Rebuilding a Strategy against Global Terror*. Princeton, NJ: Princeton University Press.

Sierra Club (2003) Statement on recent acts of violence in the name of the environment. Press Release, 25 August, www.sierraclub.org/pressroom/releases/pr2003-08-25a.asp (accessed November 2008).

Sierra Club (2018) Welcome to the Sierra Club! No date, www.sierraclub.org/welcome/ (accessed July 2018).

Silbey, Susan S. and Patricia Ewick (1998) *The Common Place of Law: Stories of Popular Legal Consciousness* Chicago: University of Chicago Press.

Silva, Sebastián (2009) Gira presidencial en paises bajos: Michelle Bachelet: "En Chile no hay presos políticos Mapuches. *Azkintuwe Noticias*, 26 May.

Starr, Amory, Luis A. Fernandez, Randall Amster, Lesley J. Wood and Manuel J. Caro (2008) The impacts of state surveillance on political assembly and association: A socio-legal analysis. *Qualitative Sociology*, 31: 251–70.

Stavenhagen, Rodolfo (2003) *Report of the Special Rapporteur on the situation of human rights and fundamental freedoms of indigenous people, Mr. Rodolfo Stavenhagen*. Submitted in accordance with Commission resolution 2003/56. Geneva: UN Commission on Human Rights

Sudnow, David (1965) Normal crimes: Sociological features of the penal code in a public defender office. *Social Problems*, 12(3): 255–76.

Support Eric (2011) Background. No date, http://supporteric.org/background.htm (accessed September 2011).

Support Peter (2007) Peter's support sponsors. 21 February, http://supportpeter.com/updates.htm (accessed October 2010).

Tamanaha, B.Z. (2001) *A General Jurisprudence of Law and Society*. Oxford: Oxford University Press.

Terwindt, Carolijn (2009) The demands of the "true" Mapuche: Ethnic political mobilization in the Mapuche movement. *Nationalism and Ethnic Politics*, 15(2): 237–57.

——(2011) Were they tortured or did they make that up? Ethnographic reflections on torture allegations in the Basque Country in Spain. *Oñati Socio-Legal Series*, 1(2).

——(2012) *Ethnographies of Contentious Criminalization: Expansion, Ambivalence, Marginalization*. Submitted in partial fulfillment of the requirements for the degree of Doctor of the Science of Law at Columbia Law School, https://academiccommons.columbia.edu/doi/10.7916/D8H70NWM.

Thompson, E.P. (1975) *Whigs and Hunters: The Origin of the Black Act*. New York: Pantheon.

Tilly, Charles (1997) *War Making and State Making as Organized Crime: Roads from Past to Future*. Oxford: Rowman and Littlefield.

—— (2003) *The Politics of Collective Violence*. Cambridge: Cambridge University Press.

——(2007a) *Explaining Social Processes*. Boulder, CO: Paradigm Publishers.

——(2007b) *Contentious Politics*. Boulder, CO: Paradigm Publishers.

Toledo Llancaqueo, Víctor (2007) Cronología de los principales hechos en relación a la represión de la protesta social Mapuche, Chile 2000-2007. *OSAL* (Buenos Aires: CLACSO) 8(22).

Univisión (2009) ¡ASI DE CARADURAS! Gobierno de Chile niega en la ONU que abuse de su ley antiterrorista contra Mapuches ... Dice que sólo son 16 VECES en menos de diez años. Unas cuantas no más. 24 September, www.mapuexpress.net/?act=news&id=4719 (accessed September 2010).

Unzalu, Andoni (2008) ¿Qué es el delito de terrorismo? *Bake hitzak*, 68(April).

Urquia, Iñigo (2017) Así era el negocio del impuesto revolucionario: ETA logró millones de euros extorsionando a 10.000 personas. Eco-diario.es, March.

US Embassy in Santiago (2010) Myth vs. reality in Chile's Mapuche conflict. Diplomatic cable, 09SANTIAGO826, http://213.251.145.96/cable/2009/09/09SANTIAGO826.html (accessed December 2010).

Van den Broek, Hanspeter (2004) Borroka: The legitimation of street violence in the political discourse of radical Basque nationalists. *Terrorism and Political Violence* 16(4): 714–36.

Van Reenen, Piet (1979) *Overheidsgeweld: Een sociologische studie van de dynamiek van het geweldsmonopolie*. Alphen aan den Rijn: Samsom Uitgeverij.

van Swaaningen, René (1999) Kritische criminologie. In E. Lissenberg, S.V. Ruller and R. van Swaaningen (eds) *Tegen de regels III: Een inleiding in de criminologie*. Nijmegen: Ars Aequi Libri.

Vanderpool, Tim (2001) Eco-arson sets off sparks in desert: Phoenix luxury homes are among US construction sites targeted by eco- terrorists. *Christian Science Monitor*, 9 February.

Vargas, José Luis (2010) Comités ONU preocupados: Expertos critican aplicación de ley antiterrorista contra Mapuches en huelga de hambre. *Observatorio Ciudadano*, 26 August.

Vercher Noguera, Antonio (1991) *Antiterrorismo en el Ulster y en el Pais Vasco*. Barcelona: PPU.

Villanueva, N. and N. Colli (2011) ETA exigio al gobierno que frenara los macrojuicios contra su entorno. ABC.es, 1 April.

Villegas Díaz, Myrna (2008) *El derecho penal del enemigo y la criminalización de las demandas Mapuche*. Informe Final, Santiago de Chile, Universidad Central, www.pensamientopenal.com.ar/system/files/2011/07/doctrina29871.pdf (accessed 30 July 2019).

Vold, G.B., T.J. Bernard and J. Snipes (1998) *Theoretical Criminology*. New York: Oxford University Press.

Waddington, P.A.J. (1998) Controlling protest in contemporary historical and comparative perspective. In D. Della Porta and H. Reiter (eds) *Policing Protest*. Minneapolis: University of Minnesota Press.

Wallerstein, Shlomit (2007) Criminalising remote harm and the case of anti-democratic activity. *Cardozo Law Review* 28.

Walsh, Edward J. (2000) The Animal Enterprise Protection Act: A scientist's perspective brings the law into focus. *Lab Animal*, 29(2).

WATU Acción Indígena (1997) Letter to Antonio Castro Gutiérrez, investigative judge on the "Lumaco" case, 29 December.

Weber, M. (1972) *Gezag en bureaucratie*. Rotterdam: Universitaire Pers Rotterdam.

Whitehurst, Lindsay (2015) Charges for controversial "ag-gag" dropped. Associated Press, 12 January, www.ksl.com/?nid=157&sid=33074971 (accessed January 2019).

Wiener, Martin J. (1990) *Reconstructing the Criminal: Culture, Law, and Policy in England, 1830–1914*. Cambridge: Cambridge University Press.

Woodworth, Paddy (2017) In 1973, I applauded an ETA killing. Not now. *Irish Times*, 8 April.

Yoldi, José (2009) Cárcel para la alcaldesa de Hernani por enaltecer el terrorismo. *El País*, 5 June.

Young, Peter (2005a) Peter's statement to the court. 8 November, http://supportpeter.com/111705-3.htm (accessed September 2011).

——(2005b) Interview with Peter Young. *No Compromise* 28.

——(2008) Peter Young: Imprisoned for activism. Speaking Engagement at New York Law School, New York City, 29 October.

——(2010) Judge denies motion in Animal Liberation Front case. *Animal Liberation Frontline*, 12 January.

——(2011) Fugitive moves to third on most wanted terrorists list. 2 May, www.voiceofthevoiceless.org/fugitive-moves-to-third-on-most-wanted-terrorists-list/ (accessed September 2011).

Zulaika, Joseba and William A. Douglass (1996) *Terror and Taboo: The Follies, Fables and Faces of Terrorism*. London: Routledge.

Zwerman, Gilda and Patricia Steinhoff (2005) When activists ask for trouble: State–dissident interactions and the New Left cycle of resistance in the United States and Japan. In C. Davenport, H. Johnston and Carol Mueller (eds) *Repression and Mobilization*. Minneapolis: University of Minnesota Press.

Interviews

28	Oñati, June 2008	Member prisoner support organization Etxerat
29	Madrid, June 2008	Defendant in case against Gestoras pro Amnistía
30	Madrid, June 2008	Member of political party Eusko Alkartasuna
31	Madrid, June 2008	Threatened by ETA and paying "revolutionary tax"
32	Bilbo-Bilbao, June 2008	Activist with Gesto por la Paz
33	Madrid, June 2008	Swiss sympathizer with MLNV
34	Bilbo-Bilbao, June 2008	Non-political youth from small Basque village

Chile (C)

1	Santiago, Oct. 2002	Lawyer for Mapuche community in Ralco case
2	Alto Bío Bío, Nov. 2002	Mapuche community member
3	Temuco, Dec. 2002	Employee at the National Forestry Corporation
4	Temuco, Jan. 2003	Vice-regional governor of the 9th Region
5	Temuco, Jan. 2003	Director of Programa Orígenes
6	Temuco, Jan. 2003	General director at Millalemu forestry company
7	Temuco, Jan. 2003	Commercial manager, Magasa forestry company
8	Temuco, Jan. 2003	Land administrator, Mininco forestry company
9	Temuco, Jan. 2003	Lawyer for Mininco forestry company
10	Temuco, Jan. 2003	Head prosecutor, public ministry of 9th Region
11	Temuco, Jan. 2003	Spokesperson, public ministry of 9th Region
12	Temuco, Jan. 2003	Lawyer, public ministry of 9th Region
13	Temuco, Jan. 2003	Lawyer, public ministry of 9th Region
14	Collipulli, Feb. 2003	Police chief in Collipulli
15	Collipulli, Feb. 2003	Prosecutor in Collipulli
16	Temuco, Feb. 2003	Lawyer for Mininco forestry company
17	Temuco, Feb. 2003	Chef of public relations for Mininco forestry company
18	Collipulli, Feb. 2003	Private security guard for Mininco
19	Collipulli, Feb. 2003	Mayor of Collipulli
20	Concepción, Feb. 2003	Mapuche activist convicted of arson
21	Collipulli, Feb. 2003	Family members of convicted Mapuche activist
22	Collipulli, Feb. 2003	Member of Mapuche community
23	Temuco, Feb./Mar./Apr. 2003	Convicted CAM member

24	Temuco, March 2003	Member of Mapuche organization Ad Mapu
25	Temuco, March 2003	Defense lawyer
26	Traiguén, March 2003	Mapuche community member
27	Los Laureles, March 2003	President of Mapuche community
28	Nueva Imperial, March 2003	Mapuche student leader, former CAM member
29	Temuco, March 2003	Member of Mapuche organization Consejo de Todas las Tierras
30	Temuco, March 2003	Accused Mapuche activist
31	Temuco, March 2003	Employee at CONADI
32	Temuco, March 2003	Director Corps Araucaria
33	Temuco, March 2003	Forestry engineer at Bosques Cautín
34	Temuco, March 2003	Forestry engineer at Forestal Valdívia
35	Temuco, March 2003	General manager of CORMA in 9th Region
36	Temuco, March 2003	Judge in Temuco
37	Temuco, April 2003	Private landowner
38	Angol, April 2003	Son and grandson of private landowner
39	Osorno, March 2009	Mapuche activist, defendant
40	Temuco, March 2009	Daughter of a Mapuche activist
41	Temuco, April 2009	Mapuche activist involved in prisoner support
42	Temuco, April 2009	Lawyer with SOFO for private landowners
43	Temuco, April 2009	Researcher
44	Temuco, April 2009	Senior lawyer for Mininco forestry company
45	Temuco, April 2009	Lawyer for Regional Governor of the 9th Region
46	Temuco, April/ May 2009	Mapuche activist, defendant in case against CAM
47	Temuco, April 2009	Defense lawyer with the public defenders
48	Temuco, April 2009	Lawyer, Public Defense Office for Mapuches
49	Temuco, April 2009	Grandson of former expropriated farmers
50	Temuco, April 2009	Defense lawyer with the public defenders
51	Temuco, April 2009	Prosecutor at the regional office of the 9th region
52	Ercilla, April 2009	Mapuche activist, community spokesperson
53	Temuco, May 2009	Mapuche activist, prior conviction
54	Temuco, May 2009	Director of CORMA
55	Temuco, May 2009	Director of SOFO
56	Angol, May 2009	Lawyer for Provincial Governor of Malleco
57	Temuco, May 2009 (×2)	Former CAM member, prior conviction
58	Victoria, May 2009	Convicted Mapuche activist
59	Labranza, May 2009	Former CAM member, prior conviction
60	Ercilla, May 2009	Four Mapuche community members of Lumaco
61	Collipulli, May 2009	Mapuche activist, community spokesperson

62	Collipulli, May 2009	Mapuche activist, defendant in case of arson
63	Temuco, May 2009	Mapuche activist, defendant in case of arson
64	Temuco, May 2009	Defense lawyer
65	Angol, May 2009	Mapuche activist, prior conviction
66	Temuco, May 2009	Mapuche activist, family members in prison
67	Victoria, May 2009	Activist, visiting Mapuche activists in prison
68	Ercilla, June 2009	Mapuche activist, community spokesperson
69	Temuco, May 2009	Employee Observatorio Ciudadano
70	Temuco, May 2009	Son of a Mapuche activist
71	Angol, May 2009	Supporter of defendants in case of arson
72	Los Angeles, June 2009	Defendant in case of arson

United States (US)

1	Sacramento, CA, Sept. 2007	US attorney
2	Sacramento, CA, Sept. 2007	US attorney
3	Sacramento, CA, Sept. 2007	Defense lawyer
4	Sacramento, CA, Sept. 2007	Prisoner supporter attending a trial
5	New York City, Oct. 2007	Animal rights activist
6	New York City, Oct. 2007	Lawyer and anti-AETA activist
7	New York City, Oct. 2007	Social justice activist
8	Washington DC, Oct. 2007	Defense lawyer
9	Washington DC, Oct. 2007	Defense lawyer
10	Washington DC, Oct. 2007	Journalist and environmentalist activist
11	New York City, Nov. 2007	Executive director National Lawyers Guild
12	New York City, Nov. 2007	Defense lawyer
13	Trenton, NJ, Nov. 2007	US attorney
14	Trenton, NJ, Nov. 2007	Defense lawyer
15	New York City, Oct. 2008	Animal rights activist, convicted under AEPA
16	New York City, Nov. 2008	Animal rights activist and press officer ALF

Trial Transcripts

All documents and audiotapes mentioned here are on file with the author.

Spain

Case publishing ETA-communiqués Luis Felipe
- Verdict Audiencia Nacional, 9 January 1980.
- Verdict Tribunal Supremo 2nd bench, 3 March 1981.

Case Sumario "18/98"
- Indictment, Juzgado Central de Instrucción No. 5, Audiencia Nacional, 19 November 2004.
- Verdict Audiencia Nacional, 19 December 2007.

Case Gestoras pro Amnistía, Sumario 33/2001
- Auto de procedimiento, Juzgado central de Instrucción No. 5, Audiencia Nacional, 29 October 2002.
- Conclusiones provisionales, prosecutor Enrique Molina, Audiencia Nacional, 10 June 2005.
- Field notes trial, April–June 2008, Audiencia Nacional.
- Verdict Audiencia Nacional,15 September 2008.
- Verdict Tribunal Supremo, 13 October 2009.

Case Jarrai/Haika/Segi, Sumario 18/01 and 15/02
- Conclusiones provisionales, prosecutor Enrique Molina, Audiencia Nacional, 27 December 2004.
- Expert report about the criminal justice response to the Kale Borroka, 20 December 2002, Bilbao, submitted during the trial.
- Concluding statements of the prosecutor, Juzgado Central de Instrucción, No. 5, Audiencia Nacional, 11 April 2005.
- Verdict Tribunal Supremo, 19 January 2007.

Case Egunkaria, Sumario 44/2004
- Auto del procedimiento, Juzgado Central de Instrucción No. 6, Juan del Olmo, Audiencia Nacional, 4 November 2004.

Case Kale Borroka
- Diligencias previas 271/05-A, Juzgado Central de Instrucción No. 5, Baltasar Garzón, Audiencia Nacional, 19 October 2007.

Case flag wavers, Sumario 67/2007
- Verdict Audiencia Nacional, 15 November 2007.
- Dissenting opinión, Judge Ramón Sáez Valcárcel, 4/2007.

Case Mayor Hernani, Sumarios 19/2008 and 35/2008
- Diligencias previas, 19/2008 on 25 January 2008.
- Auto de procedimiento, Audiencia Nacional, Madrid, 3 April 2008, 35/2008.

Case on the illegalization of political parties ANV (Acción Nacionalista Vasca)/ PCTV ([Partido Comunista de las Tierras Vascas)
- Field notes on trial, Supreme Court, Sala 61, Madrid, June 2008.

Case Portu and Sarasola
- *Portu Juanenea and Sarasola Yarzabal v. Spain*, 1653/13, [2018] ECHR (European Court of Human Rights) 174, 13 Feb. 2018.

Chile

Case Consejo de Todas las Tierras (Rol 24.486)
- Verdict Court of Appeal Temuco, 6 September 1994.
- Comisión Interamericana de Derechos Humanos (CIDH/ IACHR), report No. 9/02 about admissibility, Petition 11.856 Aucán Huilcamán and others, Chile, 27 February 2002.

Case Lumaco (Rol 2-1997, against Lumaco community members and A. Salazar)
- Official request by the governor of the 9th Region, Oscar Eltit Spielmann, requesting the Appeals Court to apply the State Security Law, 2 December 1997.
- Judicial decision on preventive detention, Antonio Castro Gutiérrez, 17 December 1997.
- Letter from WATU Acción Indígena to investigative judge, 29 December 1997.
- Defense statement by lawyer José Lincoqueo, Court of Appeal Temuco, 5 January 1998.

Case A. Fuentes (Rol 2.052 99)
- Verdict Court of Appeal Temuco, 5 March 1999.

Case Temulemu (Rol 875-02)
- Verdict Court of Appeal Temuco, 4 June 2003.

Case *Lonkos* of Traiguén (R.I.T. 2-2003, against P. Pichún, A. Norin and P. Troncoso)
- Declaration before the police by landowner Rafael Figueroa about arson of his house, 3 August 2002, Traiguén.
- Audio proceedings trial, 31 March–9 April 2003, Tribunal de Juicio Oral en lo Penal de Angol.
- Field notes on trial 31 March–9 April 2003, Angol.
- Verdict Tribunal Angol, 14 April 2003.
- Verdict Tribunal Angol, 27 September 2003.

- Comisión Interamericana de Derechos Humanos (CIDH/ IACHR), report on admissibility, 21 October 2006.

Case Ancalaf (Rol 24.486, against V. Ancalaf)
- Verdict Appeals Court Concepcion, 4 June 2004.
- Comisión Interamericana de Derechos Humanos (CIDH), Interamerican Commission of Human Rights (IACHR), report about admissibility 2 May 2007.

Case CAM (R.I.T. 80-2004, against members of CAM)
- Declaration on 28 May 2003 before the local prosecutor in Temuco by Gustavo Adolfo Aranela Salazar, working for private security company ASS Ltda in *Fundo* Poluco Pidenco for forestry company Mininco.
- Audio proceedings trial, 21 June–29 June 2005, Tribunal de Juicio Oral en lo Penal deTemuco.
- Verdict Tribunal de Temuco, 27 July 2005.

Case Chequenco (R.I.T. 143-2008, against 11 members of community Chequenco)
- Audio proceedings trial, 19 February 2009, Tribunal de Juicio Oral en lo Penal de Angol.

Case Cayupe (R.I.T. 16-2009, against C. Cayupe)
- Audio proceedings trial, 16 April 2009, Tribunal de Juicio Oral en lo Penal de Angol.

United States

Case Rod Coronado 1995
- Sentencing Memorandum, 31 July 1995, Western District of Michigan, Southern Division, available at: www.scribd.com/doc/5496556/Animal-Liberation-Front-Rod-Coronado-1995-Sentencing-Memorandum (accessed 9 August 2011).

Case SHAC 7 (USA v. Stop Huntingdon Animal Cruelty USA, Inc. et al.)
- Indictment, 27 May 2004, New Jersey.
- Summations, stenographic account, District Court of New Jersey, 27 February 2006.
- Trial transcripts first instance, stenographic account, February 2006, District Court of New Jersey, Appendix I–VI, including jury instructions.
- Tape of Joshua Harper speech at a Washington college, 17 October 2002, Appendix V, cited in: government exhibit 8018.

Case Operation Backfire (USA v. D. Thurston, K. Tubbs, K. Tankersley, S. Meyerhoff, C. Gerlach, S. Savoie, N. Block, D. McGowan, J. Paul, J. Zacher)
- Terrorism Enhancement Hearing, Reporter's Transcript of Proceedings [Kristi L. Anderson, Official Federal Reporter], 15 May 2007, US District Court of Oregon, Ann L. Aiken, judge presiding.

Case Eric McDavid
- Transcripts of trial, Sacramento, September 2007, https://supporteric.org/court-documents/ (accessed 29 July 2019).
- Field notes trial first instance, September 2007, Sacramento.

Case AETA4 (United States of America v. J. Buddenberg, M. Khajavi, N. Pope aka N. Knoerl, and A. Stumpo)
- Order dismissing indictment, Northern District of California, San José Division, 12 July 2010, www.greenisthenewred.com/blog/wp-content/Images/100712_aeta4_dismissed.pdf

Case Tim DeChristopher
- 'Prosecution: Sentencing Recommendations for Tim DeChristopher', 19 July 2011, www.peacefuluprising.org/prosecution-sentencing-recommendations-for-tim-dechristopher-20110719
- 'Tim's official statement at his sentencing hearing', 26 July 2011, www.peacefuluprising.org/tims-official-statement-at-his-sentencing-hearing-20110726

Index

Vidal, Esmirna 6–7, 223
Viehl, William 190, 197, 240
violence
  law and 49–50
  public support of 135–6, 139
  social contract and 25–6, 33–4,
    40–3, 49–50, 77, 85–6, 94,
    223–4, 239
vivisection 37, 204, 205, 214, 215
voice 235–6

Waddington, P.A.J. 67

Wallace, Edward 68–9, 70
WATU Acción Indígena 154
Weber, Max 49
website administrators 206, 210–15
White, James Boyd 49
Wiener, Martin J. 49
wood theft 172, 175

Young, Peter 69, 102, 104–5, 106, 196,
  220–1

Zuloaga, Jesús María 96